Foxfire 2

ghost stories, spring wild plant foods, spinning and weaving, midwifing, burial customs, corn shuckin's, wagon making and more affairs of plain living.

edited with an introduction by
ELIOT WIGGINTON

Anchor Press/Doubleday
Garden City, New York
1973

Eliot Wigginton, faculty advisor to *Foxfire* Magazine, teaches journalism at the Rabun Gap-Nacoochee School in Georgia. "Wig," as he is known to his students, is currently working to extend the *Foxfire* concept of education and oral history to other communities.

The Anchor Press edition is the first publication of *Foxfire 2* in book form. It is published simultaneously in hard and paper covers.

Jacket and title page photos courtesy of John Hill.
Jacket and cover designs by Jim McWilliams.

Portions of this book first appeared in *Foxfire* Magazine, Copyright © 1970, 1971, 1972 by the Southern Highlands Literary Fund, Inc.

Anchor Press edition: 1973
ISBN: 0-385-02254-9
Library of Congress Catalog Card Number: 70–163087
Copyright © 1973 by the Southern Highlands Literary Fund, Inc. and Brooks Eliot Wigginton
All Rights Reserved
Printed in the United States of America
First Edition

This book is dedicated to high schools kids like Carlton, Karen, David, Barbara, Stan, and thousands like them across this nation—all searching, all groping, all testing for the touchstone, the piece of serenity, the chunk of sense and place and purpose and humanity they can carry with them into a very confusing time.

ACKNOWLEDGMENTS

Hundreds of people have helped us, and to those people—they all know who they are—we literally owe our survival. A list of them would encompass everyone from parents who have let us send their kids into the mountains alone, to school administrators who have let us take kids away from their normal routines, to journalists who have given us an immense amount of support through their publications, to people who have generously donated money, time, energy, advice, and expertise.

But rather than detail those people, I'd like to dedicate this space to a man who, perhaps more than any other, drastically affected the future of our experiment. That man was the director of the National Endowment for the Humanities' Education Division—Herb McArthur.

Foxfire was three years old, and I had spent the better part of a year seeking additional financial support. As testimony to that struggle, I refer you to a manila folder in my office packed with letters from foundations and organizations—most of which I had visited personally—saying, in essence, that they liked the idea but could see no way to help us. Herb listened to me one day in his Washington office, liked the *Foxfire* idea, and saw a way to help us out. The end result of that collaboration was two grants totaling nearly twenty thousand dollars that moved us about eight giant steps forward by allowing us, among other things, to purchase videotape equipment, darkroom equipment, send kids to New York on exchanges, and hire Suzy—our first paid employee.

Herb has agreed to resign at the request of Ronald Berman, the newly appointed NEH head who, according to the September 4, 1972 issue of *Time* has vowed to return the NEH to a "strict constructionist" view of the humanities (supporting such things as a television series on Shakespeare's plays) and away from "Classic Comics—culture simplified and castrated." All well and good. But it frightens me to think that this might also mean that other stumbling experiments like ours will be passed over in favor of "professional studies professionally run."

Herb's genius was that he could recognize and encourage highly experimental, often risky projects—but projects having the look of a winner about them—and urge that they be assisted. In a day when most of us find only financial rejection at the state and local level, the only place we have left to turn is to larger foundations with directors like Herb. I can only hope for all our sakes that somewhere there are more of them around.

BEW

CONTENTS

Acknowledgments   6
Introduction   8

Maude Shope   18
Sourwood Honey   28
Beekeeping   32
Spring Wild Plant Foods   47
Happy Dowdle   95
Making an Ox Yoke   112
Wagon Wheels and Wagons   118
Making a Tub Wheel   142
Making a Foot-powered Lathe   164
From Raising Sheep to Weaving Cloth   172
How to Wash Clothes in an Iron Pot   256
Anna Howard   266
Midwives and Granny Women   274
Old-time Burials   304
Boogers, Witches, and Haints   324
Corn Shuckin's, House Raisin's, Quiltin's,
    Pea Thrashin's, Singin's, Log Rollin's,
    Candy Pullin's, and . . .   362
Kenny Runion   378

Appendix   393
Index of People   408

INTRODUCTION

O
ne evening a couple of years ago, with some cicadas making a deceptively comfortable racket outdoors, and the mountains easing from green to blue to purple, I sat down alone at a desk full of papers and photographs and notebooks and articles torn out of magazines and loose paper clips and Bic pen tops and empty film cans and general trash like that; and I shoved it all around and got enough flat space to make an introduction to a book some high school kids and I had put together. That was the first *Foxfire Book*.

It was no piece of cake—that introduction. Mostly it was hard because I was trying to tell a lot of people who had never heard of us who we were and what we were doing. That's done now. This evening I sit down alone at the same desk, having just made another flat space and nodded to the mountains, prepared to do it all again; and I feel some sense of relief at not having to tell over again the story of *Foxfire*. Tonight I just feel like talking some on paper.

A lot has happened down here since that first introduction. But the cicadas outside are at it again tonight just like they were before. They haven't changed. The world goes on. There's something there to wonder at . . .

Meanwhile, there's this second book that on the surface is about the same thing the first one was about—namely, one group of people and how they dealt. Simple. But I suspect that if you really got into the first volume, you know already it had to do with a lot more than that. Perhaps you're the kind who once knew a grandfather who was extraordinary, maybe for no other reason than that he didn't give a flying damn that he was poor as Job's turkey as long as everyone he cared about was dry and warm, and that there was hot food on the table, and a couple good neighbors, and time to hike up into that cove above the cabin to see if there were any four-prongers this year in the 'sang patch. Or maybe for the fact that he was one of those rascally scoundrels who ran a liquor still in a basement right in the middle of town and vented his smoke out the same chimney the courthouse used. Like that.

Or maybe you know people like Suzy and Harry. Suzy works with us. I don't remember just how it happened except that she was a VISTA here, and when she was done with that, we got her. And she married Harry from Virginia who learned how to make pots from Bob Owens and drove a beat-up Chevy pickup on its fourth transmission and grew a beard. And Suzy used to come in to work every day with great plum-colored bruises on her legs where she had fallen down between the floor joists of the house they were building by themselves in a pine thicket near Tiger. And she was always laughing, and the kids would crowd around and want to help—and she and Harry let them.

Or you know and probably care deeply about some high school kids, and maybe this kind of thing has happened to you. Then you'd understand the day when I was in the office and Suzy was in the outside room and I heard her laughing—as usual—except she was really cracked up this time, and so naturally I had to go out and see what was happening, and she said just be quiet and listen. And Carlton, one of the tenth grade kids, had been in the darkroom alone for an hour and I had forgotten—and God he was missing his English class —and this string of muffled swear words suddenly drifted through the darkroom door. Yep. Carlton was still in there—oh, hell, that English class—trying to make a double exposure print for Karen's and Betse's burials article. And he was trying to figure out how to do it and burning up all this printing paper and coming closer and closer to getting it just right and talking to himself explaining what was wrong like there were seventy-eight people watching. And Suzy had been listening to the struggle, laughing, when—Bam—out he came with a dripping wet print and a *There how does that grab you*—and it was beautiful, and we used it on the cover of the magazine that had that article in it (and in the book). And Suzy and I were both laughing, and then Carlton cracked up too. And we slapped him on the back and he punched us and we laughed some more. And then he went to English.

And when he got to English, he had to write five hundred times, "I will not be late to class any more."

And the teacher read some poems aloud that nobody listened to, so she spent the whole hour reading to herself while the kids hacked off —or slept. Sort of like us in church five minutes into the sermon. You know.

All that's true. And I guess if you really understand what this book is about, you've had some of that happen to you because this book is *really* about those kids like Carlton and what they did in between algebra problems. See, this isn't really a "How to Survive in the Woods" manual, although it does show how one specific group of people in one specific time and place did survive. I just want to explain that to some of you who may be irritated because we haven't told you how to vent your outhouse yet. See, mostly this book is about school, and about community, and about people, and about the great adventure life can be when lived intensely. And about the fact that instead of celebrating with our kids the infinite variety and ingenuity of nature and man, we are still allowing them to be drowned in the Franco-Prussian wars.

Sometimes, on cicada nights like this, I do a lot of thinking. Mostly it's thinking about stuff that's happened since the first *Foxfire Book* came out—about letters we've gotten, schools we've seen, groups we've visited and talked with. We made some good friends through that book —friends who intuitively understood what we were saying, knew they were saying it too (though in different ways), and got in touch. And sometimes I am overwhelmed by optimism when I watch them at work with those fragile, humane experiments like the Opportunity II school in San Francisco, The Young Film Makers and the *Fourth Street i* and the Teachers' and Writers' Collaborative in New York City, and Interlocken's Crossroads America Program. And I know good things are happening to the kids involved. I *know* it's making a difference.

But inevitably the optimism I feel when I dig in with those people and share their adventures—inevitably that is tempered by the sounds of human cicadas that endure and drone on and on endlessly into the night.

"I will not be late to class any more."

And they never understand.

Sometimes I lie awake at night and think about all that. Strange stuff to think about, I know; and I probably wouldn't except that it constantly colors my life and the lives of kids I care about.

What do I say, for example, in answer to the stacks of letters I get from teachers asking questions like, "My pupils are so listless, so uninterested. How can I motivate them?" Or, "I would like to start a project like yours. Would you please tell me exactly how to go about doing so from beginning to end?" How can I answer questions like that, knowing that the only way it can work is for the teacher to push back the desks and sit down on the floor with the kids and really listen to them for the first time, and see what they can all come up with *together* that *might* work in the context of their own particular school and community—and they try to find ways to make it work for as long as it seems worth doing—and then find another. Knowing all the while most teachers won't bother to do that. Knowing they want texts and learning kits and packets that tell them how. Knowing they're missing the greatest adventure of all. And so are their kids.

How do you get to those teachers?

And what do I say to kids who ask me for one good reason why they should stay in school and stay straight when they've just been humiliated in front of their classmates for answering a question wrong, or just been punished for doing something that deserved no punishment (or something they didn't do), or just flunked a course by one point —a course they'll now have to repeat. Or a kid who's on the verge of running away?

What do I say to those faces?

And what do I say to a state's education organization that's trying to prevent the teaching of journalism by any teacher not properly credentialed in that area, knowing I never had a course in journalism or folklore in my life? What do I say to them, knowing our magazine has been written about in virtually every publication of any note in this country—but has yet to be mentioned, after seven years of operation, in our own state's education publications (and there are several). I should think that at least half the time of such organizations would be devoted to ferreting out projects of some potential worth, helping them when they need it most (as we did often during those first three years), and putting them in touch with others who can act as support, as valid critics, and as invaluable resources. We operate in vacuums.

What do I say to them?

I lie awake and think about that stuff. I can't help it. And I am filled with dread at the thought that that mentality will prevail, driving out the next Pat Conroys, Herb Kohls, Jim Herndons, and Jonathan Kozols in the process—along with the fragile, humane experiments. Because I know that if it's a lost struggle, everyone loses: the kids, the society that gets them next, and the teachers who scurry back to the safety of their texts and shelve their imaginations and their enthusiasms and their dreams for better times.

Then I remember Myles Horton—constantly engaged in causes bigger than himself—and what he says to people who lie awake at night: "You must not worry about things you have no control over. Make peace with yourself, choose your battle carefully, fight there and there alone to make things right, and leave the rest." And that makes a certain amount of sense. If our battle is to go roaring into a school, try to change it, and get fired in the process, then that's one thing. But I am rapidly reaching the point where I believe my battle is with a tiny group of kids who happen to be working on a magazine called *Foxfire,* and with what happens to them in the process of that involvement. And that is all I can afford to worry about. They are my challenge now. Period.

Perhaps that's all any of us can do. Choose one small piece of turf, be honest with ourselves, choose our approaches, stay in touch, remain constantly open to new ideas and new approaches, shut up, go to work, and hope for the best.

That is what I find myself doing. For the record, then, and for those who are still reading and curious, and for those who have written and asked, these are the principles I operate by today. They will change in time, but for now these are my touchstones.

First, I've found that the world of most of my kids is filled with so much negative energy imposed from outside sources that they have no choice but to withdraw into themselves and their circle of friends for sanity, safety, and some sense of belonging. Examples come to mind immediately: the shopkeeper who automatically suspects the kids are going to steal; the waitress who automatically assumes the kids are going to make a mess and be a pain in the neck; the dormitory, home, or classroom where, whenever the kid hears an adult call his name, he recoils, wondering, "What am I going to have to do now?" or, "What have I done this time?" Or where a kid is met at the door with that special gaze designed and perfected through years of practice that says, "I'm here, see? Any trouble and you're going to wish there hadn't been, and I'm not kidding." The air is charged with it.

How many times have I seen the effects of a great day evaporate like mist before the door of a classroom or home? A fourteen-year-old gives a talk before a group of 450, is mobbed afterwards by people wanting to ask questions, thank him, or get his autograph on the article he wrote in the last *Foxfire;* and that night, giddy with happiness and accomplishment, he is met at home by a mother who chews him out for forgetting to make his bed that morning. He says, "But, Mom, let me tell you what just happened to me." And she says, "I know already. You got caught smoking, right?"

And then those adults wonder why there's no communication; wonder why the kids don't want to come home at night. What choice have we given them?

I've been building a six-sided log house on the side of a mountain near here. Kids help me all the time, of course—nearly every day—and some of the finest experiences of any of our lives have happened there. We have no blueprints (read curriculum guides), so when someone gets a brainstorm and suggests we move a window, or shove a wall two feet farther out, or stick in a skylight, we often do it. A couple of weeks ago six of us got the last wall log up, notched and secured, and mounted the first floor joist for the second floor. It was a moment we'd been working toward for months; and when we finished, we charged down the mountainside to The Villager, a local restaurant, for a celebration. Kate, who owns the place, let me cook up some stuff for them, and we all laughed and ate and laughed—really did it up right. But I made sure I got them back to the dorm that night in plenty of time for study hall.

The next day I was treated to a display of real anger by the dormitory houseparents. Mostly it centered around the fact that the kids had come in noisy for study hall, and they just weren't going to have any more of that. Instead of sharing that experience with those kids, they had landed on them, saying that if it happened again, they'd make a rule that the kids would either have to be in a full half hour before study hall, or just not go outside before study hall at all. Here we go again.

The obvious corollary is that not only do we too rarely share a kid's ideas and joys and triumphs, and not only do we too rarely put them in situations where they *can* triumph, but we also do not trust them. They cannot be in such and such a place unsupervised. They cannot be left with this decision. They cannot be expected to carry out that task. And so we retreat behind rules that bind them up.

To say kids *cannot* be trusted is the most personally damning statement any adult can make, for it simply reveals either that he can neither create nor endure the kind of atmosphere in which a kid can try and perhaps fail (read learn) and yet not be damned; or that he is not an inspiring enough individual to make them want to participate *with* him as responsible partners in a common goal.

I'm not just spouting idealistic jargon. I've seen it work the other way. The Hill School, for example, where kids can work alone on independent study projects in most of the campus buildings far into the night; or another school I know of where the kids even have the responsibility of deciding at the end of the year which teachers get re-hired; or our school where an inspired work supervisor has turned over the supervision of the campus work crews to the kids.

Too many of us fall short of that love and patience and self-confidence it takes to work with kids as equal partners. We must do better. There is so little joy in the world of most kids. The recognition of worth and accomplishment is so strained and so stingily parceled and our condemnation so freely given that it completely overwhelms the elation of any positive, shared experiences. I find it no mystery at all that kids tune us out.

And if you think I'm exaggerating, you're probably part of the problem.

Second, I believe that in most cases the most rewarding and significant things that happen to a kid happen outside the classroom: falling in love, climbing a mountain, rapping for hours with an adult who is loved or respected, building a house, seeing a part of the world never seen before, coming to some deep personal empathy with a kid from another background and culture, or genuinely understanding some serious community or national problem.

These are all things that may *later* give him the motivation necessary to *want* to be able to write correctly and forcefully, or *want* to know history, or *want* to understand the complexities of nature and man through biology, botany, psychology, anthropology, or physics. But we too often ignore these events, seeing them as "irrelevant" or "froth." Until they are acknowledged as important and relevant to the student's existence, all he does inside those walls is doomed to seem meaningless and without reason. What we must realize is that the walls of those buildings we imprison kids in now must come crashing down, and the world must be their classroom, the classroom a reflection of their world. The two must work as one.

The purpose of our schools, then, must be to help our kids discover who they are, their loves and hates, and the stance they are going to take in the face of the world. It becomes our responsibility as teachers to put them in situations where this testing can go on; to create for them memorable experiences that they will carry with them like talismen and come back to touch a thousand times during the course of their lives. I'm convinced, for example, that a student learns more about himself and life generally in three days spent with an Aunt Arie (who went no further than the fourth grade) than in four years of high school English.

We've gotten everything mixed up. We saw a man in a factory say, "I can guarantee that if you put piece A and piece B and piece C together according to this blueprint, you will get the following result, and I can guarantee it will happen every time." We saw that, and it seemed good.

And so we took it to our schools. "Put text A and kit B and qualified teacher C before the students of this land, and we can guarantee they will all read at level D at the end of one year." We tried that, and it was not good.

But now we cannot stop. We have substituted understanding *Silas Marner* for understanding the communications (no matter what form they may take) of others. We have substituted the dates of the Spanish Armada's great battles for an understanding of history and how it works and how the past affects the present. We have substituted the use of clay molds of little figures and the copying of pretty pictures for creativity in art. All in the style of technology. "These tools and these ingredients and these instructions will yield these results. Follow them. At the end, you will have a well-educated student, ready to think for himself and take his place in society. This we can predict." And it does not work. And we are reaping the harvest now.

We have ruled out the possibility of anything worth while, new, or creative coming out of random behavior, play, or the testing out of a kid's own ideas in any area from art through zoology. And so we have eliminated those activities. And we expect our kids to learn from their mistakes.

We have ruled out the possibility of a student's being able to make competent decisions regarding his life, his environment, his conduct— even his bed time—so we make those decisions for him. And we expect him to be able to walk out of our schools self-confident, ready to make competent decisions regarding his life, his environment, his conduct . . .

We have separated him from his world—have made it irrelevant to our tidy curricula—and yet we count on him to know what to do with that same world, and have creative solutions for its problems, when our time with him is done. Amazing.

And third, I'm afraid we've become a nation of nomads with no sense of that security or serenity that comes from being able to say, "Here is where I belong. Here is my place, my time, my home, my birthright, my community. Here I am loved and known, and here I love in turn."

It happens all around us. *Foxfire* has had four different editors at Doubleday. The first three have left, one by one. It happened to me personally. My mother was from Poughkeepsie, New York; my father from Marietta, Ohio; my stepmother from Washington, Pennsylvania. I was born in Wheeling, West Virginia; raised in Athens, Georgia; educated in Pottstown, Pennsylvania, Ithaca, New York, and Baltimore, Maryland; and I now work in Rabun Gap, Georgia. I've learned a lot from all of that, but still I have no more idea of where I fit in space and time and community than if I had just landed inside a meteor from Pluto. I make my home where I am.

And it happens to my students. Over half of them move away permanently. They are giving this county away. Our tax assessors are all land developers from outside the area. Parents have no family left to sell the farms to, so they sell them off and watch "second home" extravaganzas take their places. Kentucky Fried Chicken is proud to announce its arrival . . .

The only way I can see to get our kids committed to our neighborhoods and our communities is to get them so involved in their surroundings that they become determined that the community's destiny will be in *their* hands, not in the hands of commercial rapists. They must feel that they are essential to the future of their homes. The alternative is to watch them leave, creating a vacuum filled, in our county's case, by ten thousand summer lots all priced so high that even if those kids *wanted* to come back someday they couldn't afford to.

Until we put together the article on shuckings and house raisings (in this volume), none of us realized the extent to which people used to be dependent on and responsible for each other. We knew that once there *were* shuckings, but these sounded somehow remote—curiosities of a long-gone day. Now that we've done some real work on the subject, I realize how widespread and pervasive and varied and common these practices were. They were a part of everyone's existence here—and they were a constant part—not a once-a-month rarity.

Somewhere along the way, we've lost something fine. Perhaps in our search for personal satisfaction and pleasure, we've dug so deeply into ourselves that we've forgotten each other. The extent to which neighbors are strangers is frightening, and the extent to which we've blocked out and structured and programmed most of our time for ourselves may be tragic. It may mean that we truly *have* lost our sense of community, and in the process killed our interdependence forever.

It's a mad cycle. We get jobs to support our families. They take our time. Our time gone, we do less together. We see our neighbors less and less frequently, and a gulf is formed. With the loss of contact comes loss of friendship, and with the loss of friendship/dependence comes hesitance at reopening the contact (you have to work at being friends), and with the hesitance comes suspicion. We read about crime and dope and . . . I wonder if . . . ?

Soon we are a community of isolated islands ("Who are those people who just moved in?" "I don't know. We ought to go find out someday.") and the damage is done. We need only look at a friendship quilt (*The Foxfire Book,* page 143) to see how great the loss.

Now I'm not suggesting that everyone should suddenly get together and have a pea thrashing. A barn raising in the middle of suburbia is likewise farfetched. But as our leisure time increases, and as we search for new ways to fill it, surely we are inventive enough to be able to find ways to work/play/create together as communities.

There are a few hopeful, tentative signs. Community-wide trash cleanups, for example. Or neighborhood parks and recreation areas built and designed for the community by the community. Or food cooperatives. But they are often tentative, groping, short-lived.

Too often we fail to see any common bonds between ourselves. Maybe if we set about with our kids creating some fertile ground for those bonds, we'll find how close our interests and our instincts and our needs as human beings really are. And maybe we'll find again the rich wisdom in that sense of shared responsibility and love that once existed.

Until that time, we may have to resign ourselves to a world where our kids flee home leaving their parents behind: lonely, embittered, bewildered islands on a whole wide street full of people.

As I said, I'm far from having all the answers for myself or anyone else. But those things I believe. They are the platforms from which I work in Rabun Gap. I am convinced that we, as adults, must constantly cling to, affirm, and celebrate with our kids those things we love: sunsets, laughter, the taste of a good meal, the warmth of a hickory fire shared by real friends, the joy of discovery and accomplishment, empathy with the Aunt Aries and their triumphs and sorrows, the constant surprises of life; and we must hope that, as teachers, in the process of that celebration and that empathy, we will build in our students' souls such a reservoir of warmth and hope and generosity and energy and self-assurance that it would carry them through hell. That is surely what those who do not have that reservoir will face.

Foxfire is one means I have stumbled upon to help with that building. It is not enough by itself. There are hundreds of other ways. But with Myles Horton in mind, it is the way I have chosen, for me, for now. It isn't going to work for all my kids, but I believe it's worked for some; and I'm constantly revising to make it work for more.

And I have to believe that if a man is doing that, then, though cicadas ring forever in his ears, he may not be praised, but he at least will not be damned; for he is doing everything he can in his small part of the globe to help, in his small way, to set things right.

BEW

MAUDE SHOPE

Maude Shope is one of our newest contacts. She was born in North Carolina within seven miles of where she lives now, and she steps right out of an age that is long gone. She's been to corn shuckings ("Oh, that was a big thing, y'know; goin' to shuck out a man's corn"), log rollings, has spun wool, sewed clothing, raised twelve children, done midwife work, walked to church and school—and a thousand other things; even at the age of seventy-six, she hasn't slowed down much. And neither has her thirty-two-year-old mule, Frank. When she claimed she still rode him, we looked at her in disbelief, I guess. So she proved it, as the photographs show.

When she's not being visited by family, or visiting with her granddaughter (who attends Western Carolina University) and her son-in-law who live just up the dirt road, she stays alone in a tiny frame house.

The grass hasn't grown greener up at Maude's, and she has never won any world titles or medals, but if there were ever one to be recognized for just plain, simple, old-fashioned ways, Maude would surely be a prime candidate. She lives rough, but she has pride, dignity, warmth, a joy and enthusiasm for life that is boundless. And she has our respect and affection.

BARBARA TAYLOR and SHEILA VINSON

Maude began by telling us about her childhood: We didn't have

PLATE 1   "I never did try t'drive a car. My mule is th'way I got around. Used t'ride him t'Otto [North Carolina] t'get groceries. I've drove him all th'way t'Franklin and back years ago. 'Course you couldn't do it now. There's too many cars on th'road. I've had him since he'uz eighteen months old. He'll be thirty-two in February. You can drag wood with him—anything y'want t'do. He'll do any kind of work you want done. Yes, sir. He's something."

th'things that children's got now, but we didn't have'em and we didn't look fer'em. When we'uz children, we'd all get out'n'play, y'know. Instead of a horse, we used t'have a stick and ride that around. As fer dolls, oh, had one doll apiece in our life. And we thought we'd got somethin'. We saved eggs and bought our dolls—give a quarter apiece fer'em. And Mama made'em dresses th'next mornin'. Well, that'uz worth more than a ten dollar doll would be now.

We thought Santa Claus, up t'when we was great big young'uns, brought us stuff. I know one Christmas, we couldn't wait, hardly. And they wouldn't let us get into things, and we felt of th'stockin's we'd hung up. Oh, we didn't know what was in'em, and we *couldn't* get into'em till just before daylight.

PLATE 2

PLATE 3

And we used t'walk t'school. Now, y'know, grownups and children don't have t'walk as fer as from here t'th'creek hardly. Now we used t'go and stay all night with our neighbor's boys and girls when we'uz children. Mama'd let us go, and we thought it was th'greatest thing there was, y'know—git t'go t'somebody's house and stay all night. And us and them children'd play—oh, we thought we had th'biggest time. We'd git into this sandy place—old gray sand. If we could git into that sandy place, we was havin' our fun!

And I did farmwork and housework. Went t'th'field and worked in th'field all m'life since I was a child. I always fed th'cattle an'stock. T'tell th'truth, I'd rather work in th'field than t'work in th'house. I like t'see a purty, clean house, but I'm not too good a housekeeper.

[The subject of children led us naturally into a discussion of how children should be raised now, and what advice she would give them, if she had the chance, to help them deal with today's world.] Well, I don't know. Th'first thing is t'be honest and truthful. That's about th'best thing I could think of. Live their life; be honest and truthful and not steal. That's honesty, y'know. If you're honest and truthful, you're not a'gonna' steal.

PLATE 4 "I take hay t'my stock in th'wheelbarrow. I could go out there an' call right now, 'So-o-o-o cow!' and they'd three or four of'em bawl at th'same time. And th'old mule, he'd be there."

Now I've heard, and you have too, heard people say, "I'd starve before I'd steal." Well, I don't think I would. I think if I couldn't do no other way, I'd slip me a bite a'somethin'. What I mean is, they's not many people *has* t'steal anything. You can get somethin' t'eat without stealin'. That's one thing, young'uns, you can take down. I'm not a'gonna' steal if I can get by it. I won't steal a thing. I won't lie t'you, and I won't steal. I say bad words sometimes—I don't deny it. I say nasty words sometimes, and cuss sometimes. I've done that. But stealin'r'lyin' to y', I'm not a'gonna' do it. I think that is a dirty thing t'do. I believe in bein' honest—tellin' th'truth. That's th'way I feel.

I don't live like I should. I one time belonged to th'church and prayed in public. I don't no more. I try t'live right, but still I don't live like I should, not as good as I should live. At one time, I was counted as good as anybody in th'church. But th'feelin' is just as important [as praying in public]. I don't git down on m'knees and pray, but in my mind I pray, and I do believe that there's a higher power than us. I do believe that. I can't say that there's not. [God shows himself.] He's got control of—like this mornin'. It'uz as cloudy as it could be, and we all said it'uz gonna' rain; and God done it, I suppose. We didn't. And it cleared off, and now it's a purty day. He's got His ways.

I don't read th'Bible a lot. I don't read it like I should. It's very important, though. I'd be afraid t'give th'Bible a lie or somethin'; I certainly would. I'll tell y'one thing I don't like—th'way they drag it around. I like th'old Bible better than I do this new style they've got now. I don't know if that's contradictin' th'Bible or not, but I don't think so. They change and try t'tell different things, but I'd be afraid t'try t'contradict some a'God's things in th'Bible.

I feel like I'm a Christian, and all that; but still, I'll break over and say nasty words, and I think it's a habit more'n anything. Just shore as somethin' goes wrong, I'll say, "Well, dammit." And I don't mean a bit more than—it's just habit. Just like you'll say little ol'—like, "dadburnit," or somethin'r'nother. I think it's just as dirty as sayin' th'other. So I don't think that a body's doin' th'wrong thing. Well, of course they're doin' th'wrong thing in one way, but show me one that don't do somethin' wrong. There's nobody but what does somethin' wrong. They might think they was doin' it right, but I might see it [another way]. It's just your way a'seein'. I might see that they was doin' awful dirty, and they might think they was bein' honest with ever'thin' they done.

[That's why] I feel like I can't tell you [young people what to do]. You're gonna' do as you please. But I could tell you what I thought was best. I'll tell you one thing I don't believe in. All right: if you was courtin' a boy, maybe I'd just hate him. Well, and I wouldn't have that boy if it was me. But it's *you* talkin' to'im, and you've got your feelin's, haven't you? You're gonna' do what you think is right, either way. It might be somebody I just hated. You've seen people thataway. But I don't believe in tellin' you what t'do. You do th'best you can,

PLATE 5

and do what you think is right. People say, "Well, if I'uz her, I wouldn't marry him." Well, they're not a'gonna have t'live with'im. It's *you* that's a'marryin'im. I believe in tendin' to your own business and leavin' other people alone. If you tend to your own business, you've got plenty t'do without a'tendin' t'mine and hers. Not t'say I'm perfect'r'anything.

My parents was good about lettin' us make up our own minds .They was good t'us. They was strict about makin' us mind, but they was good. Had a Christian mother and father all my life. We worked. Didn't work like slaves—I don't mean that. But we had t'work for our livin'. And they didn't 'strict us t'havin' t'belong t'th'church that they b'longed to ner nothin'. We had our privilege. They was Methodist— both of'em—and I'm a Methodist. But if we'd a'wanted t'been Baptists, they wouldn't've objected. Same way with politics. They were all Democrats, but if we'd a'wanted t'be somethin' else, they wouldn't've fussed on us.

[But they *were* too restrictive in one way, she felt.] But grown people wouldn't've talked about havin' babies'n'such as'at a bit more'n you'd go out here and shoot somebody. My gosh, we'uz taught up till we'uz great big kids [that] th'doctor brought th'little babies all th'time. We didn't know. When I'uz a great big girl, I didn't know no more about sex than a dog does. And little calves—we thought cows scratched'em out from under a stump or log out there till we was great big children. That's th'way I'uz brought up. Not you know [about sex] from th'time you're born, nearly. I believe it's better t'let children know. If y'know somethin', you're not as apt t'do somethin' wrong as you would if you didn't know it was th'wrong thing t'do. Years ago, y'know, if somethin' happened then, it was awful. But now it ain't so awful. Well, th'girls know how to behave theirselves. I think girls ought t'know what t'do and what not t'do.

And like it is by dressin'. Years back, well, if a woman had her dress up and somebody seen her knee, awfullest thing ever was. But now they don't pay no more attention for their knee than they do for their hands. And so I don't know. It's just human nature.

Now when I first come to this creek, we broke up our land with a mule and a single-footed plow. We made plenty of corn t'do us all year long—never bought no corn when I first come t'this creek. Take what we called a single-footed plow, break up th'ground and then go and lay it off, cover it with a single-foot plow, drop it by hand. Now it's changed so that my grandchildren couldn't build a fire in that wood stove 'cause they don't know how. Well, I don't know how t'drive a car, so I guess their way of doin' is just as good as mine. But I like my way of doin' th'best.

When I come t'this creek, didn't know what buyin' meat and lard was. They made their own meat and killed their hogs in th'fall of

PLATE 6

th'year. You can remember your parents killin' hogs, and maybe they still do yet, but they don't like they used to. Kill three or four big hogs, or whatever you had, and take care of your meat and render out th'lard, and have it and have lard t'do y'. But nowadays, th'younger generation—they don't know how t'go and make it, and so all they know t'do is go and buy. Well, it's like fixin' a meal. I can put me on a pot a'green beans or shelled beans or whatever I got, and cook'em here on th'fire. Nine times out of ten, nearly, they [the younger people] stop at th'store and get some canned stuff and then come in and fix their supper in a few minutes where it takes me all day t'cook a half a pot a'beans.

I don't know which is th'best. I guess a wood stove's better for *me*. It's old-fashioned, and I like it. With a 'lectric stove, you can heat one of them, y'know, and have your meal ready before y'get your first fire t'burnin' in that'n. But just for th'old-fashioned of it, I like it. And then, it heats th'house. I like it for that. It's best for *me* t'do it th'old-fashioned way, but then, I've got my way and they've got theirs.

But I think they oughta know how t'do this too. A person don't know what might happen. They might get t'where they needed t'do it and didn't know how. Like milkin' cows. They's not none of th'younger generation knows how. Wouldn't know which side of th'cow t'go to t'milk. Lots of y'don't. Well, I do. And I think because I know it, some of th'young'uns quarrel at me. I know how t'do somethin', and I just think it's better t'know how t'do that work; and they think it's better, a'course, t'do other work.

I just think ever'body's got his way of feelin'. You've got your way, and if you think you're right a'doin' somethin', well, you're just as honest as I am because you're doin' what you think is right.

Maybe there's somethin' I like t'eat, and you don't like it fer a thing in this world. I'd say, "Oh, eat this. This is good. Eat it. Eat it. Eat." Well, now, if you don't like it, you don't want t'eat it. I think that's right in lettin' th'other man have his privilege.

Some people have superstitions, and that's their business too. You've heard these old tales where if you dream a dream and tell it before breakfast, it'll come t'pass? Or th'old sayin' on New Year's mornin' that if a man comes t'your house first, you'll have good luck. If a woman comes t'your house first, throw th'broom in front a'her 'fore she comes in th'door or you'll have bad luck. That's an old sayin', y'know. And not t'take th'ashes out between Christmas and New Year. If you do, you'll have bad luck. Or eat black-eyed peas for New Year's day? I seen a piece in th'paper where someone was eatin' cabbage for

New Year. If I had cabbage *any* time through th'year, I'uz proud of it.

And some believe if th'smoke's a'goin' t'th'ground, it's a'gonna' rain. Or if it's clear fogs [fog without clouds accompanying it] through th'month of January, then there'll be frost in May. Lots a'people believes them, and that's their privilege. But I never pay no 'tention to'em.

[Changing the subject somewhat, we asked Maude what she considered her most valuable possession to be.] Water. That's important. But that comes by th'Almighty. But it's our place t'get it.

I guess cattle and stock is actually th'most important t'me. They're company. You take stock and them blamed old dogs—well, they're company to a body. A dog usually comes ahead of anything else, don't it? You know yourself that you'll hold up for your dog. If somebody was t'come in and kick that dog just t'get t'kick him, I'd fly all mad in spite of myself, I guess.

[As the interview ended, we asked her if anything really worried her.] I'll tell you what I'm afraid of. You may live t'see it. I guess I'll not. And that's that th'government will come and cut up our land— [take it from] all that's got more than a certain amount. There's s'many more people bein' born into th'world, y'know. Ain't no tellin' how many more people they is now than they was forty and fifty years ago. Well, they've got t'have a place t'live. We've got land here. In a few years they'll cut it up and they'll take off so much and sell it. That worries me. There's so many new houses put up down th'road in just th'last little while.

I don't want no city life. I like country life better. I've never lived in a city, but I don't want to. For one thing, if you're in th'city, it's a noise all th'time. Back in th'country, you got your free runnin' water and all such as that.

Why, I wouldn't swap this little shack here for th'finest house in New York. I wouldn't do it. That's just th'way I feel.

SOURWOOD HONEY

by Marie B. Mellinger

Bees are outstanding botanists. They know instinc-
tively which plants provide
the most nectar, and will visit one plant species almost exclusively as
long as it is in blossom. In the Blue Ridge Mountains, the bees are
busy from the time of the first red maple blossoms in the spring
through the last of the ironweeds and asters in the late fall. But many
mountain dwellers will tell you that the very best honey comes from
the sourwood.

The sourwood tree, *Oxydendrum arboreum*, has been called one of
the world's best bee trees. It is a member of the heath family, *Ericacae*.
It may be a tall and stately tree, often an understory tree with dogwood in groves of oak and hickory, or it may be short and shrubby on
ridges or rock outcrops. It is found from the red clay hills of the Piedmont to mountain elevations of three thousand feet.

The sourwood has long, narrow, very glossy leaves. These have a
tart, sour taste, and they can be chewed as a thirst quencher. Some
botanists describe them as being bitter. They turn brilliantly scarlet in
early autumn and paint the hills and lower mountains with color. Me-
dicinally they are a diuretic. Gathered when red, "filled with sun
power," a grasp of sourwood leaves plus anvil dust made dropsy medicine. They also yield a black dye.

The sourwood often has a curved or crooked trunk once prized for

Marie Mellinger, a local botanist, works with the Georgia Conservancy and as
a naturalist for the Georgia State Parks Department.

PLATE 7

PLATE 8

sled runners. The wood has been used for tool handles and bed posts. The dark, roughly squared bark was also used for dye and medicine. But a few say it is very bad luck to burn sourwood for fuel. This can supposedly bring on bad weather or family disasters. A sourwood limb cut to the exact height of an asthmatic child could be put under the doorstep. When the child outgrew the length of the stick, his asthma would be cured.

The sourwood tree, in early July, is covered with drooping racemes of waxy white bell-shaped blossoms that perfume the air and call all the honeybees in the neighborhood. Flowers are called "angel-fingers," and the sourwood is also known as "sorrel-tree" or "lily-of-the-valley tree." The long blossoming period of the sourwood makes it a favorite honey-producing tree. One mountain man said, "I never seen bees go crazy like they do on sourwood." Bees will work at sourwood flowers even in the rain and through most of the daylight hours. Stand under

PLATE 9

a sourwood and you can hear the melodious hum of the bees in the blossoms.

The honey is described as "larrupin' good," and a "man ain't tasted nothin' lessen he's put his tongue to sourwood honey." Many people still like the sourwood honey as well as do the bees. Maurice Brooks wrote that "sourwood honey is yellow and just a touch of the oxalic acid which the host plant contains comes through to give the sweet a certain piquancy." Sourwood is extolled as "mountain honey thick and raw, exactly as the bees made it."

In the mountains, honey was the preferred, "long sweetening" while "short sweetening" was sorghum. A drink for hot summer haymaking days was "switchell," made by mixing a half cup of honey and a half cup of cider vinegar. This was kept in a jar and four teaspoons of the mixture were added to a dipper of water for a nourishing drink.

Sourwood honey is credited with more virtues than just tasting good. It has been called a natural stimulant with a pleasant acidulous taste, very good for rheumatism and arthritis. It is often a main ingredient in homemade cough medicines combined with wild cherry or white pine, or as a stomach medicine with yellow-root and moonshine whiskey. Sourwood honey plus flaxseed was used for whooping cough, and sage, honey, and vinegar were combined for coughs or sore throats. Honey and alum relieved hoarseness. Honey could also induce sleep, help relieve fevers, or be applied to burns.

The production of sourwood honey has become a beekeeping industry that brings thousands of dollars to mountain economy and supplies honey to roadside tourist stands and grocery stores all over the mountains.

BEEKEEPING

This has been one of those maddeningly elusive topics that we run into once in a while. Four years ago, for example, we were told that Terrell Lamb's old beegums were still set up in his field. When we checked it out, though, we found that they had all disappeared. That began a search for an old beegum still in use that just ended this year in Farish Kilby's back yard over on Persimmon.

The same thing was true with bee trees. We finally located one, and we had Lon Reid's assurance that he'd cut it with us this spring so we could see how it was done; but he got sick and never was able to complete the job. Mrs. Mellinger's companion article, meanwhile, sat in our office for over a year while we followed one false lead after another—or made contact with men who could add pieces to the story, but never quite enough to complete it.

Now, however, with the help of people like Esco Pitts, Lawton Brooks, Elb McClure, Farish Kilby, Lon Reid, and many others, we think we've about got it. We still don't have those pictures of a tree being cut, but we're going to have to wait until next spring before we can try again. Meanwhile, here's what we have so far.

BEEGUMS

In the early days of beekeeping, the hives were nothing more than

PLATE 10   A hollow tree trunk used as a beegum.

twenty-four to thirty-inch long sections of hollow black gum trees—a
fact that has caused even modern hives in the mountains today to be
called "gums," "beegums," or "plank gums." Some peculiarity special
to the black gum almost invariably caused it to be hollow and thus perfect for hives (and, incidentally, for dripping lye for lye soap).

Hollow sections of the tree would be brought home and the inside
rounded out smooth and uniform with a long chisel. "Middleways" of
the gum, four holes would be bored—one at each point of the compass
—and two sticks run horizontally through the gum at right angles to
each other. These sticks acted as supports from which the bees would
suspend their brood combs. The bees would automatically save the top
half of the gum for their honey and would hang those combs from the
plank lid, or "head," that was set over the top of the gum. The head
was often held in place by a stick run through two wooden eyes (visible in several of the following plates). Then a slanted, easily remova-
ble lid was usually set above the head to keep rain from running into
the gum.

PLATE 11 Farish Kilby's bee-gums are of the earliest type. The two arrows in the middle show the ends of the crossed sticks that pass through the middle of the hollow gum. The arrow at the bottom points out a bee about to enter the gum. Note the wooden eye at the top of the gum. It holds the stick that clamps the head on.

PLATE 12 Ed Ramey nails the base onto a new gum. Note how the base extends beyond the entrance holes to provide a landing platform for the bees.

Beekeepers always set the gums on flat platforms raised well above ground level. Small rocks could be set under one edge of the gum tilting it slightly so the bees could enter; or "V"-shaped notches were cut into the bottom on one side to serve the same purpose. The platform extended several inches beyond the entrance to provide a landing area.

These gums were so satisfactory that even when the early beekeepers began using plank gums, they used the same "crossed-stick" design. The hives were childishly simple to build, and they could be easily "robbed"; one simply removed the slanted roof, eased the head up a crack, slid a long-bladed knife in the crack and sliced the comb from the head, removed the head, and cut out the honey.

There were some disadvantages, however, that became obvious when the modern "supers" were introduced. One disadvantage was

PLATES 13–15 Lon Reid's plank gums are the next step in the evolution from hollow tree trunks to modern supers. Lon's gums also have the wooden eyes for holding the heads on tightly (*13*), and the crossed stick design (*14*). To make sure the lids stay on, Lon piles rocks on most of them (*15*).

that since no comb foundations were provided for the bees, as in modern hives, the bees simply hung the combs in random fashion from the gum head. Removal was a sloppy, sticky job that fractured the combs and often drowned masses of bees. The honey thus removed was also often cluttered with debris such as dead bees, eggs and larvae from the brood chambers below, splinters of wood, ashes from the wads of burning rags used to smoke the bees, and so on.

Another disadvantage was that there was no control over what type of honey the bees collected. With supers, when the sourwood began to bloom, the beekeeper could simply add a new, empty super, and he could pretty much count on getting it filled with the almost colorless sourwood honey. The honey collected in gums, however, represented nectar from everything that had bloomed from spring to the time the gum was robbed. It was dark in color and not as delicate in flavor.

Yet another disadvantage was that since the comb stayed in the gums "from one robbin' to another"—i.e., twelve months—it was tougher and older than that of the supers which were changed regularly.

The gums sufficed, however, and it is a tribute to their usefulness that people like Farish Kilby and Lon Reid still use them today.

BEE TREES

When the new gums were ready, the next step was finding a bee tree. Sometimes one was stumbled across by accident out in the woods. More often, however, beekeepers either found a watering place or set out bait and then followed the bees home. For bait, Esco Pitts's father used corn cobs soaked in honey. He would choose a spot somewhere in the woods, chop out undergrowth and low-lying limbs to create a small clearing (or just find a natural one), place the bait on a piece of bark in the center of the clearing, and then sit down nearby to wait. In short order, if bees were anywhere in the vicinity, one would find the bait, fly back to the tree to tell the others, and soon have a supply line set up from the bait to their tree. The bees would light, fill up, rise and circle once or twice to gain altitude, and then head in a "bee-line" for home. All one had to do then was note the direction and head that way. As Esco said, "He'd course'em from that."

Often the bait was carried along and reset somewhere along the line to check direction and to see whether or not the tree had been passed yet.

Variations in style and bait abound. Some used a drop or two of sweet-smelling anise. Elb McClure used sugar water (one part sugar to one part water) or pure comb honey. Lon Reid's father used corn cobs soaked in salty water for bait, and Lon still keeps salt water near his gums: "You put the salt on th'cobs and then put water, and they suck th'salt out of th'cobs. There's not many folks, I guess, that know that, but they'll search for salt. I never did know what they done with it. Daddy said they fed it t'th'young bees. I never do put much salt. Liable t'get it too salty. I don't know, but they'll suck at it. They will. They'll just cover them cobs up if y'put salt in'em."

Joe Kilby claims that some old-timers used to put corn cobs and dirt in a bucket, urinate in it, and then leave it for a few days. When they got back, the bees would be there. And Elb agrees, saying the old-timers used to call that "stinkbait." At times, he adds, they would even feed it to their bees in early spring before the honey flow started. Soon after it started, however, "th'bees wouldn't fool with it."

Lawton Brooks used a different bait: "Well, now, t'make your bait up, y'take a little honey and some vinegar and warm water, and stir it up together—not too much—and then y'just go and get a bunch a'leaves, or find y'a stump'r'somethin' out in a kindly open place in th'woods. I bet y'a dollar I can put some out where you live in your yard and have a bunch a'bees on it in five minutes. They'll come to it. And then y'watch'em, and when one gets loaded, he'll make a circle'r'two, and then when he starts, he'll go just as straight t'his tree as you can shoot a rifle. Then y'just go th'way he went, and y'just look at th'trees when y'get out t'th'distance you think he went.

"I'll tell y'what I do when I think of it. I fix me a little can a'bait. I generally keep a can wi'me in th'summertime in my car. And when I fish, I put some out and get t'watchin' it.

"Th'best place—if you can find'em a'waterin', you can find their tree 'cause they water at th'closest place to their tree. I went down there in th'pasture one day and found some a'waterin', and they went right up across th'road and right in by a poplar tree. I sat there and, 'Know you ain't high on that hill, son, 'cause you went into th'woods too low down.' So I got my little ol'hatchet and went right down th'road. At th'little ol'tree I turned up in th'woods and I looked around a little bit—up three'r'four trees—and they'uz a big ol'dead tree a'standin' up there on th'mountain, and he went straight for it. I said, 'Oh, he's in that'un.' He was in a big ol'black oak that had a bulge on it—looked like a maul. And they'uz a split place about that big in it, and buddy, they was just a'fillin' it full goin' in and out. I found it in ten minutes. It's still up there."

PLATES 16–18   Lon found a bee tree for us, but we didn't have a chance to cut it. In *Plates 16* and *17,* the arrows show where the hole is (the arrow in *Plate 17* points out a bee entering the hole). In *Plate 18,* Lon and Merle, his grandson, sit at the bottom of the tree watching the hole.

Joe Kilby often left his bait set up overnight. When he got back in the morning, the supply line would be set up. Sometimes he would set up two bait locations—one a short distance from the other. When the lines from each were established, one had simply to follow each to the point where they intersected, and there would be the tree.

When the tree was located, a deep "X", "⚹", or "///" was almost always cut into the bark. Such a mark was understood by the whole community as meaning that that particular tree was already someone's property and thus should not be cut or interfered with. It rarely, if ever, was. As Lawton said, "They ain't supposed to [bother your tree]. Now they hardly ever do, but they's some people'll come in and cut your tree. But if you hack three marks on it, it's supposed t'be your tree. I started t'hack that'n I'uz talkin' about before, and them little devils come out and they just run me wild. I hit that tree three times. By th'time I done it, them woods was full'a bees zippin' around my head, and I took off. I went back t'see about it, but I never did cut that'n.

"I like t'hunt'em. If you ever got started t'huntin'em, you'd be a'huntin'em all th'time. It's somethin' t'do."

The time when the tree was cut depended on several things. If the beekeeper wanted the honey from the tree, he often waited until September to cut it. Then he could rob both honey and bees. This meant, however, that he would have to feed the bees during the winter months.

If he cared only about getting the bees themselves, he would cut the tree in the spring (Elb always cut them in April, and Lawton always cut his when the apple trees started blooming), get the bees, and give them plenty of time to rebuild inside their new home.

On the day the tree was to be cut, the beekeeper would carry the empty gum (and a tub if he wanted the honey) to the site. Then, using a crosscut saw or an axe, he would fell the tree—hole up if possible—wait for the bees to settle—sometimes overnight—and then cut into it. The bees, of course, would go crazy. Lots of smoke from burning rags, pine needles, or dry locust bark helped somewhat, as did protective clothing; but, as Elb said, "You can just figger on gettin' stung."

The method of cutting into the tree varied. Sometimes the tree split open when it fell, and it was easy to open it up even further. At other times, it was more difficult.

Esco Pitts told us his father usually waited a short while until the bees settled somewhat, then cut into the tree with an axe across the grain both two feet above and two feet below the hole. Then he would split with the grain and lift out a four-foot long, several-inch wide slice of trunk. Usually it would be chaotic inside with broken comb, drowned bees, and splintered wood. He would get out what honey he could—splinters, dead bees and all—bring his gum over and set it up on a platform beside the tree, find the queen in the brood chambers, gently pick her up (other bees would immediately gather on that hand), and then shake her off in front of the new gum. Both she and the attendant bees would immediately crawl into it, and the others from the tree would follow shortly.

If it was in the spring, he would then return that night or early the next morning when all the bees were inside, put a sack over the gum or plug up the hole so none could escape, and then carry it home and set it up on its platform. If it was in the fall, he would leave it in the woods until some cold fall morning when the bees were either sluggish or hibernating, and take it home.

Elb McClure used almost exactly the same method, but instead of picking up the queen, he would "herd" her toward the gum. He stressed repeatedly the need to find the queen for "that's th'mother of 'em all," and the other bees would invariably join her in the gum. To hold them there, he always cut out a slice of the brood comb or a large chunk of honey and put it in their new home with them. At "dusky dark" when all the bees were in, he'd plug the hole. The next morning he'd haul it home and, with a little luck, the bees were his.

Farish Kilby, on the other hand, when cutting a tree open, would cut three holes in a straight line about a foot apart each into the hollow, bee-filled area. The smoke was pumped into the upper hole, the honey was removed from the middle hole, and the bees (who came out the lower hole from the brood chamber) were urged into the waiting gum.

Lawton had still another method: "You can guess about how far that holler part goes. Saw it off up fer enough where y'know it ain't holler. Then come back and shave off another little part and another, and you can tell where it goes t'gettin' rotten just a'lookin' at it. When it does, quit there.

"Then go down and start on th'other end and saw up that way till it looks like it's gettin' rotten. You may not have a piece over that long [arm's length], and you may have one eight foot long." Some, he continued, if the piece was short, would simply carry that home and set it up as the gum. There was almost no way to get the honey out, though, when you wanted to rob it. And sometimes the impact of the tree falling made such a mess of the comb inside that it was almost impossible for the bees to rebuild.

SWARMS

Whenever a hive gets overcrowded, some of its bees set out in a "swarm" with a queen to found a new hive. This often happens in

April and May, and if a beekeeper is alert, he can easily add another gum to his holdings.

If the swarm was flying, old-timers in the mountains "settled" it in a number of ways. Some beat on dishpans with wooden spoons or metal forks, or rang cowbells to make them light. Esco Pitts thinks the reason this worked so well is that the queen, he thinks, emits a high-pitched noise to keep all the bees together. The ringing and clashing so confuses them that they settle to regain their bearings. Esco himself has often thrown handfuls of loose dirt in rapid succession both into and in front of a flying swarm. He claims they light and settle immediately.

Sometimes the swarm has already settled in a giant cluster when discovered. Once Esco carried a swarm that had settled on a limb, limb and all, several miles to his gums at home. Lon often carries a burlap sack and a gum to the swarm, spreads out the sack, sets the gum on it, and shakes the bees off their perch so that they land in front of the gum and go in. "Once," he says, "they'uz some settled out yonder, and I just shot th'limb smooth off with a rifle. But they flew back up and settled on th'body of a little ol'simmon tree. I didn't have nothin' but a ol'dull axe up there, and I wanted t'get'em down quick as I could as I'uz afraid they'd leave me. I've lost several swarms. That tree never did bear anyway, so I cut that just to where I could push it, y'know, so it wouldn't fall hard; and part of'em fell off on th'ground. They moved back up though. And I just spread out my cloth, and after while I just took my hand and put my fingers close t'gether, and I just raked'em off by th'handfuls by th'gum."

Lon apparently knows what he's doing. He has about sixty gums, all full, and all of the bees in them have come either from bee trees in the area or swarms that he has captured.

ROBBING

Bees were robbed at various times during the spring and summer. The important thing, of course, was to leave enough honey for the bees to get through the winter. If robbed in late spring, the beekeepers often took almost all the honey that was there since the bees would have the rest of the summer to replace what was taken. In the fall, those robbing the hives would take only a small amount of that honey that was available.

Esco Pitts's father always robbed his bees at the new moon in June. He had a long knife made from the blade of a broken crosscut saw. He would warm the blade in a fire, lift the head of his old-style gums up a crack, slice the comb free of the head with the warmed blade, and then take the head off. Then, taking another knife that had a right-angled crook in the blade's end, he would reach in between the narrow combs, slice them free at the crossed sticks and lift them out.

Farish Kilby sometimes robbed his hives three or four times a season, drawing sixteen to twenty pounds of honey from each hive each season.

Elb McClure maintained that for him, it depended on what kind of hive he had. If the hive was a gum, he'd rob it only once a year, in June, since it took the bees so long to rebuild the comb. Combs in the patent gums, however, could be rebuilt so quickly by the bees that they could be robbed whenever they were full. Elb, for example, would usually rob the early, red honey in June. Then, when the "white honey flow started around June 20," he would have the new super in place to catch the sourwood honey.

The honey from the hives was usually packed, comb and all, into cans or jars. Some was always saved for the family's use as sweetening during the winter. The rest, if a market existed, could be sold to provide a little extra spending money for the family.

ENEMIES

Bees are subject to a host of diseases and natural enemies, all of which mountain people responded to as best they knew how.

Some were harder to deal with than others. Skunks sometimes parked themselves in front of hives and gobbled the bees whole as they flew out. Bears were addicted to the honey. As Esco said, "A bear'll *sure* rob a beehive. Their wool's s'thick a bee can't sting'em." And just recently a bear overturned and destroyed a group of Elb's hives on Patterson Gap. The only remedy they knew for that was to fence in the hives.

Other natural enemies could be dealt with easily by a strong hive. A weak one, however, was in trouble. Ants, bumblebees, or weevils, for example, sometimes got in, attracted by the honey. Perhaps the worst enemy was the wax moth. It laid eggs in the gum walls that produced terribly destructive larvae. Almost the only thing that could be done when that happened was to burn the gum, bees and all, to keep the pest from spreading. If caught early enough, some mountain men either poured scalding water over them or burned sulfur in a saucer inside the gum. It killed the moths and bees both, but at least the gum itself was saved.

Kenny Runion spent some time discussing the latter curse. In his words: "There's what they call a weevil. He's about that long [half inch] and he's a worm. And he gets in there and he goes to work. He webs in there—looks like a spider web.

"Now he commences at th'top and goes down; and when he does that, you just take that gum out and set it afire. He just puts that web over there and th'honey sours. There's a miller causes it. That's a miller—like you see flyin' around a light. He goes in there and lays these eggs and this ol'worm, he'll hatch out. Then he'll go spin that web. And there never have been nothin' that I know of ever invented that would stop that. It's just a dead stand of bees when they hit.

"I've tried everything in th'world t'get shed of'em. I had a stand one time like that, and I took a razor and cut every one a'them weevils out of there. They had already went about half way runnin' th'bees out. And I put th'lid back on and I said, 'By th'way, I've got you'uns now!' In a month I looked back in there and it'uz as white as cotton. Bees done dead. Killed'em.

"And you can scald that gum. You can burn it out. And you put your bees in there and see how it'll be. Them weevils'll be back on th'same bees. Yes, sir. I went back and looked and I said, 'Great goodness!' I just took it out and set it afire. Burnt th'honeybees and all. You can't keep a miller out.

"Now when they get so far, there's another thing—what they call a roach. You know what that is. An old, slick flat bug. That thing'll run whenever you raise that lid. He goes with these weevils. And you can't spray t'kill them things. If y'do, you'll kill your bees. He follers that there worm outfit—them weevils. He may do part a'that webbin'. Keep th'strands straight, y'know.

"Now they generally hit a weak stand a'bees. They can't do much with a big stout stand. But now a weak stand is what they'll hit. And they're gone. That web, hit's stout. And that thing—he's just a little feller—he goes back'erds and for'erds that'a'way from one edge of th'box t'th'other. When he gets that done, he starts toward th'bottom. And when he gets through, them bees are shot. They're just took. There's no way a'gettin' out."

Another problem described by Esco Pitts and Elb McClure was something known as "foul brood"; so named because such a terrible odor escaped when the lid of the gum was raised. The disease, the cause of which was unknown, caused the young bees to die as soon as they emerged from the combs. Esco suspects that it was even carried on from one hive to another by swarms.

Again, the only remedy they knew was destruction. In Elb's words, "Pour y'a little gas on'em and set'em afire."

CONCLUSION

Beyond all the above, there is a multitude of brief hints and thoughts and ideas and superstitions that come from a lifetime of handling bees. A sampling:

—Bees sense when a human is afraid of them and will sting. Never fight or swat when approaching a hive or surrounded by bees. Stay calm and unruffled.

—If stung, don't grasp the stinger and pull it out. Often a poison sac is left behind at the base of the stinger, and grasping it squirts the rest of the poison into the skin. Take the blade of a knife and scrape the stinger out.

—Insecticides kill bees as well as other insects. If corn is sprayed while in bloom, bees visiting the flowers will die.

—Bee venom eases the pain of rheumatism and arthritis. Esco Pitts, when in pain from arthritis, would often get stung on purpose with good results. As he said, "I never had arthritis as long as I fooled wi'bees." Elb McClure agreed.

—Beeswax is perfect for waxing thread for quilting or sewing clothes. And Esco's father, who made shoes, sewed them with flax thread that had been coated with beeswax from their hives.

—The best honey ever produced, according to many we talked to, was that which came from the blossom of the old, now extinct, mountain chestnut.

Along with the hints and thoughts comes a natural awe at the way bees work and thrive. Lawton Brooks: "They've got bees 'at guards; they've got bees 'at carries water, and they got bees 'at makes honey. Then they got bees in'ere 'at cools their honey. They all got certain jobs. And they do their own jobs. One bee won't carry a load a'honey now and do somethin' else next. They got different bees to do what there is t'do to a gum.

"Now that's a funny thing. They got more sense than people think they do. Just like me and you goes on a job, and they put you t'doin' one thing and me another'n, and they're expectin' you t'do your job and not mine. Them bees is th'same way. They've got guards that don't do nothin' but go 'round and 'round that hole there and just watch 'at. If a ant or anything starts in, they grab it. They guard it all th'time. And they'll guard [against] you too. You get around there and they'll pop th'stinger to y'.

"And they've got'em in there that cools th'honey. You can go of a night and you can hear'em just 'wo-o-o-o-o-o-o-o'—them wings just a'goin'. You never heard such a noise at night. Specially of a hot night. And when yer gums get full'a honey, you can go out there and listen of a night and you've never heard such a sound in your life. God A'mighty. 'Wo-o-o-o-o-o'—just like they'uz billions and billions of'em. And they're a'coolin' that honey with them wings when they do that. They're all fannin'.

"And it's funny, such a scent as they've got. They can smell anything from miser'ble fur. You can put out a little bait here fer one across up yonder, and he'll come right down to it.

"They're a sharp thing. You read about'em; they're a awful sharp thing, a bee is."

Such awe is probably half the reason for keeping them in the first place, and it is echoed again and again:

Lon Reid: "I like t'fool with bees. I've worked at these so much that my shoulder'll hurt. I like t'work with'em though."

Esco Pitts: "They're an interesting thing t'study, a bee is."

Elb McClure: "Most interestin' thing you ever seen t'fool with."

We believe them. We're still going to follow someone, someday when he goes out to cut a bee tree. If our photographers don't all get chased off by angry bees, we'll have some photos for you soon. Come with us if you like.

SPRING WILD PLANT FOODS

The forests and fields of the mountains are literally filled with edible leaves, berries, and roots. Many of these have been used by the mountain people for several generations. In pioneer days, the use of wild plants to supplement the daily diet was a necessity, and many of the plants used served as tonics or medicines as well. Nowadays, with the lure of modern food markets, the use of many of the wild plants is a matter of choice, rather than need. Many of our informants say, "My mother, or my aunt, or my grandmother used that but we don't bother gathering it."

There is a revival of interest in the wild plant foods, for many who have migrated to the city are finding pleasure and good eating in returning to the country on occasion and gathering wild greens or berries. Most of the wild plants have a high vitamin and mineral content, and add greatly to the foods essential for good nutrition.

We began gathering information on this topic several years ago. Though it is not a complete handbook or guide to the woods by any means, it does reflect everything we have found so far; and everything included here has been verified and rechecked with our native informants (with the exception of those few recipes marked by an asterisk, which are recipes that came to us second-hand rather than directly from our mountain contacts).

In addition, we have enlisted for this chapter the invaluable aid of Marie Mellinger, a local botanist, who checked all our plant specimens, verified their botanical names and characteristics, tried almost every one of the recipes herself, and helped us compile all this into a chapter that would make some sense and that you might use yourselves. With her help, we've listed the plants according to their botanical order. Mrs. Mellinger also found Carol Ruckdeschel for us, a botanical illustrator, who provided us with the pen-and-ink drawings.

For those of you who intend to try to find and use some of these plants yourselves, we should emphasize that the plants named are those traditionally used here in southern Appalachia. Although they may well exist in your part of the country, you may need to consult a local plant guide to make sure. And we would also urge you to avoid plants that are becoming rare and on the verge of extinction in your areas. There will be no problem with the vast majority of these—dandelion, for example—but in this age of asphalt and summer home developments, edible plants such as Indian cucumber, wild ginger, and wintergreen have suffered terribly.

And we must issue a word of caution. John Evelyn wrote, "How cautious then ought sallet gatherers be, lest they gather leaves of any plant that do them ill." NEVER GATHER A PLANT UNLESS YOU ARE FAMILIAR WITH IT! Some plants are safe to use in small quantities, for example, sheep sorrel (Rumex) and wood sorrel (Oxalis), both rich in vitamin C. Overuse should be avoided because of their high content of oxalic acid. Sometimes one part of a plant will be safe to use, such as the stems of rhubarb, while the leaves must be avoided. Some plants are safe only after cooking.

One mountain man told us that people used to follow the cows in the spring of the year, to see what they would eat. This could be dangerous, for cows are notoriously stupid, and will eat the plants that cause milk-sickness, and such deadly things as wilted cherry leaves.

Most greens and salad plants used are in the mustard family and composite family. Most of the plants of the mustard family used for greens have a most characteristic mustardy smell and sharp pungent taste. Most fruits and berries are in the rose or heath family. Plants to be avoided are those of the parsnip family, for many resemble the deadly cow parsnip, or water hemlock. Someone, sometime, must have experimented, finding the edible plants by trial and possibly fatal error. Now there is no necessity for that. Descriptions, drawings, and photographs of the edible plants all help you to determine their identity.

There is almost nothing better after a long winter (and remember, most greens are best when young and tender) than a mess of dandelion, lamb's quarters, or cress. Absolutely nothing equals a dish of wild strawberries freshly gathered in a sunny meadow, with all the goodness of sun and rain within their tart sweetness. Have fun in the gathering, and good eating!

SPRING TONIC TIME

After a long winter, spring was the time to refresh the spirit and tone up the system with a tonic. The mountain people used teas as beverages and as tonics. They would gather the roots or barks in the proper season, dry them, store them in a dry place, and use them as they wanted them. People used sugar, honey, or syrup to sweeten the teas. Common spring tonics were sassafras, spicebush, and sweet birch.

Lovey Kelso told us, "We had to have sassafras tea, or spicewood, to tone up the blood in spring, but I never cared for either."

Sassafras (*Sassafras albidum*) (family *Lauraceae*)
    (white sassafras, root beer tree, ague tree, saloop)

Sassafras is usually a small tree, growing in clumps, in old fields and at woods' edge. It is one of the first trees to appear on cut-over lands. In the mountains, however, sassafras may grow to sixty feet tall. Twigs and the bark of young trees are bright green, older bark becomes crackled in appearance. Leaves are variable in shape, being oval, mitten-shaped, or three-divided. Leaves, twigs, and bark are all aromatic. The greenish-yellow, fragrant flowers appear in early spring and are

PLATE 19   Sassafras in spring

followed by deep blue berries. The so-called "red sassafras" is identified by some botanists as *Sassafras albidum* variety *molle,* and has soft hairiness on the leaves and twigs. The recipes that follow can be used with either variety.

Twigs, roots, or root bark are used for tea, candy, jelly, and flavorings. Leaves are dried and used to thicken soups. Blossoms are also boiled for tea.

Sassafras has a long history of use as food. It was one of the first woods exported to England where it was sold as a panacea for all ills, guaranteed to cure "quotidian and tertian agues, and lung fevers, to cause good appetite, make sweet a stinking breath, help dropsy, comfort the liver and feeble stomach, good for stomach ulcers, skin troubles, sore eyes, catarrh, dysentery, and gout." There was even a song used to advertise sassafras: "In the spring of the year when the blood is too thick, there is nothing so fine as a sassafras stick. It tones up the liver and strengthens the heart, and to the whole system new life doth impart."

In the mountains sassafras has always been used as a beverage and a tonic. There is an old saying: "Drink sassafras during the month of March, and you won't need a doctor all year." Sassafras was a blood purifier and tonic and a "sweater-outer" of fevers. Red sassafras is best, but as someone said, "Red is hard to get nowadays. The mountains used to be full of it."

Sassafras is best gathered in the spring when the bark "slips" or peels off easily. Florence Brooks told us, "Find a small bush, pull up roots and all, or dig down by the base of a tree and cut off a few sections of root. Wash the roots and scrub until the bark is pink and clean. Peel off the pinkish bark for tea." Mrs. Norton said that "some claim the root is better but you can just use the branches." Big roots should be "pounded to a pulp."

Fanny Lamb said, "Get some sassafras when the leaves are young and tender, just eat leaves and all like you have seen the cows do. Eat leaves and tender twigs and everything."

Alvin Lee wrote, "It's a remedy for colds, and for those down in the dumps from a long winter. It's a spring tonic. 'Course some folks drink it year around." Sassafras is supposed to be used on and after February 14. With golden seal and wild cherry, it makes a very potent tonic.

Sassafras tea: gather old field roots and tender limbs in March. Boil roots and limbs and sweeten with sugar to taste. Or wash roots, beat to a pulp with a hammer. Boil, strain, sweeten, and drink with ice. Or put one cup shredded bark in quart of boiling water. Boil ten to twelve

PLATE 20 Harley Carpenter with strips of sassafras bark for tea.

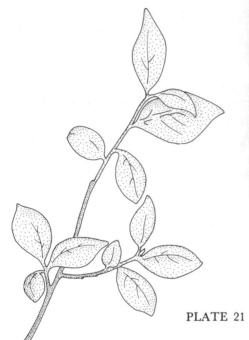

PLATE 21 Spicebush

minutes, strain, sweeten with honey or sugar. Or use one five-inch piece of sassafras root one inch thick. Shave into two quarts water; boil, adding sugar or honey. "Mighty tasty if stirred with a spicewood stick."

Sassafras candy: grate bark, boil, strain, and pour into boiling sugar; then let harden and break into small pieces.

Sassafras jelly: boil two cups strong sassafras tea and one package powdered pectin. Add three cups strained honey. Strain and put in jars. Jelly will thicken slowly.

The leaves of red sassafras make a good addition to candy and icings. Add one teaspoonful of dried and pulverized leaves to a kettle of soup, or add one teaspoon of leaves to a warmed-up stew.

Spicebush (*Lindera benzoin*) (family *Lauraceae*)
(spicewood, feverbush, wild allspice, benjamin bush)

Spicebush is a shrub growing six to sixteen feet high in rich woods, ravine-covered forests, or on damp stream-sides. It has smooth green stems and twigs, with a strong camphor-like smell. The leaves are medium green, paler below, and fall early in autumn. Honey-yellow flowers appear before the leaves in very early spring. In fall, the bush bears bright red, or (rarely) yellow, aromatic berries.

Twigs and bark are used for tea. Berries can be used as a spice in cooking. Spicebush is gathered in March when the bark slips. Mrs. Norton told us, "You've heard tell of spicewood, haven't you? Well, it grows on the branches [streams] and you get it, wash it, and break it up in little pieces. It tastes better than sassafras; it ain't so strong."

Spicewood tea: "Get the twigs in spring and break 'em up and boil 'em and sweeten. A lot of people like that with cracklin' bread" (Mrs. Hershel Keener). Or gather a bundle of spicewood twigs. Cover with water in boiler. Boil fifteen to twenty minutes (or until water has become colored). Strain, sweeten with honey, if desired, or add milk and sugar after boiling. Especially good with fresh pork.

Spicewood seasoning: gather spicewood berries; dry and put in peppermill for seasoning.

Sweet Birch (*Betula lenta*) (family *Corylaceae*)
(black birch, cherry birch)

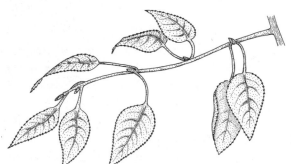

PLATE 22   Sweet birch

The sweet birch is a common tree in the deciduous forests of the mountains, growing to ninety feet in rich ravines, along with tulip poplar and red maple. Bark on young trees is a red-brown, but becomes very crackled on old trees. The slender twigs smell like wintergreen. Catkins appear before the leaves in very early spring. Leaves are oval, tooth-edged, and deep green in color. Small seeds are eaten by many species of birds.

Buds and twigs are favored "nibblers" for hikers in the mountains, and will allay thirst. Twigs and root bark are used for tea, and trees are tapped so sap can be used for sugar or birch beer. At one time, the sweet birch provided oil for much of the wintergreen flavoring used for candy, gum, and medicine. The inner bark is an emergency food if you are lost in the woods, for it is rich in starch and sugar.

Sweet birch bark tastes quite good, and may easily be peeled off to chew like chewing gum.

Sweet birch tea: cover a handful of young twigs with water; boil and strain. Sweeten with sugar or honey. The birch is naturally sweet so needs very little extra sweetening. Good hot or cold. Or bore a hole half-inch thick into tree. Insert a topper or hollow toke of bark; hang a bucket under end of toke to collect sap. Drink plain, hot or cold.

Birch beer: Tap trees when sap is rising. Jug sap and throw in a handful of shelled corn. Nature finishes the job.

Morel (*Morchella esculenta, M. crassipes, M. angusticeps*)
   (sponge mushroom, markel, merkel)

PLATE 23   Morel

The mushroom most commonly gathered in spring, and a delight to eat, is the morel, *Morchella*. There are various signs to tell it is time to go morel hunting, but usually you look for them after a warm rain, when the dark blue violets bloom. A favorite place is under old apple trees.

All are wrinkled and pitted, and a light oak-leaf brown color. Avoid mushrooms having folds instead of pits. True morels are hollow. *Morchella esculenta* is found under old apple or pear trees when oak leaves are mouse-ear size. Look for the fat morel, *M. angusticeps*, in oak, beech, or maple forests when the service berry (*Amelanchier*) is in bloom. *M. crassipes* is found in swampy ground, almost always with jewelweed (*Impatiens*). These mushrooms are especially favored by people of Pennsylvania Dutch descent. They consider them the best of all edible mushrooms and use them in sauces, gravies, and soups. Morels can be dried for winter use. Hang them strung on twine, with a knot between each mushroom to keep them from touching. Hang in a dry place. Before using dried morels, soak in milk to restore freshness, or grind into mushroom powder.

Fried morels: soak in salt water. Slice crossways in rings. Dip in egg and corn meal, and fry at medium low heat. Or put one pint of morels in pan with egg-sized piece of butter. Sprinkle on salt and pepper. When butter is almost absorbed, add fresh butter and enough flour to thicken. Serve on toast or cornbread.

Stuffed morels: soak one-half hour in salt water; parboil lightly. Stuff with finely chopped chicken or cracker crumbs and butter or margarine. Bake at low heat for twenty minutes.

Merkel omelet: let stand in salt water one hour. Chop fine; mix with eggs, salt and pepper, and fry in butter.

Merkel pie: cut in small pieces. Cover bottom of pie dish with thin bits of bacon. Add layer of merkels, salt and pepper; then layer of mashed potatoes. Put in layers of merkels and potatoes, finishing with potatoes on top. Bake one-half hour.

SPRING GREENS

Before the days of vitamin pills and supermarkets, the first warm spring days brought people out of doors to gather the new green leaves of a group of plants known collectively as "potherbs," "greens," "garden sass," or "sallet." All of the wild greens offer much good and nutritious food full of minerals and vitamins. It is necessary to know and recognize these plants at an early stage of growth; they must be gathered while very young and tender, for they become strong and

PLATE 24   Dock (foreground), poke (left rear), and dandelion.

bitter as they increase in size. Pick lots of very tiny leaves as greens "cook down" considerably.

Some of the greens that are especially good are sheep sorrel, dandelion, poke, dock, lamb's quarters, and mustard. How do we know? We've tried them, and they beat any spinach that comes canned or frozen, or even fresh from the garden.

Asparagus (*Asparagus officinale*) (family *Liliaceae*)
(sparrowgrass)

Asparagus is a cultivated vegetable that frequently escapes and runs wild along roadsides or in old fields, or persists around old farm sites. The mature plant looks like a miniature evergreen, with needle-like, finely appressed leaves. Small yellow lily-like blossoms appear on the ends of the branches followed by bright red berries containing the seeds. These seeds in ancient times were sometimes roasted as a coffee substitute.

PLATE 25   Teresa Tyler with asparagus.

The edible part of asparagus is a green-purple, thick shoot, used before the leaves or branches appear. Pliny the Elder urged eating them for good health, and they are equally valuable for good nutrition today.

Asparagus is most flavorsome if cooked immediately after it is gathered. A favored potherb, it should always be cooked in as short a time and with as little water as possible. Add butter, or hard-boiled egg and serve on cornbread, or add vinegar and olive oil, salt and pepper, and put on parsley or chives, if desired.

Wild onion (*Allium cernuum*) (family *Liliaceae*)
     (nodding wild onion)

This is a small plant with grass-like leaves, but with a strong onion odor. It grows in colonies in grassy places, usually in open fields or low spots. This wild onion has a nodding flower head with white, cream, or bright rose-colored flowers. If often forms top bulbs.

Meadow onion (*Allium canadense*)
     (meadow shallot, meadow garlic)

A small plant, the meadow onion measures eight to twenty-four inches high, with flattened, grass-like leaves and star-shaped white flowers. It also forms top bulbs. The whole plant has a strong onion odor. It is found in meadows and open woods.

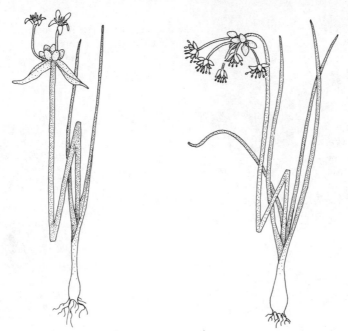

PLATE 26 *Allium canadense* (meadow onion, left) and *Allium cernuum* (wild onion, right).

The young leaves, bulbs, and top bulbs of both of these wild onions are edible, and can be used in the recipes, either separately or combined. Leaves and bulbs can be used to flavor soups, or top bulbs can be pickled.

Wild onion sauce: gather wild onions and cress. Chop fine. Mix with vinegar and a little sugar. Let stand several days before using.

Pickled onions: gather the little onions that form on the flowers. Put in jar and cover with vinegar. Add spoonful of sugar. Let stand several days before using.*

Fried onions: cut wild onions in pieces, dip in flour, fry in fat until brown.

Ramps (*Allium tricoccum*) (family *Liliaceae*)
(wild leeks)

Ramps grow to twelve inches high, with broad, lily-like leaves. They grow from a small, strong-scented bulb. After the leaves die down, stalks of greenish-yellow flowers appear. Ramps grow in rich woods, ravines and coves, usually under maple. There is a great deal

PLATE 27 Lake Stiles took us into the forest in search of ramps, found some, dug them with a hoe he had brought . . .

PLATE 28 . . . and cleaned one off for us to try.

of disagreement as to their tastiness; it seems people either love them or hate them. One gentleman said, "They's not for ladies or those who court them."

Maude Shope said, "Ramps, well to tell you the truth, I've never been where they've growed. They grow out here in these mountains. But I've seen them; they've been brought here, a kind of onion-natured thing, or garlic. A lot of people in the spring of the year, they go crazy for a mess of ramps." And Harv Reid told us, "It is a sort of wild onion. They just grow around in certain places. It is sorta' dark where they grow, like around the little streams where they come down. They grow up just like this little ol'onion they call multi-plier onion. We used to gather them when we used to live back up yonder. They is plenty of them here."

In a discussion on ramps:

Mrs. Norton: "I never could stand'em. I never did gather'em. There was plenty of wild onions in there just a mile off, but you can boil'em and they just nearly make you sick they're so strong. They say ramps is lots worse."

Mr. Pennington: "I've had ramps from North Carolina; a friend brought me some down one time and we ate'em for about a week. I like'em."

Mrs. Norton: "Yeah, lots of people just love'em. They go ramp-hunting every spring."

Mr. Pennington: "You know they have a festival up here for them; it's a big deal up here."

Mrs. Norton: "Everybody goes out in the spring of the year and hunts in these coves for ramps. Now you can smell'em all over here."

Fried ramps: parboil three minutes, drain, throw water away, add more water, cook until tender, drain. Season in frying pan with melted butter. Serve covered with bread crumbs. Or fry in grease along with tuna fish and/or eggs, or add potatoes, salt, pepper for flavor. Clifford Connor says, "Most important, go into solitary in the woods somewheres, stay for two or three weeks, because nobody can stand your breath after you've eat'em."

Ramp soup: cut one pound of beef in small pieces, add salt and water, and boil. Skim. Add ramps, carrots, and potatoes cut in small pieces. Take out meat and eat separately. Put vegetables through sieve and serve hot. Or cook beef or venison and add celery leaves, bay leaves, three cloves, and thirty-six ramps. Take meat out and serve separately. Lift out ramps and serve broth with rice. Or add fried ramps to beef stock. Season with black pepper and serve.

Ramp salad: chop up young leaves into tiny bits. Eat raw, or cook and add vinegar when ready to eat. Or add a little to any salad; or chop fine, parboil, drain and cool, and mix with mayonnaise and serve with trout.

You can also add one-half cup chopped fine to mashed potatoes just before serving.

Wild garlic (*Allium vineale*) (family *Liliaceae*)
　　(wild onion)

Wild garlic is common in fields, along roadsides, and in lawns, where it emits a strong odor when being cut. Leaves are slender, round, and hollow. The wild garlic seldom flowers but when it does

PLATE 29   Kenny Runion pulls a wild garlic and shows the students how to clean it.

it has pale pink or white flowers. Stems usually set top bulbs. This is an evil-smelling weed, troublesome in pastures where it causes the cows to give garlic-flavored milk.

All parts of wild garlic are edible, and said to be very good for you, especially to ward off germs. If used at all, a little bit goes a very long way. Gather tops in winter or very early spring when young and tender.

Seasoning: wild garlic can be used fresh. It is sliced and put in with food, especially meats, while they are cooking. To preserve, dry the bulbs, powder, and store in closed container. Or grind the garlic and mix with salt. Very powerful!

Garlic vinegar: peel garlic bulbs. Stand in one pint vinegar for ten to fourteen days, tightly covered.

Nettles (*Urtica dioica, U. chamaedryoides*) (family *Urticaceae*)

Both species of nettle are very similar, with minor botanical differences such as numbers of stinging hairs. Both are rather coarse plants, growing to three feet tall, in rich woodland coves or along streams and river bottoms. Stems are hollow, ringed with sharp,

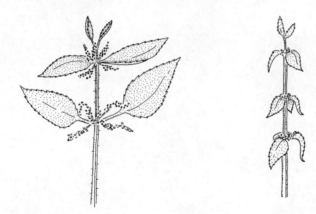

PLATE 30 Nettles: *Urtica dioica* (left) and *Urtica chamaedryoides* (right).

needle-like hairs. Leaves are oval, toothed, and opposite on the stems. Greenish flowers appear in the leaf axils.

The stinging hairs can cause a painful smarting, followed by a red rash. Nettles were once used to cure scurvy, to treat gout and ague, and for the "stings of venemous insects." Nettle greens are rich in vitamins A and C, very high in protein, and make delicious greens. They must be gathered with stout gloves. Repeated cookings, pouring off the water each time, washes away the stinging hairs.

Nettle soup: gather plants in early spring. Cook a long time to destroy the sting. Strain through colander. Add milk, chopped onion, and black pepper. Or pull nettles out of ground. Cut pinkish shoots that grow below surface. Cook in soup. Thicken with butter, flour, and two egg yolks. Season with salt and pepper. Also add shoots to chicken soup.*

Baked nettles: cook nettles a long time. Strain off liquid. Chop fine. Add ground beef, rice, and seasoning. Bake at low heat until firm.

Dock (*Rumex crispa*) (family *Polygonaceae*)
 (pike plant, curled dock, yellow dock, white dock)

Dock is a common weed that grows in fields, yards, and around barns. It is about knee-high, and has leaves six to eight inches long. Leaves have crinkled edges. Flowers appear in a green spike in May and June, followed by seeds that turn dark brown and look like tobacco.

PLATE 31   Dock

The closely related patience dock (*R. patientia*) and the speckled dock (*R. obtusifolius*) are common in waste places. Patience dock has reddish, or red-veined leaves, while speckled dock has narrow, spotted leaves. Swamp dock (*R. verticillatus*) is found in very wet, swampy places. The leaves of all dock species are edible when very young and tender. They are very rich in vitamins A and C. The long yellow roots of dock are used for medicine, boiled into tea and used as a bitter tonic. Dock greens eaten in spring will thin and purify the blood. Cooked with meat, dock leaves are said to make the meat cook more rapidly. Seeds can be munched for a snack.

Greens: leaves of dock are sometimes cooked by themselves, but more often in combination with other leaves, such as horseradish, mustard, or turnip greens. Wash thoroughly. Parboil until leaves turn a lighter green. Pour off water, wash two or three times. Then either fry in hot grease and salt for three to five minutes, or bring to a boil in fresh water, season and serve.

Hot greens on toast: to one pint of cooked dock, add one table-spoon chopped onion, two tablespoons horseradish, and one cup sour cream or a little vinegar. Season with salt and pepper. Serve on toast and top with fried bacon.*

Stewed dock: to several cups of cooked dock, add two cups to-matoes, and onions browned in fat. Simmer and serve. Top with cheese, if desired.

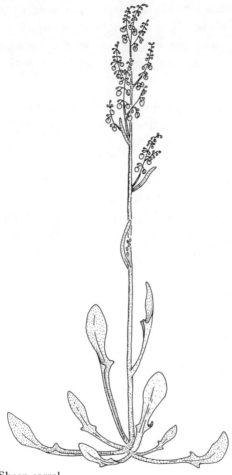

PLATE 32   Sheep sorrel

Dock soup: cook young leaves, drain off water and strain. Add milk, onion, butter, and two tablespoons flour. Cook slowly one-half hour.

Sheep sorrel (*Rumex acetosella*) (family *Polygonaceae*)
      (sour grass, sour dock, redtop, sourweed)

Sheep sorrel is a common weed of fields and roadsides, with reddish stems from six inches to two feet tall, and creeping roots. The leaves are arrow-shaped and often red-tinged. Flowers and seeds appear in reddish spikes. Pale sheep sorrel (*R. hastatulus*) with pale green leaves and pale pink flower heads is common along roadsides in the Piedmont. Sheep sorrel leaves were once used to bind up boils or carbuncles. Leaves are edible and rich in vitamin C but should be used sparingly after they are more than several inches long. Sorrel leaves are used as a potherb, as a sauce, and mixed with other greens in salads.

Sorrel soup: one pound bruised leaves, one-fourth cup butter or margarine, two egg yolks, dash of salt and pepper, one-half cup chopped onion, one cup cream, three cups chicken broth. Chop sorrel and onion together (or ramps, if available), simmer in butter until wilted, add eggs and cream. Bring to a quick boil. Serve.*

Or dice three potatoes and one onion. Fry lightly in fat. Chop one handful of sorrel, lamb's quarters, and creases. Combine. Cover with water, simmer until potatoes are soft. Put through sieve. Add salt, pepper, and milk. Heat and serve.

Or wash sorrel leaves, cover with water, simmer thirty minutes. Strain. Add milk, chopped onion, butter, and flour. Serve hot.

Sorrel omelet: wash and dry young leaves. Chop fine. Add to eggs, with some onion. When omelet is cooked, sprinkle more fresh sorrel leaves on top.*

Sorrel sauce: cut leaves fine. Steep in vinegar, drain, mix with melted butter. Serve on fish, scrambled eggs, or potato salad.

Sorrel stuffing: chop sorrel. Mix with crumbled cornbread, salt and pepper. Stuff large fish. Bake until tender.

Rhubarb (*Rheum rhaponticum*) (family *Polygonaceae*)
    (pieplant)

Rhubarb is a cultivated plant that will persist for years around old house or garden sites. It has ribbed stems, red or bright green in color, topped by large, broad, deep green leaves. Leaves are said to be poisonous. Flowers are white in terminal racemes. The stalks are gathered in early spring and cooked into sauce, or used for pies or conserves. RHUBARB IS INEDIBLE, RAW!

A dried rhubarb root on a string around your neck will ward off the stomach ache.

Sauce: peel the bark off the stalk; cut it up and stew it like applesauce with sugar.

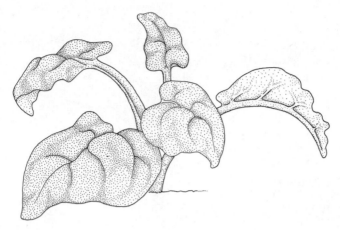

PLATE 33   Rhubarb

Rhubarb pie: cut stalks just above ground. Slice into half-inch pieces. Cook with a little water over low heat in uncovered pan, stirring often, until rhubarb is the consistency of applesauce. Sweeten with honey or syrup. Layer in large flat-bottomed pan with half inch of rhubarb sauce, layer of split biscuits, layer of rhubarb, etc., finishing with layer of biscuits. Chill and eat with milk or cream.

Pan dowdy: combine rhubarb sauce with crumbled, left-over white or yellow cake. Place in pan and bake slowly at low heat. Nuts or raisins can be added.

Turk's delight: gather rhubarb flowers. Soak one-half hour in salt water, drain and dry. Dip in batter and fry in hot fat. Drain. Dip in sugar and eat hot.

Rhubarb jelly: Wash and slice three pounds rhubarb. Add one cup water and bring to a boil. Reduce heat and simmer ten minutes. Strain through cheesecloth. Add three pounds of sugar (about seven cups) and bring to a rolling boil. Add one bottle liquid pectin. Cook, stirring, one more minute. Pour in glasses. Jelly should harden in three to four hours.

Pigweed (*Amaranthus hybridus*) (family *Amaranthaceae*)
    (red-root pigweed, careless weed, soldier weed, wild beets)

Pigweed is an annual, one to eight feet tall, found in waste places everywhere. Like most of our common weeds, it is a native of Europe. Opposite, oval leaves are often tinged with red, and stems and

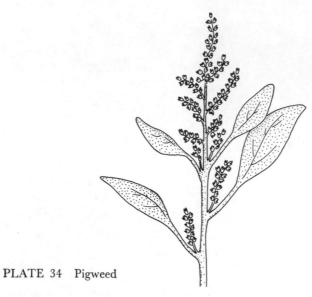

PLATE 34   Pigweed

roots are bright red. Flowers and seeds appear in a green spike. Green
pigweed (*A. viridis*) and spiny amaranth (*A. spinosus*) are also common in waste places. Green pigweed has green stems and roots, and
spiny amaranth has spines at the bases of the leaves. Pigweed has a
very mild flavor. Young leaves of pigweed are delicious cooked alone,
or mixed with stronger mustardy greens. Wash, cook lightly, drain,
and add butter, salt, pepper, and a dash of vinegar. Or cook like
turnip greens with fatback. In ancient times, pigweed seeds were
gathered and cooked into mush, or sprinkled on rolls instead of poppy
seeds.

Lamb's quarters (*Chenopodium album*) (family *Chenopodiaceae*)
    (goosefoot, pigweed, wild spinach, fat-hen, frost-blight, bacon-
    weed, white goosefoot, mealweed, meldweed)

    This is a two-to-six-foot annual weed, a native of Europe, common
in waste places. Stems are succulent and ridged, sometimes red or
purplish in color. Leaves are scalloped and frosted blue-green, or
rarely red-tinged. Flowers are greenish and insignificant.
    Good king henry (*Chenopodium bonus-henricus*), also known
as blitum, smiddy, or markery, is sometimes cultivated as a potherb,
and has become naturalized in many places. It is very similar to
lamb's quarters in appearance, but reddish in color. Leaves are very
mealy.

PLATE 35   Lamb's quarters

Young leaves of lamb's quarters are used as greens, and as someone said, "If they think it's spinach, they think it's good." It is very similar to spinach in texture and taste, and like spinach very rich in iron and potassium. The whole plant can be used if it is under six inches high, or just the leaves picked from older plants. In Europe at one time, seeds were ground into meal, or used on top of rolls.

Lamb's quarter greens: cook in a little water. Drain off water and cover with white sauce made of flour, milk, salt, and pepper. Add lemon and butter, or bacon bits and vinegar, if preferred. Or gather one gallon greens (lamb's quarters and dock), wash and boil for ten minutes. Drain and add one cup water and four tablespoons grease. Cook covered until tender. If preferred, cook with a streak of fat and streak of lean.

Baked lamb's quarters: cook, drain, chop fine. Put in baking dish, top with egg and grated cheese. Cook until cheese is melted.*

Pokeweed (*Phytolacca americana*) (family *Phytolaccaceae*)
   (poke sallet, gorget, pigeonberry, cancer jalap, inkberry, scoke)

Pokeweed is a large, handsome plant, a native American, that grows to eight feet tall in disturbed soil. Stems are large, often red-tinged. The narrow, alternate leaves may be red-tinged. Drooping white flowers are followed by shiny, wine-red berries on bright red stems.

PLATE 36 Poke, young . . .   PLATE 37 Poke, mature

ALTHOUGH THE BERRIES LOOK VERY PRETTY, THEY
ARE SAID TO BE POISONOUS AND SHOULD NOT BE
EATEN. Pokeweed shoots are edible when very young and ten-
der but should be avoided when stems become red and plant is over
a foot high. Berries were once used for ink or dye. ROOTS ARE
ALSO POISONOUS AND SHOULD BE AVOIDED.

Poke shoots resemble asparagus. They are probably eaten more
frequently than any other wild food in the mountain area. Dr.
Neville said to be sure to eat at least one mess of poke each spring. It
was "worth all the medicine you could buy. Don't eat poke sallet
raw; if you do, you'll get poisoned. The antidote is to drink lots of
vinegar which will kill the poison, and eat about a pound of lard. Poke
sallet eaten in the spring revives the blood."

Dr. Dover said, "Anybody that gets sick from eating poke, I'll treat
them free."

Mrs. Carrie Dixon said, "Poke sallet is the best spring tonic you can
find. My ma used to send us young'uns looking for it as soon as the
frogs started croaking in spring."

Poke is rich in iron and vitamin C. Pansey Slappey writes that "it
is rich in iron from the red clay of Georgia, but also has phosphorous
and other minerals."

Mrs. John Hopper doesn't like poke. "It's just not one of those
things that I eat. People'll tell you without a seasoning it'll kill you,
but it won't do it, 'cause Miss Hambidge never eats seasoning on
anything and she eats it. It ain't never killed her. The berries won't

kill ya either but I wouldn't advise ya just to eat'em. I seen a woman whip her little kid because it wet the bed, and they told her to make it eat ten pokeberries every day for ten days, but I don't know what success she had. I'm not whipping anybody and making them eat pokeberries."

Poke greens: collect tender young shoots of poke six to eight inches high, in the spring. Do not cut below surface of ground as root is poisonous. Wash and cook leaves and stems together, parboiling two times (pouring off water each time after boiling a few minutes). Boil in third water until tender, salting to taste. Drain and top with slices of hard-boiled egg. Or put three tablespoons grease in iron fry pan, add salt. Fry greens. You can scramble three eggs in it, or cook with a streak o'fat and streak o'lean. Or add little spring green onions. Or add pepper sauce or apple vinegar.

Poke sallet: put greens in a boiler of cold water; wash two or three times. Drain off all the water. Fry in pan of hot grease. Add half teaspoon of salt. Let cool. Beat two eggs and stir in after greens have cooled. Serve with vinegar or pickle juice.

Fried poke stalks: cut whole poke plant off level with ground when young (four to seven inches high). Wash. Slice like okra. Roll in a mixture of salt, pepper, flour. Fry in grease until brown on outside and tender on inside.

Poke soup: take leaves and stalks when about six inches high. Boil, adding meat gravy and a little corn meal to thicken, until tender.

Poke-tuna roll: spread cooked poke leaves flat; put tuna fish along middle. Roll leaves to enclose the tuna fish.

Poke pickles: collect very young stalks, scrape, remove leaves, and pack in jars. Combine one cup vinegar, half cup sugar, one tablespoon salt, one stick cinnamon, several whole cloves. Boil, pour over poke, and seal.

Pokeberry wine: [While many people believe pokeberries are poisonous, Mrs. Carrie Dixon swears the wine is good medicine for rheumatism.] Gather ripe pokeberries, wash, and place in crock. Cover with cheesecloth and let set until it ferments. Strain off juice and sweeten to taste. Take a spoonful when your rheumatism acts up.

Purslane (*Portulaca oleracea*) (family *Portulacaceae*)
    (pussley, pigweed)

A common weed in gardens or cultivated fields, purslane grows

PLATE 38   Purslane

flat on the ground, with thick radiating stems, and small, pinkish fleshy leaves. Small yellow flowers in the leaf axils open only when the sun is shining. Seeds are in small lidded capsules.

Purslane is rich in vitamin C. The whole plant is edible before flowering, and adds bulk to other greens. Someone said, "It tastes sort of indefinite." Young shoots can be added to soups as a substitute for okra, or pickled. Poultices of purslane were once used for inflammation of the eyes.

Pussley casserole: cook, drain, and chop fine. Add eggs and cracker crumbs, or crumbled cornbread. Bake. Top with grated cheese just before serving. Or put the cooked greens in baking dish with bread crumbs, onion or poke greens, and beaten egg. Bake at low heat.

Fried purslane: cook lightly, drain, chop, and mix with corn meal and beaten egg. Fry in drippings or bacon grease. Or fry bits of ham or salt pork, add vinegar and brown sugar, and simmer. Add chopped pussley. Serve hot.

Pussley salad: wash well and chop fine. Mix with salt, oil, and vinegar. Add cress or peppergrass for sharper flavor. Or add purslane to cress and dandelion, serve with vinegar and chopped hard-boiled egg.

Pickled pussley: cook wild onions with vinegar and one-quarter cup ground mustard seed. Simmer, strain, pour over pussley tips.

Pussley dumplings: chop fine. Mix with biscuit dough, salt, pepper, and butter. Make into balls, drop into soup or stew.

Chickweed (*Stellaria media*) (family *Caryophyllaceae*)
    (birdseed, starweed, starwort, winterweed, satinflower, tongue grass)

PLATE 39   Chickweed

Chickweed is a naturalized native of Europe, grows all year, and can be gathered in the winter months. It is an annual growing to eight inches high, with weak stems, and succulent, bright green leaves. Flowers are small, white, and star-shaped.

The whole plant is edible before flowering, and a good source of vitamin C in winter time. It can be used as a potherb, or in salads, or in soup instead of okra. It is good mixed with sheep sorrel, or peppergrass, or more sharply flavored plants. It was once believed to be a medicine to heal and soothe cancers.

The closely related mouse-ear (*Cerastium*) is also edible, but less flavorsome as the whole plant is covered with woolly hairs.

Creamed chickweed: parboil, strain, chop fine. Reheat with milk, butter, salt, and pepper.

Peppergrass (*Lepidium virginicum*) (family *Cruciferae*)
    (bird's pepper, poor man's pepper, tongue grass)

PLATE 40   Peppergrass

Peppergrass is an annual weed, naturalized from Europe, and common in waste places. It grows to twenty inches tall with branched stems and small leaves. Tiny white flowers are followed by flat, peppery seed capsules. Young leaves are used in greens or raw in salads, and the seeds as a substitute for pepper.

Garden cress, or tongue grass (*Lepidium sativum*), is sometimes planted in gardens, and escapes or runs wild. It has bright green, very peppery leaves, and round flat peppery pods. Seeds of both cresses can be ground and mixed with vinegar and flour as a substitute for mustard.

Greens: peppergrass is good with poke salad. It is not quite as tender as poke salad, and must be cooked five to seven minutes, when used in combination. Or mix it with other greens such as dandelions, lamb's quarters, mouse-ear (chickweed), dock, or wild lettuce. Just cook peppergrass like cresses or turnip greens.

PLATE 41   Shepherd's purse

PLATE 42   Wild radish

Peppergrass sauce: mix seeds with vinegar and a little salt. Use as a sauce on fish.

Pepper substitute: "You know the wild pepper plant? It blooms and has seed on it, just like little seeds in the pod of peppers, and you use that for seasoning." Use in salads or on tomatoes (Mrs. Mann Norton).

Shepherd's purse (*Capsella bursa-pastoris*) (family *Cruciferae*)
>   (mother's heart, caseweed, St. James wort, poor man's pepper, topwort, clapper)

Shepherd's purse is another common annual weed, growing to eighteen inches high. Flowers are white and followed by flat, heart-shaped seed capsules.

The young leaves can be cooked and added to salads; or the seeds used in salads, or ground and mixed with vinegar as a substitute for mustard. Use in the same manner as peppergrass in any of the same recipes.

Juice of shepherd's purse on a piece of cotton will stop a nosebleed.

Wild radish (*Raphanus rhaphanistrum*) (family *Cruciferae*)

Wild radish grows to five feet high and is found in waste places. Leaves are coarsely toothed. Flowers are white or pale violet or yellowish with darker veins. Seeds are in a jointed pod.

Young leaves are used in salads with cooked greens, or in meat sauce. Young pods are cut up in salads.

Mustards

All of the mustards can be lumped together in terms of edibility, and any of them can be used in any of the recipes. Cultivated collards, turnip greens, and cultivated mustard varieties can escape or naturalize and grow wild in old garden spots. All these members of the mustard family are characterized by having flowers with four cross-like petals, and a smarting taste. All of the mustards contain vitamins A, B, B-2, and C, and minerals very important to health. Leaves of all should be gathered when plants are very young and tender. Their pungent odor will identify the plants at once. Most of them are best if first cooking water is drained off. They are good "blood purifiers" and much-favored spring tonics.

PLATE 43   Kenny Runion with wild mustard.

White mustard (*Brassica hirta*) (family *Cruciferae*)
   (pale mustard, kedlick)

An erect, winter annual, occurring in cultivated fields and low places, white mustard is a native of Europe naturalized in this country. Leaves are rough, hairy, and greatly dissected. Pale yellow flowers are followed by bristly seed pods. Rich in vitamin C and sulfur, young leaves are used in salads, greens, and in sandwiches, and seeds ground up for mustard or mustard sauce.

Black mustard (*Brassica nigra*)
   (warlock)

This is another native of Europe, very weedy in cultivated fields. Leaves are large and very coarse, and strongly flavored. Clusters of four-petaled flowers are bright yellow. Leaves are edible when very young and tender. Seeds, when mature, are ground for prepared mustard. In olden days, black mustard was used in love potions to overcome lassitude in females.

Indian mustard (*Brassica juncea*)
   (Chinese mustard)

This mustard is very similar to white mustard, but the leaves are smooth and covered with a bloom. Flowers are bright yellow. The leaves are edible when young.

Charlock (*Brassica kaber*)
    (field mustard, kedluck, shellick, hevuck, field kale)

An annual weed, charlock grows to two feet high and is naturalized in waste places. Leaves are yellow-green, rough, coarsely toothed, and are very strong smelling. Bright yellow flowers are followed by hairy pods. The leaves are edible and rich in vitamin C.

Greens: parboil greens, drain, and cook again. When you cook mustard, the secret is to add some sugar to a big pot of greens to take out the bitterness. Add chopped onion, salt and pepper, or bits of fatback and grease. Another favorite recipe for mustard is to take three large ham hocks; two chopped medium onions; one quart water; three pounds greens; three tablespoons bacon fat; one teaspoon salt; one-fourth teaspoon red pepper flakes; and freshly ground black pepper. Boil the hocks and onions slowly for over an hour. Chop greens in small pieces; add to ham hocks; add seasonings; cover and simmer one hour until greens are tender. Then serve with cornbread.

Mustard buds: gather buds just before they open. Cook, drain, serve with sauce made of prepared mustard and mayonnaise. (Tastes like broccoli.)

Prepared mustard: grind mature mustard seeds; mix with flour, water, and vinegar. Serve with meat or fish.

Flavoring: add tiny young mustard leaves to sandwiches, or put in deviled eggs.

Mustard flowers: gather newly opened blooms. Cook in boiling water. Remove from heat, add butter or bacon fat.

Mustard-ramp soup: clean and wash leaves. Heat one quart milk, almost to boiling. Meanwhile melt bacon fat in skillet, add chopped ramps, cook until brown. Add salt, pepper, flour, and mustard. Cook five minutes. Add milk and simmer.

Water cress (*Nasturtium officinale*) (family *Cruciferae*)

Water cress is a perennial, introduced from Europe and naturalized in cold, limestone-based streams. Stems grow to ten inches and recline weakly. The dark green leaves are small and scalloped and very pungent to taste or smell; they are often used raw in salads to give a

PLATE 44 Dean Beasley with a clump of water cress she has just picked out of a nearby stream for noonday salad.

spicy, tangy flavor. Small white flowers appear in April and May. The whole plant is rich in iron and vitamins A, B, and C, and is prized for salads, sandwiches, or soups. Raw cress, chopped fine, mixed with mayonnaise and served on whole wheat bread, makes delicious sandwiches.

Horseradish (*Armoracia rusticana*) (family *Cruciferae*)

Horseradish, native to Europe, is planted in gardens, but it also persists around old house sites, or naturalizes in rich ground. It has large, rather crinkled roots, somewhat like those of dock, but pungently flavored and odorous. Flowers appear in midsummer on high branched stalks. The deep, white, very pungent roots are edible, and supposed to be an excellent spring tonic. They were once used for dyspepsia, rheumatism, scurvy, and hoarseness, made into a tea of one teaspoon ground roots to one cup of boiling water. Eating horseradish is a spur to digestion. It is also supposed to expel kidney stones.

Some people say the young leaves are edible; others say that they are not good to eat. They are extremely pungent and could probably be used only when very young and tender.

PLATE 45   Horseradish

Relish: dig roots in early spring. Grate and cover with vinegar. A little salt and pepper may be added, or a touch of sugar. Beets may be added for color. Dill seeds or honey may be added if desired.

Horseradish sauce: three tablespoons butter, one tablespoon flour, one and one-half cups boiling beef stock and horseradish to taste are mixed together until smooth. Serve over meat or fish.

Mix very young leaves with purslane or pigweed. The liquid makes good pot liquor with corn pone.

Food preservation: "It looks quite a bit like mustard, but the roots are as hot as any red pepper you ever saw. You know, we didn't have a lot of refrigerators to keep things in back then. They'd get it and wash it and slice it up and put it in pickles to keep them from having that mold that comes over the top of them when they set" (Mrs. Selvin Hopper).

Creases (*Barbarea verna*) (family *Cruciferae*)
    (dry land cress, upland cress, herb barbara, St. Barbara's cress, bitter cress, poor man's cabbage, scurvy grass, yellow rocket, rugula)

PLATE 46   Jake Waldroop with a clump of young creases from his cornfield.

   This cress grows to two feet high in damp ground, along streams, and in old fields. It is a common weed naturalized from Europe. Dark green, divided, basal leaves appear in late fall, and can be gathered all winter. In late spring the plant has a stalk of bright yellow, four-petaled flowers. Seed pods are one inch long, slender and slightly curved.

Winter cress (*Barbarea vulgaris*) is very similar in appearance, with large, more deeply cut leaves.

This plant was named for St. Barbara's Day, December 4, for one could gather the green leaves from December on. The leaves are sharp-tasting, very like water cress, and can be cooked or used raw in salads. The Barbareas are sometimes cultivated under the name "upland cress."

Mrs. Norton told us, "They bloom yeller all over a cornfield, that's creases. They have the same seed on them as mustard." The root is a tiny bulb but Ethel Corn says, "That part ain't fit to eat."

Greens: pick, wash, and boil in water with piece of fat meat until tender, cooking slowly. Or parboil them. Take out of water and put in frying pan with grease. Fry five minutes with a little salt. Pick more greens than you think you need, as they shrink. Serve with vinegar or dill pickles, or cook and season as you would spinach. When greens are older, cook in two waters, throwing cooking water away. Aunt Arie Carpenter likes to put in a piece of middlin' meat in the morning to boil. Boil that for at least two hours, or as long as it takes to get it tender. Take the grease off the meat; add it to a pot of water and bring to a boil. Add cleaned creases and boil for thirty minutes. Mustard may be done the same way.

Cress salad: toss together lightly, two cups finely cut creases, one-fourth teaspoon salt, one tablespoon salad oil, one tablespoon salad oil, one tablespoon vinegar, one tablespoon French dressing. Or chop young leaves, mix with sliced radishes, oil, and vinegar.

Sandwiches: add chopped cress leaves and peppergrass seeds to sandwiches.

Fried creases: fry fatback meat in heavy pot, preferably old black dinner pot. Have creases washed. Take meat out, leaving grease in pot. Shake out creases and drop in hot grease, mixing thoroughly with grease. Add just enough water to keep from sticking to pot. Add salt, as desired, and cook about twenty minutes, or until tender. Stir often.

Cooked buds: gather buds of cress. Pour boiling water over buds. Let stand half minute. Drain. Cover with fresh boiling water. Boil three minutes. Drain. Season with salt, pepper, and butter. (Tastes like broccoli.)

Spring cress (*Cardamine hirsuta*) (family *Cruciferae*)

Spring cress is found growing in all damp places, with a purplish stem, and many basal, finely cut leaves. The stem is topped with a cluster of very small, white, four-petaled flowers. Seed pods are very slender.

PLATE 47   Spring cress

Bitter cress (*Cardamine pensylvanica*) is very similar, and is found in wet places, often growing in the water.

Bulbous cress (*Cardamine bulbosa*) also grows in wet places, with long round leaves and white flowers. It grows from a bulb-like root.

The foliage of all the Cardamine cresses can be used in greens or salads, and can be substituted in any recipe using creases. Leaves are especially good raw in salads.

Toothwort (*Dentaria diphylla*) (family *Cruciferae*)
   (turkey mustard, turkey salad, turkey cress, crinkleroot, pepper-
   root)

A small plant with creeping stems, toothwort has three-parted leaves veined with white. Stems and underside of leaves may be purple. The white, four-petaled flowers grow in a cluster and are very showy. Both the leaves and the bulbous roots are edible. Turkey mus-

PLATE 48   Turkey mustard

tard grows in rich woodlands, deciduous coves, and along mountain streams.

Dentaria laciniata, crowfoot or turkeyfoot, has leaves divided into narrow segments. This grows in colonies in rich woodlands.

Peeled roots or young leaves add flavoring to salads, but a very little goes a long way. "You talk about something strong, it's strong. It grows on branches and tastes like tame mustard. It can be used as a tonic for old people in the spring," said Harley Carpenter.

"It's a right tasty little weed," said Delia Williams. "It will remind you of mustard quite a bit."

Greens: pick leaves. Cut up in bite-size pieces and wash thoroughly. Place in bowl, pour hot grease over them, salt and serve. A quart basket of leaves will make two or three servings. If desired, pour a little vinegar over them. Or cut up the leaves and put bacon gravy over them and salt.

Brook lettuce (*Saxifraga micranthidifolia*) (family *Saxifragaceae*)
(branch lettuce, St. Peter's cabbage)

PLATE 49   Lawton Brooks with brook lettuce.

Brook lettuce is found in very wet seepage slopes, springheads, on rocks in streams or on stream banks. It has four-to-six-inch dark green, succulent leaves that are irregularly scalloped on the edges and slightly fuzzy. Young leaves are used in salads.

Myrtle Lamb told us, "It is kind of a long-leaf thing, and grows in the wettest damp places, where moss grows. As it gets older, it gets a red cast to it."

Mrs. Norton said, "It's kind of sticky when its gets old, so you have to get it when it's real young."

Salad: Myrtle Lamb likes to take brook lettuce and cut it like tame lettuce, and put onions in it, and hot grease on it. Then sprinkle salt and pepper over it. Or just pour hot grease over it so that it wilts. It can be eaten like wild mustard or turkey mustard.

Blue violet (*Viola papilionacea*) (family *Violaceae*)
   (johnny-jump-up)

The blue violet is common in meadows, lawns, and damp, open woodlands. It grows to eight inches tall, with heart-shaped, deep green leaves, and long-stemmed, deep blue flowers. There is a cream-colored form, and the common form with blue and white flowers, called "confederate violet" and naturalized around many home and farm sites.

Violet leaves and flowers are both edible. The blue wood violet (*Viola cucullata*) is very similar, with darker blue flowers, and found in rich woodlands and wet places along streams. Leaves and flowers of

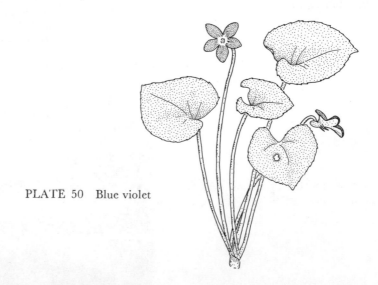

PLATE 50   Blue violet

both species can be used in any recipes. Leaves are very rich in vitamins A and C. Many people mentioned mixing them in with other greens such as wild mustards, creases, or lamb's quarters. Leaves and flowers are also used in tea, and in a medicine supposed to induce sleep, and to "comfort and strengthen the heart."

Violet flowers have long been used in fancy confections, candied or sugared. In the last century, a gift of candied violets was a "message of love."

Greens: wash and cut up leaves of blue violets. Cook with a little water twelve minutes. Serve butter over them, or cook with bacon or fatback. Or mix violet leaves with dandelion greens or milkweed shoots and top with bacon and chopped-up hard-boiled eggs. Or mix with lamb's quarters or pokeweed and cook as above.

Violet salad: add chopped violets to other spring greens for salad, or use alone with vinegar and bacon.

Violet jelly: cook violet flowers with boiling water. Strain, add sugar, pectin, and juice of half a lemon. Simmer until it jells.*

Sugared violets: cook two cups sugar, one-half cup water, a dash of cream of tartar. Stir until sugar grains. Dip fresh violet blossoms (free from stems) and place on platter to dry.

Violet syrup: cover violet blossoms with water. Let stand two days. Strain. Cook with honey and juice of lemon. Stir well. Bring to boil. Put in jars and seal. Good for colds or coughs.

Milkweed (*Asclepias syriaca*) (family *Asclepiadaceae*)
  (silkweed, cottonweed)

Milkweed is a stout perennial, growing in colonies, to five feet tall. It has large, oval, opposite leaves, and stems and leaves exude a milky juice. It is found in dry fields and on roadsides. Rough pods contain silky-winged seeds. Young shoots are edible when very young, before leaves unfold. Young pods can be used as a substitute for okra, and flowers are cooked into sugar.

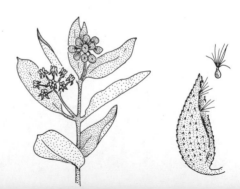

PLATE 51   Milkweed

In Tennessee and Kentucky, milkweed is considered a tonic, greens "good for what ails you."

Fried milkweed: cut shoots in small pieces, boil fifteen minutes in salted water. Drain. Fry in small amount of fat. Add in eggs, salt and pepper, and cheese, if desired.

Milkweed soup: shoots—gather shoots while young and tender. Do not gather after July. Wash, cook, drain. Add more water, rice, bacon drippings, salt, pepper, or wild onions. Cook over a slow fire until done. Pods—boil a hambone, add young milkweed pods cut in small pieces, several wild onions or ramps, and a handful of rice. Cook slowly. Add salt and pepper before serving.

Cut milkweed shoots in small pieces. Drain. Serve on toast, topped with hard-boiled egg and bread crumbs. Add onion, if desired. Or add bacon or fatback; or top with cheese sauce.

Milkweed greens: cook one pound very young stalks in water with salt and butter, covered for ten minutes. Drain. Add more butter and chopped wild onions.

Ground Hog Plantain (*Prunella vulgaris*) (family *Laviatae*)
   (selfheal, square-weed, heal-all)

A common, naturalized plant, found everywhere along paths and in waste places. Stems are square with green leaves, and spikes of purplish flowers. Mrs. Ethel Corn said, "It looks sort of like rabbit plantain, only the leaves are darker green and bunch up more." She said to put them in and boil them with a piece of hog meat.

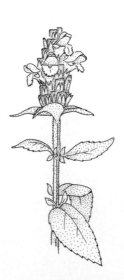

PLATE 52   Ground hog plantain

Mrs. Norton said, "There is a wild ground hog mustard, they call it, and it grows little and low on the ground, and it's got a round leaf. It has a bloom comes up, it's a purple flower. But you have to get it real quick, for if you don't, it's gone." When we asked, she said, "How do you fix it? Just cook it with your wild mustard or anything. We always used the sheep sorrel to make it sour like vinegar. Didn't have much vinegar then, you know, so they used that."

PLATE 53   Broadleaf plantain

Broadleaf Plantain (*Plantago major*) (family *Plantaginaceae*)
  (dooryard weed, great plantain, Englishman's foot, devil's shoe-
  string, hen plant, birdseed, waybread, rabbit plantain)

Plantain is a very common dooryard weed, a native of Europe, and naturalized in this country. It has large round, basal leaves and a spike of greenish flowers and seeds. The leaves are edible when young, rich in calcium, and make excellent greens, especially when added to mustard.

English plantain, or ribwort (*Plantago lanceolata*), is known in the mountains as white plantain. Leaves can also be eaten, but leaves of rabbit plantain are preferred.

Plantains are rich in vitamins A and C.

Greens: pick leaves. Pull off stems, parboil fifteen minutes. Drain and rinse. Boil again in fresh water with fat meat until tender. Or fry in a small amount of grease five to ten minutes after boiling and draining. Or, Mrs. Norton suggests, "You take blackberry leaves, wild plantain leaves, and wild mustard, and cook them together and see what you get."

Salad: cook plantain leaves, chopped fine, in salt water. Add a pinch of sugar. Mix with other greens in salads. Or, "Cut it up and eat it like lettuce. Pour hot grease on it," says Mrs. Tom McDowell.

Corn salad (*Valerianella radiate*) (family *Valerianaceae*)
     (lamb's lettuce)

A common plant of early spring, with opposite, narrow, light green leaves and heads of small white flowers. *Valerianella locusta* is similar, except leaf edges are wavy, and flowers are a very pale blue. Young leaves are edible "used any way you'd use lettuce."

Valerian tea, a mild sedative, is made by boiling leaves in water. Let them stand twelve hours to draw, then strain and drink sparingly.

Chicory (*Cichorium intybus*) (family *Compositae*)
     (succory, blue-sailors, bunk)

Chicory is naturalized from Europe and found along roadsides. It has dandelion-like basal leaves, and stems that exude a milky juice.

PLATE 55   Chicory

PLATE 54   Corn salad

Bright blue flowers open every morning and close again by noon.

Young leaves are eaten like lettuce or endive, and roots are also edible, often added to coffee or used as a coffee substitute. Leaves are extremely high in vitamins A and G and in calcium.

Chicory with mustard sauce: cook young leaves until tender. Cover with a sauce made of one-fourth cup sugar, one-half teaspoon salt, two egg yolks, one cup scalded milk, two tablespoons vinegar, one tablespoon mustard. Blend until thick in a double boiler. Serve over the drained chicory.*

Panned chicory: melt two tablespoons fat and add chopped chicory greens. Cover and steam for fifteen minutes. Add one tablespoon flour, a small amount of cream, salt and pepper. Let simmer five minutes more.

Chicory coffee: wash and peel roots. Grind and roast in oven. Add to, or use instead of, coffee.

Wild lettuce (*Lactuca graminifolia*) (family *Compositae*)

PLATE 56   Ral Henslee with wild lettuce.

Wild lettuce is a tall plant, found in open woods, and in damp places. Leaves are dentate, usually a bright blue-green color, and very smooth to the touch. Small, dandelion-like flowers open briefly in bright weather. They may be blue or whitish or pale violet. *Lactuca hirsuta* and *Lactuca canadensis* are very similar, differing slightly in leaf shapes, or in flower color, for flowers may be violet, white, or yellow. Tall lettuce (*Lactuca floridana*) grows to six feet tall, with a hollow, leafy stem, and white or pale blue flowers. Leaves of all species of wild lettuce are edible when young and tender. Every species will emit a milky juice when leaves or stems are broken.

Wild lettuce must be gathered and eaten in the early spring when the plants are young, as the older plants get tough and wormy. Ethel Corn told us, "It grows mostly in poor ground where it ain't tender. When you get it, it has a flavor like tame lettuce, only it don't look much like it, and it's a whole lot better."

Mrs. Keener said, "It's slick when it first comes up, the leaves are. And it don't resemble lettuce at all, but it tastes like it. It's a little bit tougher. You find it all along fence rows, or anywhere. It comes up in early spring, that's when you get it; when it grows up tall, it's too tough."

Mrs. Norton said, "You break a leaf off and if it's kinda milky, that's wild lettuce."

Salad: cut up greens and wash. Cut green onions in it and pour hot grease over it. Also good with vinegar, oil, and salt. Mrs. Irene Gray says, "It sure did taste good!" Try frying bacon until crisp and crumbly. Add brown sugar and vinegar and pour over chopped wild lettuce leaves. For extra flavor, add chickweed or mustard.

Greens: pick young leaves (before they are eight inches high). Wash, and cook with very little water. Add butter, salt, pepper, and bits of bacon and bacon grease.

Dandelion (*Taraxacum officinale*) (family *Compositae*)
    (blowball, peasant's clock, cankerroot, down-head, yellow gowan, witches' gowan, milk-witch)

Dandelions are common on lawns and in fields and along roadsides. Stems grow three to fourteen inches and are hollow. Dark green, dentate basal leaves emit a milky juice as they get old. The golden yellow flowers are one to two inches across. Dandelion is a native of Europe, naturalized all over America.

Edible parts include the young leaves, the flower buds, and the

PLATE 57   A clump of dandelion.

scraped roots. Dandelion greens are very rich in iron and vitamin C. Frederic Klees says a Dutchman has to eat dandelion salad on Maundy Thursday to stay healthy all the year. Some authorities say the roots are inedible, and all traces of root must be cut away when preparing greens for cooking. Gather much more than you think you need, for they cook down. Some cooks add a pinch of soda when cooking dandelions. Mrs. Norton says, "You can use dandelion in tossed salads, the kind with feathery leaves; it makes what you call a wild salad."

Greens: gather when young, wash, and boil about twenty minutes in water with fatback added; or drain and fry in grease. Season with salt and pepper. Or after cooking, drain off water, and heat with small amount of vinegar. Add small chunks of fried salt pork, heat, and eat. Or cook lightly in salted water. Drain. Mix milk, butter, one egg, and vinegar together. Cook to just a boil and pour over greens.

Hot greens on toast: cook greens slightly; drain. Add bits of fried bacon and bacon grease. Serve over toast.

Dandelion bud omelet: gather one cup dandelion buds before flower color shows. Fry buds in dab of butter until they pop. Add four eggs, salt and pepper. Top with raw leaves, finely cut before serving.

Salad: wash and pat dry one-half cup unopened flower buds and one bunch tender leaves. Fry two strips bacon, toss buds in hot bacon grease until they open. Drain. Mix with leaves and bacon; add three tablespoons oil and vinegar. Or wash young dandelion leaves and chop fine. Add salt, vinegar, and olive oil. When mixed, add one tomato cut in pieces, or cooked lima beans. Toss. Or mix chopped dandelion with chopped ramps or wild onion; top with bacon, bacon fat, and vinegar.

Green drink: cook chickweed and dandelion, each alone. Put through a sieve, add cider vinegar, and drink for a tonic.

Coffee substitute: gather dandelion roots. Peel. Roast until dark brown; grind. Use as substitute for real coffee.

Dandelion wine: pour one gallon boiling water over one gallon dandelion flowers. Let stand until blossoms rise (twenty-four to forty-eight hours). Strain into stone jar. Add juices of four lemons and four oranges, and four pounds of sugar, plus one yeast cake. Stir four or five times a day until it stops fermenting. Keep well covered. In two weeks, strain, bottle and cork tightly.

Tall coneflower (*Rudbeckia laciniata*) (family *Compositae*)
    (cochan, coach-ann)

Tall coneflower grows in wet places, with finely dissected, smooth green leaves, and later in the season, tall stems of yellow, daisy-like flower heads with green, cone-shaped centers. This is a close relative of the brown-eyed susan, and the wild ancestor of the garden golden globe.

Leaves are edible when young and tender. Mrs. Ethel Corn told us, "You find it along branch banks. It looks like golden globe flowers, and it will run up when it goes to seed. You have to watch when picking it, for the wild parsnip looks similar to it, only it's more whitish-leaved than that."

Mrs. Hershel Keener said, "There's a plant that grows along this branch called coachie-ann; now I don't know how you spell it, and it's got such an odor when it's cooking. You can boil it just like you do poke, and season it real good, but I don't like it."

Greens: pick when tender and parboil until tender. Wash until water is clear, squeeze water out. Put in pan with grease and fry.

PLATE 58   Kenny Runion with cochan from a neighbor's cornfield.

Or after cooking, chop fine and add salt and margarine and top with chopped boiled eggs.

RECIPES FOR MIXED GREENS

Many different kinds of greens can be combined in salads, or in recipes for cooked greens. Any mild-flavored green can be combined with the sharper tasting mustards and cresses, and add bulk.

Mixed greens:

Get together a mess of poke, dandelion, lamb's quarters, violet leaves, and sour dock, and mix together. Cook, drain, and season with bits of fried salt pork, and a little vinegar.

(or)

"When I was small, my people used to pick wild mustard, narrow-leaf dock, and lamb's quarters. Mix it all together and fry in grease," says Mrs. Al Webster.

(or)

Parboil poke, then cook with ham hock like turnip greens. Dandelions are done the same way. Thistle, wild lettuce, whiteweed, narrow- and broad-leafed dock, pussley, wild violet leaves, wild mustard are all cooked like turnip or mustard greens.

Canned greens:

Most wild sallets can be canned. Mix mustard and wild turnip greens, or buff sallet and mustard mixed, or with creases. Fix and precook until tender. Put in jars, add water, seal, and cook thirty minutes in pressure cooker.

Mixed green salad:

Take equal parts of dandelion, shepherd's purse, peppergrass, curly dock, poke shoots, and sorrel. Chop fine. Add wild onion to taste. (Poke shoots must be cooked first.) Make a dressing of oil and vinegar, and flavor with garlic, mustard, salt, and pepper. Serve on a bed of wild dock or lettuce leaves.
     (or)
Toss one cup chopped cress, one cup chopped dandelion, one-fourth cup ramps or wild onions together with French dressing.
     (or)
Three slices bacon, cut fine. Three tablespoons vinegar, dash of salt, one cup chopped cress, one cup dandelions, one cup wild lettuce. Fry bacon, add vinegar and salt, pour over greens, and toss.
     (or)
Mix water cress, sorrel, purslane, wild onion, and dandelion leaves, chopped fine. Fry bacon bits, pour bacon bits, grease, and vinegar over greens.
     (or)
Wash chopped sorrel, sour dock, dandelion. Put in pan with diced onions or ramps, pour dressing of vinegar, sugar, salt, pepper, and bacon over greens, and toss.

Wild strawberry (*Fragaria virginiana*) (family *Rosaceae*)

Wild strawberries grow in colonies, or beds, in open, sunny places, in old fields, along roadsides, or damp meadows. Stems are three to eight inches high, with three divided fuzzy leaves. Small, white flowers

PLATE 59   Wild strawberries

appear in early spring, followed by the delicately flavored, red strawberries.

Strawberries are rich in iron and in vitamin C. They have a
wonderfully tart goodness for "eating out of hand," or they can be
used in jams, jellies, pies, preserves, desserts, cakes, or ice cream.
Some people are allergic to strawberries and may get a rash from
eating them. The berries are small and it takes a lot of work to ac-
cumulate enough for a pie, or a batch of jam, but they are well worth
the effort, and taste better for it. Someone said, "If it is four o'clock
by the time you get your clothes on, it will be light enough to pick
strawberries."

Strawberry leaves are used to make a delicately flavored tea, said
to be good for bladder infections.

Jam: put a quart of berries in a pot, add a cup of sugar, and
bring to a boil, stirring gently. Boil three minutes, add another cup
of sugar and boil three more minutes; then add a final cup of sugar,
skim off foam and put in jars and seal. Or boil for five minutes
one cup strawberries and one teaspoon vinegar. Add one cup sugar
and boil fifteen minutes; skim while hot. Set aside to cool all day or
overnight before putting in jars. Or cook four pounds of berries in
porcelain kettle. Boil juice first. Add two pounds sugar, and boil
again. Skim and put in jars.

Wild strawberry preserves: To a quart of strawberries, add one cup
of sugar and three tablespoons water. Boil slowly fifteen minutes. Let
stand overnight. Next morning, bring to boiling point and pour in
jars while hot. Or dissolve nine cups sugar in one cup water, add

eight cups berries and boil fifteen minutes. Skim; seal in jars. Or boil equal weight berries and water for ten minutes. Set overnight. Pour in shallow pans, cover with glass. Set in sunlight until it thickens, then pour in jars.

Canned strawberries: fill hot jars two-thirds full with berries. Make a syrup of one quart of water, one cup sugar, and fill jars. Berries are not cooked.

Strawberry leather: mash ripe berries to pulp, spread on platters. When dry, dust with sugar and roll up like a jelly cake into pieces. Pack into clean jars.

Strawberry gelatin: use one package red fruit gelatin, one cup boiling water, one pint wild strawberries. Dissolve gelatin in boiling water, add berries, chill. Serve with cream, and garnish with whole berries.

Strawberry mallow: use two cups wild strawberries, one-half cup sugar, few grains salt, half pound marshmallows cut up, one cup cream. Mix together and chill. Top with whole berries.

Strawberry pie: use three cups flour, one cup lard, one teaspoon salt, one egg, five tablespoons cold water, one tablespoon vinegar, strawberry filling. Sift flour, mix with lard, salt, cold water, and vinegar. Mix well and roll out dough; put in greased pie pan. Bake fifteen minutes. Make filling of one cup crushed strawberries, one-half cup sugar, two tablespoons cornstarch, and one cup water. Cook into a syrup. Fill pie crust with fresh strawberries, pour syrup over top and serve. Or use one quart berries, one and one-half cups sugar, one tablespoon flour, one-fourth pound butter. Cook berries a few minutes, put in deep pie pan or dish, cover with a short biscuit crust, dot with butter, and bake until crust is brown. Or put a layer of strawberries in a pan, sprinkle with sugar, then a layer of biscuit dough; keep layering until almost to top of pan. Bake until top is brown.

Strawberries and pieplant (rhubarb): cook pieplant with sugar; just before it is done, add a cup of strawberries, let cool and eat.

Strawberry leaf greens: the leaves of wild strawberries were sometimes eaten along with blackberry leaves, fried in grease, or boiled in water with fatback added.

HAPPY DOWDLE

Thad Dowdle got his nick-name because, "I was always in a good humor, I reckon . . . You just as well laugh as to cry 'cause nobody don't care nohow. That cryin' don't do no good. Don't do *no* good."

Even at eighty-six years of age, "Happy" hasn't slowed down much. Neither has his wife. And his memory is as vivid and as clear as that of a young man.

The oldest of seven children, he went to school, but "They all got a better education than I ever got, fer I was always havin' t'do somethin' around home. I had no chance t'go t'school. I finished th'fourth grade, but that was all." While he was a boy, he traded horses and cattle to make a little money, but when he was eighteen years old he went to the logging camps in Washington state, stayed there four years, came home and married and went back, bought a house and became a foreman at one of the logging camps near Hamilton, Washington. "They built a cabin for us t'live in up there, and we was gettin' along fine. I had about twenty of th'prettiest white-legged chickens you ever saw nearly. And we lived just above th'plant."

But just when things seemed to be going smoothly, trouble hit. A friend tipped him off that another man was visiting his wife pretty regularly. That was the only way he would have ever found out, for he could only get home on Saturday nights. The rest of the week he was tied up at the camps.

On his next trip home, he told his wife that he would not be coming home the following Saturday night as they had to work overtime at the camp. The following Saturday, he eased up to the house. "About ten or eleven o'clock in th'night, I come in and th'doors is all locked. So I commenced a'callin' her and I couldn't get no answer. I had a dinin' room and a kitchen off from th'main part of th'buildin', and I heard a racket start through there. I got t'th'kitchen door, but I didn't get there *quite* till there was a man run out. And I shot at him three times and he jumped th'fence. I didn't hit him, I guess.

"So I wadn't goin' t'live with a person like that. Me a'workin' like a dog and a'bringin' in th'livin' there and tryin' t'give her th'best of things she wanted. And I said, 'Well, now. What'a you think I am anyhow?'

"She says, 'Well, that there boy just come t'see me.'

"I says, 'Well, he's been a'comin' pretty regular. I've been hearin' of it.' And I says, 'If you think more of him than you do of me, I'll take th'baby and I'll go back to North Carolina.'

"She says, 'Well, you can't do that.'

"I says, 'Well, we'll see whether I can't or not.' I said, 'Now you picked you another home. Now hunt it out and see which end is better.' I says, 'Me and you is *done,* woman—right now!'"

He sold the house. When she balked at letting him take their three-year-old daughter, he said, "I've laid off and bit my tongue and ever'thing else t'keep from shootin' you, but I will if you just fool with me this mornin'." She packed the child's clothes, he gave her two hundred dollars, and he and his daughter returned to North Carolina where he began trading out of his own barn in Franklin.

We talked to Happy and Sarah—his second wife—literally for hours, on three separate interviews. Here is some of what they told us, excerpted from ninety-two pages of transcript. The story begins with his return to these mountains after years of travel.

GREG STRICKLAND

Happy: They's a lots a'things about th'city I don't like. You're hemmed up in little bitty huts, and it takes a pretty good moneyed man t'buy a nice home in th'city. Out here, you can turn your kids loose, and they can play around here with nothin' t'bother'em, but if they'uz in th'city, they couldn't.

Sarah: They ain't much place they can play in th'city, except in their back yard, and they have t'fence'em in *then* t'keep'em corralled. I wouldn't know anything about th'city, and *I'm* proud I don't.

Happy: Yeah. I've always liked th'country life. You've got a little ol'place special of your own. You can do whatever y'want'a do there. You ain't got t'run t'nobody and ask'em what t'do and all this stuff.

Sarah: I think you got more freedom in th'country than you would have in th'city. And then when y'went out on your porch, y'ain't a'thinkin' they's somebody watchin'y' all th'time. I wouldn't like that. And they're just simply friendlier in th'country. Them city people don't even ask you to come in. They don't have time t'fool with y'. If you want anything, you have t'tell'em what y'want right at their door; and if they don't have time, they'll say, "Well, come back some other time," or so on.

Happy: Yeah. People are friendly and nice—that is, people who have got and stayed up here. And it's a better place t'grow up in. Now you take when I was boy, somebody'd make us a little home-made wagon t'pull around. Maybe have y'a goat and put to it. We'd have th'best time around here with that goat and wagon, and th'neighborhood boys'd come, and they'd have th'best time. And we'd make pop guns out'a elders and play with them. We'd make sling-shots—take and cut out a piece a'leather, y'know, and cut holes in it and put rubber to it. Shoot with it around th'barn or at home.

And there was money enough t'get along. I had a uncle over here in th'Patton Settlement. If y'had a few dollars, you could raise you some yearlings and stuff. I'd gather up a bunch like that—go t'a neighbor's house and if he had one t'sell, I'd buy it if I could, y'know. And I'd bring it in and put'em together, and my uncle would come over there and buy th'whole bunch, and I'd make a little on it.

And I'd help him drive'em over across th'gap yonder inta his settlement. Yeah, I done that when I was just a boy. When I had'em together, I'd send word to'im. There wadn't no telephones then, y'know.

And my father trained me up t'handle all kind of stock. When I was seven'r'eight year old, I'd take care of'em. He trained me that. And if I didn't do what I was told when I was just a chunk of a boy, he'd cut th'limb off. That's what they called it. Th'apple trees up there had lots'a limbs. He'd jerk off one of'em and take it to me.

He trained me t'be honest. Their word was their bond at that time, and y'didn't have t'put up no bond when y'went t'borry money. It was your name. Your neighbor would loan y'money and just take your word. But y'can't do that now. He said, "Thad, if you die in

PLATE 60

PLATE 61

PLATE 62

PLATE 63

th'poor house, try t'be honest. Do what you promise anybody, and don't try t'defraud nobody." I had a good ol'daddy. And mother too. Shore did.

He taught me how t'plow, how t'take care of horses, how t'harness'em and how t'work'em. And we kept cows and things there. We'd go and help mother milk, y'know, and stuff like that. He learned us all that stuff.

He had a country store there, m'father did. Good long while. And after I got big enough, we had a covered wagon, and we'd go around th'country here and go t'people's houses and buy their chickens, put'em in this wagon, and th'next mornin' go out t'Talullah Falls t'sell'em. Then we'd bring back a load a'goods for our store, y'see, when we left. We made lots'a trips like that.

We bought a hunderd and some turkeys once. A man down in Georgia come up and wanted'em. Wanted these turkeys. We drove them turkeys in th'road from here t'Talullah Falls. They'd go t'jumpin' up on th'fences and be goin' t'roost, and we had t'stop there. Yeah—that's true. Took two days, y'know, with th'turkeys. They'd get tired, y'know, and we'd go slow. But they'd all stay t'gether nearly. We never lost a turkey. We started down th'road, and a turkey'd run t'th'side, y'know, and he'd run back. We had a covered wagon. It kept them kind'a t'gether, y'know. Drove along behind'em all th'time.

After I got big enough t'drive a team—oh, I'uz fourteen'r'fifteen years old—he'd let me drive. After I got onta th'roads'n'ever'thing, and Daddy got kind'a down with th'rheumatism, he said t'me one mornin', he says, "Thad? You reckon you can make it t'th'Falls'n'-back?"

I said, "Yeah, I can make it."

Said, "You afraid t'camp out?" (We had t'camp out one night on th'road, y'know.)

I said, "No, I'm not afraid t'camp out." I had a big bulldog there at home. I said, "I'll take him with me, and th'first person that'll tackle me, he'll eat him up." And he would too.

So I made a trip one day, and got over there to th'Falls, and they'uz some men all around there—had a big dog with'em—and they kept their eye on me. I happened t'notice'em, y'know. I was waitin' there t'check up th'stuff I'd took there t'sell this man, y'know.

And they'uz a'watchin' me close.

Along in th'evenin' I figured on comin' back up th'road about seven'r'eight miles that night. They was lots'a pretty campin' places all up th'creek there, y'know. So I come on after I'd went t'th'depot and got what I had t'get.

I come on, and they was a road come this'away, and they'uz a little branch come down here, and on th'other side a'this branch there was a pretty campin' place. We'd generally camp there if we'uz t'happen t'be there at th'right time. So I drove out.

I watered m'mules and fed'em and built me up a little fire and fried me some eggs and sausage and stuff fer supper, and made me some coffee. And I'uz sittin' there eatin'—had m'stuff sittin' on m'lunch box. And here come that big dog out in th'road that I saw at th'Falls. And I thinks t'm'self, that's th'dog I saw down there with them men. Might'a been a man'r'two held up along through there, but I didn't know.

But anyhow, they wadn't but a few minutes an'at dog come back trottin' along 'at road, and directly I heard th'brush a'kinda cracklin' in there. They was a lot a'dead ivy bushes in there that had fell, and you'd step on one of'em and they'd crack like a whip, y'know. And I heard one of'em fall.

I had a good pistol. I said, "Who are y'there. What'r y'doin' around here anyhow?"

And nobody said a word, and nobody moved. And I think if 'at dog comes back by here again, I'll shoot th'son-of-a-gun. And I hadn't no more got it out'a m'holster and here he come. I shot at'im, and when I shot at'im, they went t'tearing that ivy *down* a'gettin' out'a there. And I held th'dern pistol runnin' in th'ivy right atter'em.

Well, they was a big oak tree 'bout like that'un right down there. I stood behind that oak, an' m'pistol, till daylight. I never went back t'no wagon t'go t'sleep, ner nothin' else. I just stood there behind that, an' I knowed if they come t'm'camp, I'd kill one of'em'r'all of'em. But they never come back.

Next mornin' pretty early I fed m'mules and hooked'em up and got m'breakfast and give them their breakfast and got out. I got home a little bit early, but I made it back home. So I told Daddy what'd happened, and he said, "It's a wonder they didn't kill you." He says, "I ain't gonna let you go n'more."

I said, "Yeah you are too. I'm just as able t'take it as you are. I'm satisfied I am." I said, "I made it this time. I'll make it again."

"Well," he said, "if that's th'way you feel about it, all right."

So I took th'wagon there all th'time after that.

It was a hard livin', but it was good.

Sarah: They had corn shuckin's a lot. That was one thing was good. They'd gather their corn in and pile it up in a big pile—a hundred'r'two hundred bushels. And they'd gather ever'thing that could be thought of t'eat, and you went and ate all you wanted.

Th'wealthiest family in this community, they had a big water bucket full'a grape wine made out of white grapes, and a dipper in it. And my brother—he took a couple a'dipper fulls and fell down and skint both of his knees. He got high. And they walked two'r'three miles t'these corn shuckin's, and when this'un'd get through with his corn, he'd go on to somewhere else for th'next night.

Happy: They'd help one another, y'see.

Sarah: And they'd split rails—they'd help split rails t'build fences. And all th'women'ud be in th'house a'cookin' dinner and quiltin'. We'd have th'best times!

They'd visit each other and take their knittin', y'know. They'd have t'knit their stockings and socks. Lord, I learned t'knit and I wish I never had! My mother'd make me sit down ever' night. I knit till I couldn't hardly get my breath.

Happy: They used t'love one another. It ain't like it used t'be at all.

Sarah: They'd be eight in th'field a'hoein' at one time.

Happy: Now it's just so many different things that's come ahead of'em. People are enjoyin' themselves a'ridin' in th'old car'r'airplane'r somethin' like that, y'see. They'd rather be in that as t'be associated with you'r'him'r'me.

Sarah: Now they don't have time t'have a conversation even on th'streets of Franklin. And that's where I see most of my friends and schoolmates. They never come t'see'y'r'nothin', y'know. But they used to. They did. But anymore, they've given it up. Not unless you fix up a big dinner and invite'em t'come.

Happy: They loved one another better, yeah.

Sarah: You could turn your old cows out in th'woods. You had t'go two'r'three miles t'get'em of a evenin' t'bring'em in t'milk'em.

Happy: We used t'get out at Christmas time and get a bunch a'bells and ten'r'fifteen crowds, y'know, and go from house t'house sere-nadin'. Oh, we'd shoot guns and holler and ring these bells an' ever'-thing else. We had a better time then they do now. Th'young folks don't have t'fun and places t'go that we used t'have. Un-uh. Wonder why it does thataway?

Sarah: Probably 'cause there's lots more that's got more money than say, we young'uns, and it's went t'their heads where they won't hardly speak t'y' no more. I'll tell 'y', honey; they didn't have no car t'run out and get away from home.

Happy: I had a aunt that lived right across th'river from us—from where I'uz raised up there—and she'd come maybe once a week—ever' two weeks anyhow—and stay all day with Mother, y'know; and they'd talk and crochet and sit around and crochet and talk. Talk about this'n'that'n'th'other.

Sarah: Yeah. They'd knit and embroider.

Happy: Yeah. And they'd have a good time. But people don't do that no more.

Sarah: And they used t'get out and 'sang [ginseng] hunt. They'd get lots'a 'sang. Big crops. Forty dollars a hunderd. And, honey, in th'fall of th'year we used t'go out and pick chestnuts up to buy our winter shoes with. And they'uz about a dollar and a half, a dollar and seventy-five cent a bushel.

Happy: Sometimes y'got a dollar. I've bought'em fer a dollar a hunderd.

Sarah: And then y'could buy you a pair of shoes fer a dollar, and you could buy you enough cloth t'make you a dress fer a quarter. All that stuff now is three'n'four dollars.

Happy: People didn't have ever'thing in th'world. They wasn't a'cravin', y'know. But now, you take folks now; you take a family maybe down here that's got plenty a'money, and they can stare back and kinda side-swarp'y'. Well, such folks as that I don't pay no 'tention to. I just go ahead. I've always been a poor boy, and I don't owe no-body nothin', and I get along pretty good anyhow. So if they want'a 'sociate, they know it; and if they don't, why just forget 'em. That's th'only way t'do it.

Sarah: We had a neighbor over last week t'help us plant our 'taters.

Happy: Oh, yeah. Now that's th'kind'a neighbors y'used t'have. But they're old-timers kinda like us, y'know. Oh you got neighbors here that'll come and see us, and if we needed'em fer anything, they're right here; but they ain't like they used t'be so much. They don't come t'see whether you *do* need'em or not. That makes a big difference.

Sarah: I remember when my daddy had steers, and he'd hitch'em t'th'wagon and go off on Sunday and stay all day t'see somebody—have dinner with'em. And I remember very well havin' t'cross a great big creek, and them old steers'ud just a'howl over there. My daddy plowed th'steers, and when th'ground got too wet t'plow, used t'go fishin'.

Happy: Yeah. If it rained and y'couldn't work on th'crops, why they'd go fishin', or t'see their neighbors.

Sarah: Seem like they had more time then we do now.

Happy: Maybe they didn't value their time so much.

[After Happy returned from the West, he bought his own piece of land, remarried, and raised a son himself much in the same way his father had raised him.] Way it happened, they'uz an old gentleman come and bought this lot here, and he started t'put up a little house. Well, he put up a little shack. Just this room was just about what he had up. An he'uz an ol'bach, y'know—never had been married, and his folks all lived over yonder on th'other branch. He got homesick and wanted t'sell it t'me.

So he come in one night'when I come in. I talked with'im awhile. Said, "I'll tell y'what I come out here for, Mr. Dowdle."

I said, "What's that?"

Said, "I want t'sell you my little place out there."

Well, I'uz hardly able t'buy that and run m'business too. But we talked on a little bit, and I asked him then what he wanted for it. Said he wanted eight hunderd dollars. "Well," I said, "I wouldn't be interested."

So he went on back t'his cabin, and he stayed gone a couple a'nights. When I come in again, he was at th'house again. We talked there t'gether, and he said, "Uh—have y'thought any more about buyin' m'place?"

I said, "No, I never give it a thought."

He said, "I want eight hunderd dollars fer it."

I said, "I wouldn't be interested at all."

And he went off *that* time. And th'next night, here he was out there again. He said, "Uh, you never did make me no offer."

I said, "Well, I always make a man an offer, and if he can't take it, it don't make me mad."

"Well," he said, "what would y'do?"

I said, "I'll give you six hunderd dollars fer yer place."

He says, "That's awful little."

"Well," I says, "it ain't much. No, but six hunderd dollars—you don't just roll it up ever'where."

"Well," he said, "I'm gonna go back over yonder t'm'folks. When could we make th'deed?"

I said, "Make th'deed? Right in th'mornin' if y'want to. I've got yer money. When you make th'deed, yer money's ready."

"Well," he said, "we'll just go t'town in th'mornin' then and get it all done."

I said, "Suits me fine." So I moved out here; sold off part of it, and that fer way more money than I give fer th'whole thing. So I've still got this, and I'm gonna keep it long as I'm here.

I used t'get pretty high with whiskey. That was th'worst habit I had. Well, I got t'goin' with m'wife here, and she hates that worse than anything in th'world. So she said, "I don't ever aim t'go with you again if you don't quit that drinkin'."

I'd get about half high and go down in m'old Model T and ask her t'go fer a ride, and she'd say, "No, sir."

So I'd just go on, and ever' time I'd see her, I'd wave and go on like that. Well, after we'uz married, she said, "What made you do thataway?"

"Well, I'uz just a'tryin' you out t'see what you thought of me."

Then I had a son. M'boy said, "Dad, I smell liquor on you!" I had 'bout a pint and had just took a drink'r'two. I got it up and shook it good. I said, "If I'm gonna raise that boy, that'll be a poor way t'bring him up. I'm done!" So I took that bottle and poured it out right then. I've never touched it since, and that's been thirty years.

I've heard folks say that they couldn't quit this and they couldn't quit that. They can quit anything they've got a ambition t'do. And when m'boy was goin' t'growin' up, I decided that wadn't a good thing t'bring out in front a'him. And fer th'respect a'him.

It was hard t'do. Whenever you'd walk around two'r'three and smell that liquor on'em, y'know, it'd kind a'run up in yer blood. There was a barn down yonder, and sometimes they'd come in there with their bottles t'drink, y'know; and they'd ever'one offer me. And I said, "Boys, I've done drunk my part a'that!"

And it wadn't long till they quit comin' down there a'drinkin' s'much. I wanted my boy raised right. An' we had good times. Did things in th'country we couldn't do in th'city. Here at one time I had five'r'six horses. My brother-in-law had a wagon up at th'old farm, and he said I could use it if I wanted to. I didn't have a wagon, and I went up there and got it and brought it down here; and didn't we put a bow-frame on it, mother? I split out somethin' and made some bows and put a sheet over it; and I had a good saddle and bridles and halters and stuff fer m'horses, and me and m'boy took off stoppin' and a'tradin' along.

We didn't get fer th'first day—oh, fifteen'r'twenty mile—and we camped out ever'night we was gone. And th'first night we'uz camped out, I got tickled—he'uz just a chunk of a boy.

Sarah: He come back and he was dirt and hog hairs and ever'thing else! He hadn't had a bath in a week!

Happy: Only place was th'river, and it'uz too cold there.

Sarah: When they come back I got th'washpot down yonder, and I had a big pot of hot water and he went and took a good bath and cleaned his clothes. He never turned over all night. He was wore out!

Happy: Anyway, we slept on th'road ever' night; and th'first night we was gone, why her and her nephew come down there t'see how fer we got.

Sarah: When we'd go, we'd take milk and different things t'eat, y'know; and I enjoyed it, and my boy did too.

Happy: We made pretty good th'next day, and got gone a pretty good little piece. Well, I got t'stoppin' at each house along seein' if they wanted t'swap horses'r'buy one, y'know. And that kills time.

So we went along—got along pretty good. And we come one night t'where this guy had a little store. Had a pretty good barn. I decided t'shove m'horses in his barn, and we stayed around there about nearly two days. Spread out our bed in that barn loft in that hay.

And I traded a little there—traded two'r'three times—and we went on from there t'Murphy. They had a sale barn at Murphy, y'know. Ever'body kinda gathered in there a certain day, and I swapped fer a pair a'young mules. And they never had been worked too much, so I took one of'em; led'im with a brake horse. And I said, "Thad, we'll break these mules goin' home—one at a time."

So, yep, he agreed t'that, and we got along all right. We come out over t'th'top of th'mountain 'tween here and Clayton—and he'd been a'ridin' and a'leadin' up to here. An' he said, "Daddy, let me drive th'wagon awhile. I'm gettin' tired a'ridin' this horse."

I said, "All right, son." I had one a'them young mules in with a gentle horse, y'know, t'th'wagon. I said, "Son, don't turn them lines loose. You hold them lines. And watch th'brake on yer wagon."

All right. We got on down there, and sure enough, when we went t'pass the little bridge, th'mule run away with it! Yee-day! He'uz goin' s'hard I couldn't catch up with'im. So finally he got'em steered into th'bank down there and stopped'em.

I said, "Son, are y'a'hurtin'?"

He said, "No, but I'm scared t'death!" He said, "You'll drive'em from here on home!"

I said, "All right, son. That'll be all right."

So I brought'em on down here and turned'em in my pasture here, and a fella saw these young mules. And he had a pretty good pair a'horses. He come up here and looked at th'mules and made me an offer. I went and looked at his horses and we traded.

We took'em down there, and I told'im they wadn't well broke. He ought t've had sense enough t'see that 'cause they was skittish, y'know. But he took'em down there and hooked'em up first thing t'his wagon, and they run away and tore his wagon all t'pieces.

Th'next time I saw him in town he was so mad at me he didn't know what t'say. I said, "Well, you ain't got no right t'be mad at me. I *told* you these mules wadn't thoroughly broke."

"Oh yeah! But you said you'd worked'em."

"I said I worked'em both, but one of'em run away with my boy. You got t'break them mules."

And he was mad at me fer a long bit, but he got over it.

But I quit that drinkin' business on account of my son. It was just trouble anyway.

I'uz just thinkin' this mornin' about a man that just died. Al! right. This man had put that scar on my head there. That was a bad'un. Sure was a pretty'un!

We'd all went off t'th'Georgia line and got us some liquor, and we'uz comin' back and somethin' happened t'th'old car. We'uz afraid th'law'd overtake us, y'see, and we got out and hid th'whiskey up there so we could go back maybe th'next day and get it.

So this feller come on down there with his car, and he tried t'crank it and he couldn't crank it. It was just a old crank-starter car. And after we hid th'stuff and come on back down there, I said, "What in th'world's th'matter?"

He said, "What do you care!" And he jerked out that there cranker and he lamed me right in th'head. Boy, th'blood flew. That knocked me out, and that's exactly what left that scar there. That's exactly what done it. Bein' out with drunks and that's where it winds up.

And I hadn't bothered that feller, and since that he's begged'n'ever'-thing else. And ever' time we'd go t'church, he'd foller. Made a church member. Finally, ever' time he'd meet me, he'd shake hands and pat me on th'shoulder. And of course you've got t'forgive a man when he does that, y'know. And I did. We got along pretty good from then on. Never had n'more trouble.

But if I'd had my pistol that night, I guess I'd a'shot him. I had a good'un at home, but I just happened not t'have it on me or I would'a been in trouble.

But I hope that th'old feller's gone t'heaven. It's been many years now that he's been livin' like a man ought to. I think he had anyway. Don't hear no different.

[At this point, we turned the discussion toward a "good" life and what that consists of.] Well, I ought'n t'bother you, nor do no harm again' you. I ought'a be a'tryin' t'lift you up instead a'tryin' t'down you worse'n'worse. That ain't right. That ain't right, no sir. And you're not supposed t'get out and get pretty well fixed, y'know, and get t'feelin' that you're better'n anybody else. That ain't so. They's poor people that ain't got a dime'll maybe get further t'heaven than we will—if they live right.

If people'ud get more normal and not get high up on one another and treat one another right and love one another and pray for each other, that'd be th'best thing could happen. But it'll never be, I'm afraid. I'm afraid that'll never be. I don't think it could happen.

See, th'Lord made this world, and he put ever'thin' in it. And he'uz a'lookin' fer us all t'go to Him when we leave here and our spirit goes back and our body goes t'th'dust. And at Judgment Day, why we'll be there with him.

Sarah: That's what I'm tickled of and pleased of. Salvation's free. You don't have t'pay your way in.

Happy: Th'trouble t'day is churches ain't like they used t'be. I've heard preachers get up in th'pulpit and preach, and I didn't believe a word they'uz a'tellin'. Yeah. And I had some t'get up and preach, and *they* preached th'Bible.

If a man's a'goin' t'go out and preach, he'd better preach that Bible. If he don't, th'Lord won't carry him through.

Now that's a good point of people havin' a good education now. If you read that Bible pretty regular, and you know th'Bible pretty good, when th'pastor gets up there on Sunday mornin' and goes t'preachin' some stuff that ain't in th'Bible, you know it don't you? Yeah, you know it right there. Then y'lose confidence in that man. I *know* that. I've set with'em.

Y'see, that Bible was wrote on th'wall. That was wrote fer t'stand forever. Y'can't take nothin' from it ner add nothin' to it. It just means what it says in there, and that's all. Yeah. No, sir. That's it.

Sarah: They's a lot a'difference in church than what it used t'be.

They used t'have th'spirit of th'Lord t'make us shout. Y'hardly ever see anybody shout anymore.

Happy: Yeah. They lived closer t'th'Lord than people's a'doin' today. Th'Devil's a'gettin' ahead of th'Master. Th'Devil's a'gettin' along fast, y'know; and th'Master ain't a'gettin' all these folks t'do like they used t'do. That's my way a'lookin' at it. I think th'biggest thing in th'world a'sellin' more people t'th'Devil, mebbe, is this pride. Thinkin', "Well, I'm better'n you are. I don't want nothin' t'do with you." All such stuff as that. Now that's th'foolishest thing 'at anybody can have in their mind.

They ain't nobody up and down this country here that will tell you that they ever met me but what I'd speak to'em and treat'em nice. And if they wadn't so good, well, that'uz all right. Go right ahead anyway; speak to'em. Treat'em nice and go on. I ain't a'gonna brag about it, but I've got friends all over this country. Good friends too. I've got friends that if I had t'send to'em tonight, they'd be here. That's th'only way t'live, see? Only way. Yes, sir.

Sarah: Folks should treat each other th'way we like t'be treated.

Happy: That's th'way we ought'a do.

Sarah: Some people'r'ashamed they're Christians, and some aren't.

Happy: You can go t'people's houses now and visit'em on Sunday night'r'somethin', and they'll never say nothin' 'bout havin' prayer before y'leave.

Sarah: And go t'th'table and never thank th'Lord fer what He gives us.

Happy: I've had folks t'come in here and visit me—we try t'read a little Bible every night and have a little prayer and thank th'Lord fer takin' care of us through th'day—and they's many people that's left that all off. And some of'em laugh at us fer that. That's ignorance. That's ignorance right up here [tapping his head].

Sarah: We used t'have prayer meetin's in th'home, y'know, and have th'best time singin' old-timey songs!

Happy: We used t'have family prayers. Daddy'd read a little scripture and Mother'd pray. I was real young then. Dad was a pretty good reader. He went through high school. He was more educated.

Sarah: My mother taught me about th'Bible, and that they was a hell and a heaven. Lots a'people argue with y'that they ain't no hell. Today they say th'hell is here on earth.

Happy: That's what a lot of'em tryin' t'claim. Now what about people like that? Boys, it won't do! Accordin' t'my way a'lookin' at it, it just won't do.

People believed on th'Bible more then. They appreciated th'Bible more'n they do now. Yes, sir. They's lots a'folks come in here and I'd ask'em t'have prayer'r'somethin'. Or t'read some Bible t'me. They'd glance up, and mebbe they didn't want t'do it. See, now that's th'way it is.

We had some neighbors—they're not Christian—and I asked'em if either one of'em prayed. They said, "No."

I said, "Well, we have prayer. If you want t'stay fer prayer, it's about bed time. I'm gonna pray. I'm gonna read some scriptures here and we're gonna have a prayer." And they didn't come back fer th'longest time. They never come back now. Well, that's all right. If that's all they know now and all they can learn, why, I ain't responsible. I tried t'show'em what'uz right there, and I tried t'tell'em.

Never go t'disputin' that Bible, folks. You're doing th'*wrong* thing. That'uz made fer us t'go by.

Sarah: It's like plantin' by th'signs.

Happy: Well, shore!

Sarah: If you plant corn on th'new of th'moon, it grows straight up—way high up—and th'ear grows straight up too. Plant on th'full of th'moon and it won't get very high.

Happy: That's real good.

Sarah: Plant your Irish potatoes on th'new of th'moon and they lay right on top of th'ground. When they make themselves they'll be sun dry. Now on th'full of th'moon, they go down deeper.

And th'good Lord said in th'Bible that that moon and stars was set up there for th'signs of th'seasons.

Happy: That's what it's fer.

Sarah: And y'know, that man's face in th'moon is th'man who burnt th'brush pile on Sunday, and they had that face cut in th'moon. I've heard that since I was a little girl. *That's* old-timey stuff, now.

[What do you think about the men going to the moon? Did you ever think you would see that in your lifetime?] Happy: Well, no I didn't. And I don't know yet that they went. There's a lot a'red tape t'that, son.

Sarah: Well, we *did* see them up there pickin' up rocks anyway.

Happy: Ah! They can get out on some big high mountain and pick up rocks anywhere, but I'll never believe they went t'th'moon. God didn't intend that at all. Y'can make a picture a'most anything, but is it true? That's it. I don't believe. No. I don't believe it. That's a money scheme, don't y'see?

Sarah: Well, there y'are. They spent millions a'dollars t'go t'th'moon where they's little children starvin' t'death fer something t'eat. They must not a'realized that. 'Course now, naturally, we don't know what it is t'be hungry. All my life we've had plenty t'eat. But not much t'spare.

Happy: Yep. We didn't need anything.

Sarah: My mother worked in th'fields same as th'house. Our old cook maid too. And they worked in th'fields and set me down in th'shade on this old quilt! If you're poor, y'have t'make somethin' t'eat. And she made her own soap t'do th'washin' with.

Happy: Yeah. We've worked hard and tried t'be good, and we've made it all right. I got this little house here. I don't owe nobody a nickel. And I've got a little bank account and she has too. So what d'we worry fer? We're too old now t'prosper much anyhow. And we've educated that boy. Put him where he's at. 'Course he worked his way—a lot of it—too. But I didn't mind it—to roll up them sleeves and work. And pulled in a little social security and we draw that. I ain't done all I ought'a done, mebbe, but they ain't nobody thataway, I don't believe.

You know, they's lots a'folks in th'world that wonders how poor folks like us live.

Sarah: It's funny how th'rich people don't appreciate what th'Lord's given them.

Happy: They don't. They don't! And they're goin' t'have to repent fer that before they leave this old world—or do somethin' about it.

You know, I ain't as heavy up there [tapping head] as I used t'be. I can't remember like I used to. And I'm afraid if you folks live to be as old as I am you'll be th'same way. Eighty-six years old. I'm not a'braggin' now, mind y', and I hope I don't, but they ain't many a man eighty-six years old that can get around and keep what little mind he has got.

I'll tell y', they ain't many thataway.

MAKING AN OX YOKE

Recently, we began to try to find someone who could make an ox yoke for us. A yoke, as you probably know, rests on the shoulders of a pair of oxen, and attached to it are the lines or chains from a wagon, sled, plow, or whatever else is being pulled. Rarely is one seen in use any longer, but occasionally you can find one lying around an old barn, or hanging in someone's living room, or set up in an antique shop with a giant price tag attached. And it is even harder to find someone who still knows how to make one. After talking to several people about making a yoke for us, we were beginning to get discouraged. Then we were told about Tommy Barnes.

Mr. Barnes is a small, friendly man who is usually quiet. He doesn't speak much unless asked specifically about something. He lives with his wife in a small frame house in the Buck Creek Community in North Carolina. When we found him, we were warmly welcomed and immediately felt at home. He agreed to make the yoke for us and told us that if we came back in a few days, he'd have time to begin working on it. Waiting around, we were really excited about our first interview and could hardly wait to get started.

When we went back, we gathered around his workshop—a cleared-out space around the base of a large, aging apple tree in his front yard. In and around the apple tree were different parts of yokes in various stages of completion. Leaning up against the tree was an old handmade ladder, and old pieces of wood and wood chips covered the ground. Not far away lay an anvil, and in the yard were tubs of apples that had been gathered from the old tree. Sitting in the shade was a handmade bench worn from excessive use over years.

Standing there answering our questions as he worked, we felt the uniqueness of Tommy Barnes and his way of life: "The first'un I made, I had a brother. And me and him had three yoke a'cattle apiece—six yoke. And we logged all over this mountain here, and he knows how to make a yoke. But th'first man that made a yoke like this one was Beals, and he showed me how t'do it. I've made a hundred yoke at this place."

The most popular woods for yokes are ash, black gum, pine, sassafras, and yellow poplar. Tommy's favorite, however is pine: "Well, I'd rather have pine as yeller poplar. Yeller poplar sometimes season cracks, and that won't do it!" So saying, he began to hew.

STAN ECHOLS

PLATE 64

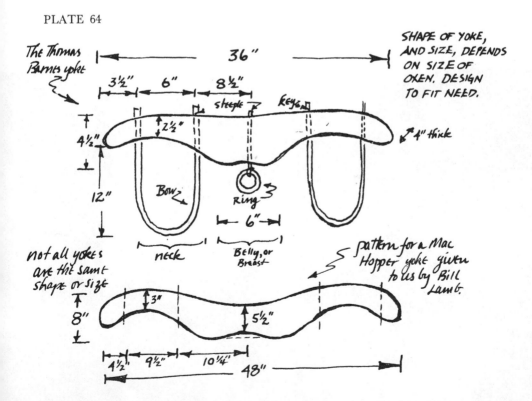

PLATE 65 Roughing out the yoke is a fairly simple process. After the size of the yoke to be made is determined (see diagrams), the sides of a piece of round stock of appropriate size are hewn off leaving a rough-hewn, rectangular block of wood. The outline of the yoke is drawn on the sides using a pattern—if one is available—or measurements. Then, with an auger, the four holes for the bows are drilled from the top surface in the proper places.

PLATE 66 Next, with an axe or hatchet, and turning the yoke from side to side as necessary, the yoke is hewn out in rough form. A drawing knife is used for the final smoothing and shaping.

PLATES 67–69 With the yoke hewn out, the next step is to make the bows.

Hickory is usually used for this because of its ability to bend easily without breaking, and because of its toughness. Often a four-inch in diameter green hickory pole of appropriate length is quartered, and the sharp, angled edges of the quarters shaved off to make pieces that are roughly round.

Now the bow is slowly and gradually bent as shown in *Plate 67* (the attaching of two stout poles to the ends of the hickory stock), *68* (the beginning of the actual bending), and *69*.

PLATE 70 Stan helps tie the bow ends together to keep it curved.

PLATE 71 The bow could be left tied if desired, and set up in the barn loft to season and "set." For our purposes, however, that wasn't necessary. Mr. Barnes simply went ahead and trimmed off any splinters . . .

PLATE 72 . . . untied the bows and slid them into place . . .

PLATE 73 . . . and then got out the steeple and nailed it into place in the bottom center of the yoke. Chains used to pull wagons and sleds are hooked to the steeple's ring. The weight of the load behind pulling on the ring holds the yoke firmly in place on the oxen's shoulders.

PLATES 74–77   With Mrs. Barnes's and Stan's help, Mr. Barnes selects a small drill and drills two holes—one on the inside end of each bow (*Plate 75*). He then saws off the ends of the bows and, using the scrap, whittles out two hickory pegs (*Plate 76*) and slides them into place (*Plate 77*). These "keys" keep the bows from sliding out.

PLATE 78   Will Zoellner, a local blacksmith, worked for years with the Babcock Lumber Company on Nantahala both driving steers for them and hewing new yokes whenever one split. He made the above yoke for us according to his own personal pattern. It is hewn out of poplar (though he also uses sassafras and sweet gum), and would have been used with heavy steers that were already broken in. The yoke measures 44 inches long, and is 7¼ inches thick at the belly.

"BEEN MAKIN' WAGON WHEELS
ABOUT FIFTY YEAR' "

"Amazing" was all I could say as I watched blacksmith John Conley fit piece by piece of our wagon wheel perfectly together. Every small detail was completed with skill and accuracy, and an ease that comes from having made his first wheel over fifty years ago. This accuracy has always been a part of John Conley's works, and it continues to be so. After he had all of the felloes sawed out and mounted, for example, he noticed that the pattern he had been using was a little off: its curvature was a little tight, thus creating a slightly scalloped circle instead of a perfectly round one. It wouldn't really have mattered, but rather than have an imperfect piece of work leave his shop, John went back one night, removed all the old felloes, cut a new pattern and new felloes, and remounted them. The next day, when we went in to watch him put the tire on, he didn't even mention what he had done until we noticed the difference. He wanted everything, he explained, "done right."

John has modernized his blacksmith shop in many ways, adding arc welders, electric drills, and a pattern lathe to cut both wagon wheel spokes and tool handles; but he was able, and willing, to show us the old methods as he worked with his newer tools. These differences are cited in the captions for the photographs that follow.

He also patiently explained many of the whys involved in the process. The spokes, for example, are oval-shaped instead of being perfectly round. This gives them a tremendous amount of additional strength.

And the reason the spokes are "dished" was also explained a number of times. This is, in fact, the touchiest part of the job. Much of it has to do with the way the hub's mortises are cut. Traditionally, the hubs (made, as the rest of the wheel, out of *well-*seasoned oak or hickory) were turned on a lathe, and the mortises (twelve for the front hubs and fourteen for the larger, weight-carrying back wheels) were cut with a wood chisel. The mortises had a half-inch slope on one side (see diagram later) to create the "dish" in the spokes. That dish curved toward the inside of the wagon so that, as more and more weight was added and the hubs were forced outward, the spokes would straighten up rather than bow out. This was especially important, too, when the wagon was riding on sloped ground. If the wheels weren't dished, then as the load shifted toward the downhill side of the wagon, the wheels would bow outward and split apart.

A pretty intricate task, all in all. And hard to explain. We hope the following photographs and diagrams make it somewhat clear.

STAN ECHOLS

PLATE 79 John used a factory-turned hub for our wheel—ready for use except for the addition of the four bands. Traditionally the hubs would be turned on a foot-powered lathe, and the slots for the spokes cut with a sharp chisel. Here, the hub is ready for the last band to be added.

PLATE 80 The steel stock for the band is chosen, measured, bent in a vise, and the ends welded together.

PLATES 81–82 Now the rough edges left by the weld are ground off. The band is next heated red-hot in the forge, driven onto the moistened hub, and then doused with water to make it contract and hold.

PLATE 83 The blocks for the spokes were cut from oak that had seasoned two years.

PLATE 84 The spokes were turned on a pattern lathe. Years ago, they would have been carved out with a drawing knife.

PLATES 85–89   The bases of the twelve spokes are now shaped, as shown in *Plates 85–89*. These are the "tenons" that fit the twelve slots, or "mortises," cut in the hub. First the draw knife cuts across the grain to the desired depth (*Plate 85*); then the knife is held parallel to the grain of the wood and struck with an axe or hammer (*Plate 86*). The back of the spoke is then sloped to work against the slope of the mortise (*Plate 87*), and the edges tapered so the tenon will slip easily into the mortise (*Plate 88*).

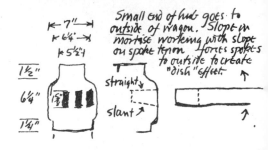

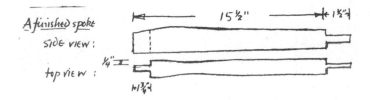

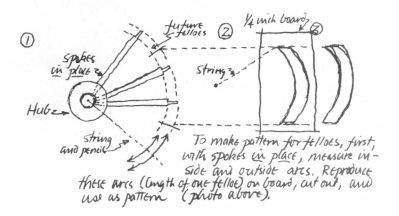

① spokes in place Hub ↘ future felloes ② ¼ inch board ③ String ↘ string and pencil ↗

To make pattern for felloes, first, with spokes in place, measure inside and outside arcs. Reproduce these arcs (length of one felloe) on board, cut out, and use as pattern (photo above).

PLATES 90–93   A pattern is made for the wooden rim of the wheel (*Plate 90*), and the six felloes marked out on inch-and-a-half thick oak stock (*Plate 91*). Traditionally, these were cut out with a felloe saw (*Plates 92–93* on p. 124).

Felloe Saw :

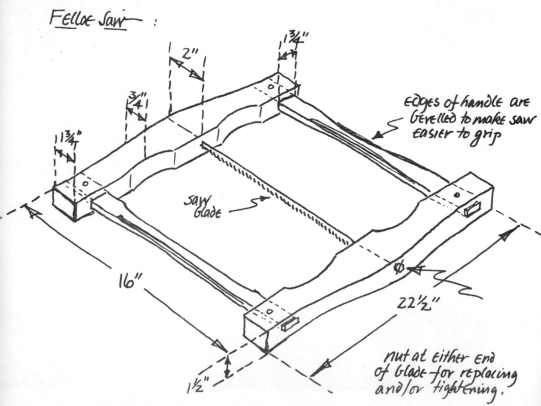

2"

1¾"

¾"

1¾"

Edges of handle are bevelled to make saw easier to grip

saw blade

16"

22½"

1½"

nut at either end of blade for replacing and/or tightening.

PLATE 94 Instead of using the felloe saw, John now uses a band saw to cut out the felloes.

PLATE 95 He drills the holes for the ends of the spokes with a drill press, rather than with the auger which would have been used traditionally. He drills the holes from the inside of the felloe.

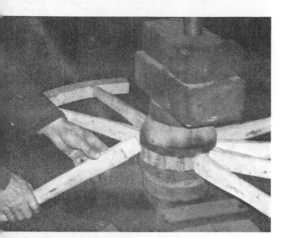

PLATES 96–97   Next the spokes are driven into the mortises in the hub. No nails or glue are needed. The slope of the mortises in the hub automatically creates the required "dish."

PLATES 98–100   Now the ends of the spokes are shaped to receive the felloes. First, a spoke pointer (*Plate 98*) points the ends to guide the spoke auger (*Plate 99*) onto a true course. The latter tool turns the end of the spoke into a dowel to receive the felloe.

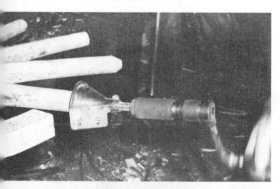
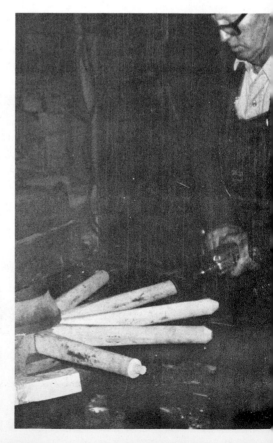

PLATES 101–102 When the spokes are ready, the felloes are laid, section by section, on the ends of the spokes, and marked on their inside curves so holes for the ends of the spokes can be drilled in the proper places. Once drilled, the felloes are mounted in place. John calls the tool he is using a "spoke puller." It pulls the spokes closer together so they can fit the holes in the inside of the felloes. As the felloe is driven on (*Plate 102*), the spokes spread back apart into their natural positions.

PLATE 103 When the felloes are in place, John takes a hand saw and saws down between each seam to insure that they meet flush, and are lined up correctly.

PLATE 104 The wheel is now ready for the metal rim.

PLATES 105–106 With a traveler, John checks the circumference of both the wheel and the metal "tire" to make sure the fit is good. The tire should be about a half-inch smaller in inside circumference than the outside circumference of the wheel itself. This insures a tight fit.

PLATES 107–109 The tire that John had planned to use on our wheel was too large, so he cut out a section (*Plate 107*), rewelded it carefully back together on top and bottom (*Plate 108*), and ground off the rough edges (*Plate 109*).

PLATE 110 Now he gets the tire red-hot in his forge. He moves the tire about a foot at a time through the flames until it has gone about four complete, very slow revolutions.

PLATES 111–113 Moving quickly, he carries the tire to the wheel, has a second person clamp down on the opposite side to keep the tire from flipping up (*Plate 111*), and pulls the tire over the rim of the wheel with a "tire puller" (*Plates 112–113*).

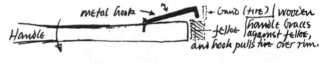

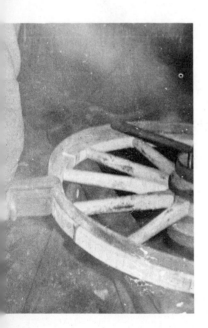

PLATE 114 As the wood smokes from the heat, he pounds the tire down evenly all the way around and douses it repeatedly with water to finish the job.

PLATE 115   The finished wheel.

THE FOXFIRE WAGON

After the wheel was finished for our collection, and we had marveled at the ingenuity of the construction, we naturally thought about what a job it must have been to make a complete wagon using only hand tools. We went to talk to Will Zoellner, who used to make wagons, to see if he could show us how.

He did even better. He had just located a wagon he had made in 1926, and he offered to get it for us if we wanted it. The wagon had changed owners five times since its construction, and it had come back to Will several times for repairs. This time he repaired it for the last time as it is now in our museum, never to change hands again.

Will went over every piece in detail with us. The following photographs and diagrams provide a pattern which will yield an exact duplicate of Will's model.

PLATE 116   Will Zoellner

PLATE 117   Karen Cox takes notes as Will describes the wagon structure.

PLATE 118   This photograph illustrates the rear axle assembly. See diagram in
Plate 119.

Rear Axle Assembly (looking from rear of wagon)

= standard
A = Rear bolster
B = coupling pole & hounds
C = Rear axle

The wagon shown here was made completely by Will Zoellner, a local blacksmith. He forged most of the metal parts himself (except for the actual nuts, the four standards, and the hound plates). The wooden pieces were hand hewn out of white oak (except for the hickory coupling pole) with an axe, adze and drawing knife.

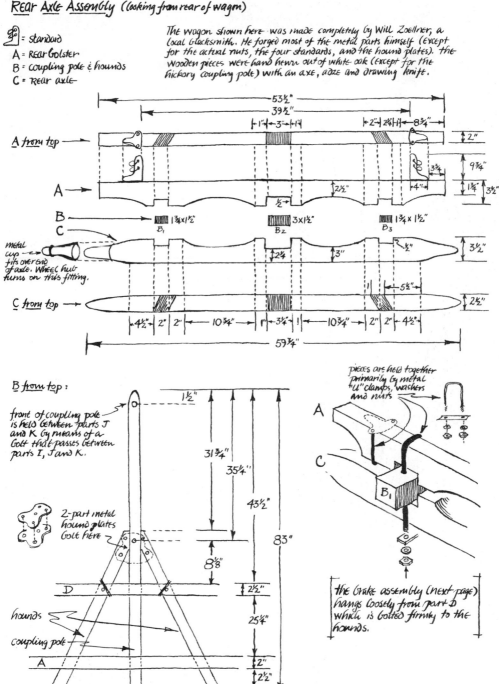

A from top →

A →

B
C

metal cup fits over end of axle. Wheel hub turns on this fitting.

C from top →

B from top:

front of coupling pole is held between parts J and K by means of a bolt that passes between parts I, J and K.

2-part metal hound plates bolt here

hounds

coupling pole

A

B₁   B₂   B₃

pieces are held together primarily by metal "U" clamps, washers and nuts

A

C

B₁

the brake assembly (next page) hangs loosely from part D which is bolted firmly to the hounds.

PLATE 119

PLATE 120   Brake assembly. See diagram in *Plate 121*.

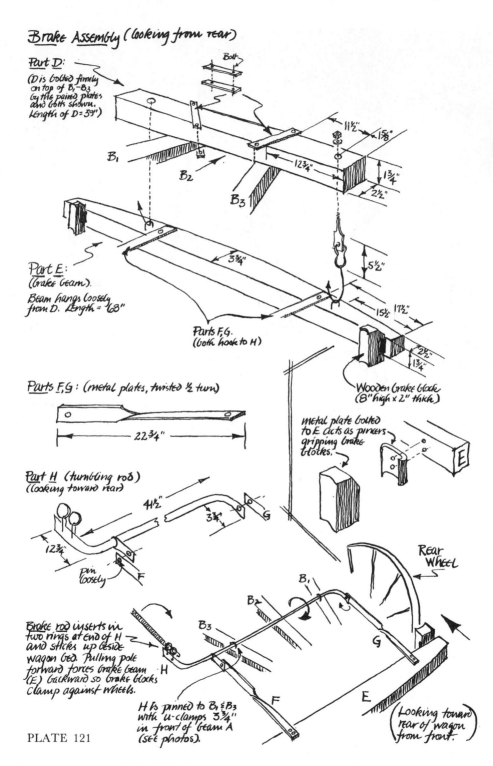

Brake Assembly (looking from rear)

Part D:
(D is bolted firmly on top of B₁-B₃ by the paired plates and bolts shown. Length of D = 39")

Bolt

11½" 1⅝"

B₁

B₂

B₃

12¾"

1¾"

2½"

3¾"

Part E:
(Brake beam).
Beam hangs loosely from D. Length = 68"

5½"

Parts F.G.
(both hook to H)

15½" 17½"

2½"
1¾"

Parts F.G : (metal plates, twisted ½ turn)

22¾"

Wooden brake block
(8" high × 2" thick)

metal plate bolted to E acts as pincers gripping brake blocks.

E

Part H (tumbling rod)
(looking toward rear)

4½"

3¾"

G

12¾"

pin loosely

F

Rear Wheel

B₁

B₂

B₃

G

Brake rod inserts in two rings at end of H and sticks up beside wagon bed. Pulling pole forward forces brake beam (E) backward so brake blocks clamp against wheels.

H

F

E

(Looking toward rear of wagon from front.)

H is pinned to B₁ & B₃ with u-clamps 3¾" in front of beam A (see photos).

PLATE 121

PLATE 122   The front axle assembly. See diagram in *Plate 123*.

Front axle assembly (looking from rear)

I = rocking bolster   K = front axle
J = sand bolster   L = slider

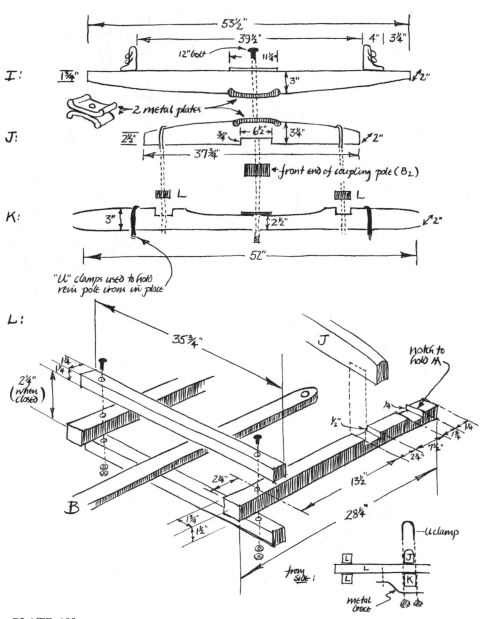

"U" clamps used to hold
rein pole irons in place

PLATE 123

Shaft Assembly:

Part M: (shaft brace)
(view is from rear / same
angle as previous diagram)

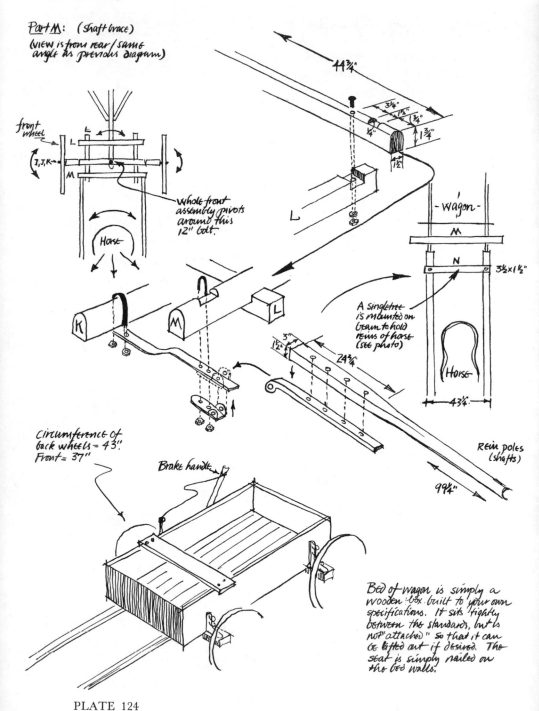

front wheel

I, J, K —

M

L

Whole front
assembly pivots
around this
12" bolt.

Horse

44¾"

3¼"
1½"
3¼"
¼"
1¾"
1½"

- Wagon -

M

N

3½ x 1½"

A singletree
is mounted on
beam to hold
reins of horse
(see photo)

Horse

43¼"

K

M

L

3"
1½"

24¾"

Rein poles
(shafts)

Circumference of
back wheels = 43"
Front = 37"

99¼"

Brake handle

Bed of wagon is simply a
wooden box built to your own
specifications. It sits tightly
between the standards, but is
not "attached" so that it can
be lifted out if desired. The
seat is simply nailed on
the bed walls.

PLATE 124

PLATE 125   The entire wagon seen from the front.

MAKING A TUB WHEEL—
SAM BURTON SHOWS US HOW

I remember saying, "I could probably work the rest of my life and not come up with anything like that." Those were my exact words when I saw what Sam Burton had made with one section of a huge white pine and two black locust pegs. He had used only a hammer, a chisel, a chain saw, a tape measure, an auger, and an axe, but his skill with these was amazing.

As all of us watched and talked and played with Mose and Booger (Sam's two dogs), he went to work, barefoot, chopping and cutting and marking and hammering and telling us stories all the while:

"I had a hog up here that weighed about three hunderd pounds. I said, 'Major, I got a hog up here I want t'kill tomorrow.'

"He said, 'Why tomorrow?'

"I says, 'Th'moon's a'shrinkin' so th'meat'll shrink.'

"He rared back and laughed. He says, 'Th'moon only controls one thing.'

"I says, 'What's that?'

"He says, 'It controls th'oceans.'

"I says, 'If it controls as big a thing as th'ocean, it probably controls that pig I got up there too!' On th'growin' of th'moon —when it's sure enough growin'—there's no kiddin' about it. You can kill a hog and his meat'll puff. If th'moon's in th'last quarter a'shrinkin', hit'll shrink up. Hit'll all fry away. All

th'grease'll come out. 'At makes sense. When you render
th'lard out, you can tell. If th'moon's growin', when your
cracklin's come out, they'll be soft and puffy."

We stayed all day, and he had just gotten started on the buckets
of the wheel. Then we had to stop because it was getting late in
the day and Sam had other work to get done.

Sam called us whenever he had time to work on the wheel. We'd
go over and watch and talk. He always worked patiently, like the
real craftsman he is.

It took time, and lots of it, but soon the wheel was done. It is
a beautiful thing—totally handmade. Sam says he would like to
get some yellow poplar and make another wheel from that. "I
wouldn't mind taking as much as two months . . ." That kind of
attitude—plus the respect we learned not only for good tools kept
sharp and clean, but also for a good piece of wood—made the whole
thing quite an experience.

The latter point was especially well illustrated when Sam came
across a piece of wire imbedded firmly in the center of the wood. No
matter which way he chiseled and cut, the wire followed him.
Getting it out so that it wouldn't dull his tools was a process that
took the better part of an afternoon, and we tape-recorded most of
his comments. Here, in sequence, are many of his statements regarding the wire he was fighting with:

"Looks like a piece a'metal here. I done hit it with th'circle
saw when I was cuttin' out this piece a'timber. It growed in
where somebody hung it on when th'tree'uz young. That's
th'reason th'Forest Service, when you go t'a campground,
don't want you t'carry a hatchet or a nail. Wire's just as bad
wrapped around a tree. I'm goin' t'see if I can work it out. If
I can, I'll start drillin'. If I can't, I'll have t'cut around it. I
actually hit a railroad spike one time [when he was running a
sawmill]. I'd done squared th'log down. Them saw rings and
discs just went ever'where! [He pulls a piece of the wire out
after chiseling around it.] They wrapped it around this limb.
It probably goes all th'way t'th'center. Depends on how big
th'tree was when they hung it up on it. No tellin' what th'diameter was. It must've been about four inches when it was
wrapped on there, and th'tree just grew on. Now that's a
shame t'do that to a good piece of wood! . . . If air could'a
hit it, rust would've eat it up by now. I'll have t'sharpen this
chisel again anyhow, but I don't want t'ruin it by hittin' that

anymore . . . Hope I 'bout got that piece a'wire. I guess I
have. No. See where that wood's dark there? I guess inside
there's another piece of it. I hit it in this bucket, and I'll hit it
in th'next'un. That wire'uz wrapped around that tree when
it'uz small. It wadn't nailed t'th'tree at all. Grandpa Watts
taught me how t'make these wheels. If he'd a'run into this
wire back in his days, he'd a'gone and got another tree. Back
then you could find timber . . . Look. That's hay balin' wire.
That's exactly what that is. They tied somethin' t'this tree
with that hay balin' wire . . . I don't know what I'm goin'
t'do with this wire yet [several hours later]. I cut it again. I
believe I'm goin' t'get it. But I'll likely hit it again. It goes on
down in there. And y'see? Right here's a resin pocket. That's
because th'wood was bruised somehow while it was growin'
. . . That tree was actually three inches in diameter when that
wire was hung around it. You can see where it's colored
th'wood blue. It couldn't a'been hung over waist high . . .
That wire makes a lot a'work; it sure 'nough does . . . That
wire just follows me around ever'where I go. I can't get shed
a'it."

Finally Sam did get "shed a'it," but listening to him fight it, we
learned more about wood than from any text we had ever read. And
we won't be wrapping wire around young trees anymore—that's for
sure.

For those of you not familiar with a tub wheel, it serves exactly the
same purpose as either an overshot or undershot mill wheel. Once very
common in this area, it is now almost extinct, as are the men who can
still make them. In fact, we know of not one single mill where a wheel
of this type is still in operation. Luckily, at the Grandpa Watts mill
near Clarkesville, Georgia—a fine old building now the studio of Glen
and John LaRowe and the home of their shop, the Mark of the Potter
—we found the remnants of a tub wheel still in place (*Plates 155–
161*). We also got word there of Sam Burton, who had made the one
that now lay, rotting, in the basement. The rest you know.

The instructions for making such a wheel can be found on the
following pages. There are several pieces of information that should
be noted before starting.

First, the wheel illustrated here is made of two slabs of wood. That's
because there aren't any trees left big enough to allow it to be made
out of one. A wheel of larger diameter can be made out of three
pieces joined together in exactly the same fashion as illustrated on the
following pages.

Second, such wheels were usually made out of soft wood like pine or poplar. The theory was that the water striking the wheel carried sand. If the sand struck soft wood, particles would become imbedded in the wood itself, and it wouldn't be long before the surfaces would be coated with sand and thus be more resistant to further wear. Sand striking hard wood will not become imbedded in the wood, but will continue to sand it away until the blades are almost paper thin.

Third, the buckets are shaped so that their openings in the bottom of the wheel are larger than their openings in the top. Sam explained the reason for this: "You make th'buckets bigger at th'bottom so they'll not hold water. It'll drop on out and be out a'th'way. After you use that water, th'quicker you can get through with it, th'better you are at not havin' to carry it. If you don't fix it where it'll [the water] drop out, th'bucket'll come back around t'where th'spout hits it again and if it's full a'water, you hadn't got any power. Now they made one over here at Hiawassee, and when it'd come back around, it wouldn't pull. When it come back around, th'buckets was all full. If it's carryin' its first load back around, it's pullin' somethin' it doesn't need. That water's gotta dump out right away as th'wheel turns."

Fourth, the wheel is set so that it turns from east to west. As Sam said, "Th'wheel goes th'same way th'sunrise does. All millstones turn that way. If they don't, there's somethin' wrong. Most ever'thing, even a tap, turns that way."

Fifth, if you make such a wheel, it should be cut out of green wood and kept in water to prevent cracking. Ours is soaking in polyethylene glycol, thanks to suggestions by Dr. Sam Stanley of the Smithsonian and Dr. Joe W. Clark, Pathologist. That should save it.

MIKE COOK

PLATE 126   Sam begins by cutting a slab of white pine (seven feet long by eighteen inches wide by nine inches thick) into two thirty-seven-inch-long slabs. He sets the excess aside.

PLATES 127–128 With the boring auger shown in detail in *Plate 127,* he drills two holes in the side of each slab. The holes are two inches in diameter and six inches deep. These holes will hold the pegs that will pin the two slabs together, so their locations must be plotted *exactly* before drilling. To do this, Sam finds the dead center of the two sides that will be drilled. Then, on a line exactly bisecting the width of the slab, he locates two points, each six inches from center. The two points, then, are exactly twelve inches apart, and on a line that passes through dead center on each slab. Doing this to two sides gives the locations for the centers of the four holes to be drilled.

PLATE 129 With the holes drilled, Sam sets the slabs together, drilled sides up, to make sure the holes align properly.

PLATE 130 He then cuts two pegs out of black locust to fit the holes. The pegs are approximately eleven inches long and one and three-quarters inches square. He trims off the corners slightly with the axe but leaves the pegs more square than round. This way, they will jam more tightly into the holes and hold far better than if they were simply round dowels. This is the same technique used whenever pegging log cabins together.

PLATE 131 Next, he drives the pegs into place in one of the two slabs. *Note:* In later steps, when the buckets are being cut out, these pins will be cut into. By that time, however, the two slabs will be held together by two iron hoops.

PLATE 132 The slab with the pegs in place is now lifted onto its mate, pegs and holes are matched . . .

PLATE 133 . . . and the slabs are driven together.

PLATE 134 Sam now finds dead center of the top surface. He drives a nail through a stick of scrap wood into dead center, measures out eighteen inches from dead center on the stick, and drives a second nail through this point. With the point of the second nail, he scribes a circle thirty-six inches in diameter on the top surface.

PLATE 135 Now, using the same method, two more circles are scribed (see arrows)—one measuring seven inches and the other fifteen and a half inches from dead center on the stick . . .

PLATE 136 . . . and the outlines for the first buckets drawn (see measurements in *Plates 152* and *154*).

PLATE 137   With an axe, he hews the wheel out round.

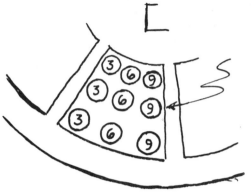

numbers in holes show how many inches deep holes should be drilled.

PLATE 139

PLATE 138   He now begins work on the buckets themselves. Nine holes are drilled in each bucket as shown.

PLATE 140 Working only on those four buckets that cut *across* the grain, Sam roughs out the buckets with an axe and . . .

PLATE 141 . . . smooths them up with a hammer and chisel. The holes which he drilled both lighten the work he has to do and act as guides to tell him how deeply into each bucket he may cut without ruining it.

PLATE 142 As he progresses, he continually checks and rechecks his measurements to make sure he is shaping the sides of the bucket correctly.

PLATE 143 In the second bucket, Sam finds a piece of wire sticking out of the middle of the wood. Here he tries to ease it out without dulling the edge of his chisel.

PLATE 144 With the top halves of the first two buckets roughed out, Sam turns the wheel up on its side and outlines the bottom halves. For measurements and a diagram of the bottom side of the wheel, see *Plate 154*.

PLATE 145 The outline drawn, Sam eases the wheel over bottom side up and begins to chisel from the bottom. The rows of holes he has drilled all the way through (the row of nine-inch holes) act as a guide, as do the lines he has drawn. While working, he goes slowly and carefully so as not to cut through one of the blades. He must also be careful to slope each one correctly.

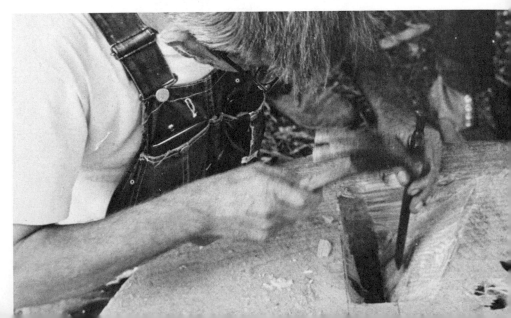

PLATE 146 With the four buckets that cut across the grain roughed out, Sam now takes two iron wagon wheel rims, each thirty-six inches in diameter, builds a fire around them (one can use hickory, corn cobs, or anything else that burns evenly and well), and gets them red-hot.

PLATES 147–148 The hoops are then carried to the wheel, red-hot, with hooks, eased over the top, and pounded into place with hammers. Often the hoops are so hot they set the wood afire.

PLATE 149 Steam boils off the heated iron band as Sam sprays it with water to cool it and make it contract. As the bands contract, they pull the two halves of the wheel so tightly together that even if the pins holding them get completely severed while the buckets are being cut (as happens in a forty-eight-inch wheel that is made with three separate slabs), it will make no difference. If the finished wheel is kept wet or treated while green with polyethylene glycol, it will keep without air-cracking or splitting for years. The bands on, Sam can now cut the four remaining buckets. These buckets, which run with the grain, might split if cut earlier.

PLATE 150 As the wheel nears completion, Sam points out certain features to Mike Cook, who has videotaped the whole process.

PLATE 151   The finished wheel from the top side.

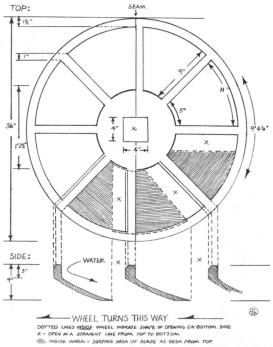

PLATE 152

PLATE 153   The finished wheel from the bottom side.

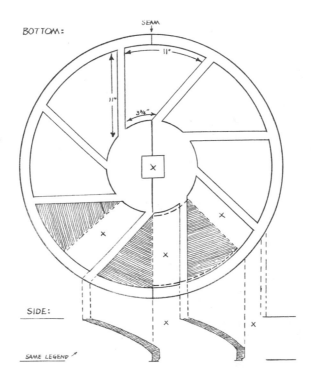

BOTTOM:

SEAM

11"

11"

3¾"

×

×

×

×

SIDE:

×

×

SAME LEGEND

PLATE 154

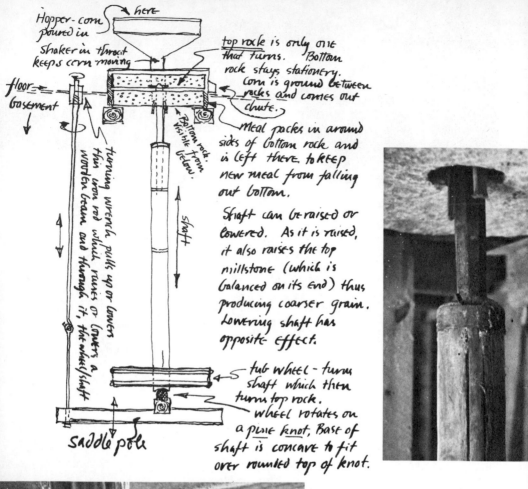

Hopper-corn poured in here

Shaker in throat keeps corn moving

floor—basement

top rock is only one that turns. Bottom rock stays stationery. Corn is ground between rocks and comes out chute.

Meal packs in around sides of bottom rock and is left there, to keep new meal from falling out bottom.

Shaft can be raised or lowered. As it is raised, it also raises the top millstone (which is balanced on its end) thus producing coarser grain. Lowering shaft has opposite effect.

turning wrench pulls up or lowers thin iron rod which raises or lowers a wooden beam and through it, the wheel/shaft

Bottom rock. Visible from below.

shaft

tub wheel - turns shaft which then turns top rock.
wheel rotates on a pine knot. Base of shaft is concave to fit over rounded top of knot.

saddle pole

PLATES 155–157 The Grandpa Watts mill near Clarkesville, Georgia, still has the ruins of an old tub wheel in place. It was made by Grandpa Watts, the man who taught Sam how. This diagram attempts to show how the wheel fits into the whole assembly. The shaft is shown passing through the bedstone (the bottom millstone) in *Plate 156;* and passing through the tub wheel in 157.

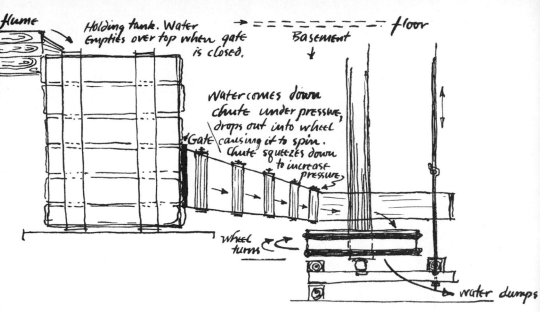

Flume

Holding tank. Water
empties over top when gate
is closed.

Basement

floor

Water comes down
chute under pressure,
drops out into wheel
causing it to spin.
Chute squeezes down
to increase
pressure.

Gate

wheel
turns

water dumps

PLATES 158–159   This diagram shows the holding tank and chute assembly
in the Watts mill. The chute is also shown in *Plate 159*.

PLATE 160 Sharpening millstones as they get worn through use is one of the trickiest jobs involved in running a mill. The fans are recut periodically by slowly and painstakingly pecking away at them with a hammer like the one Sam is using. Sam never "beats" on the rock—he just taps lightly hour after hour until the sloped surfaces of the fans are just right.

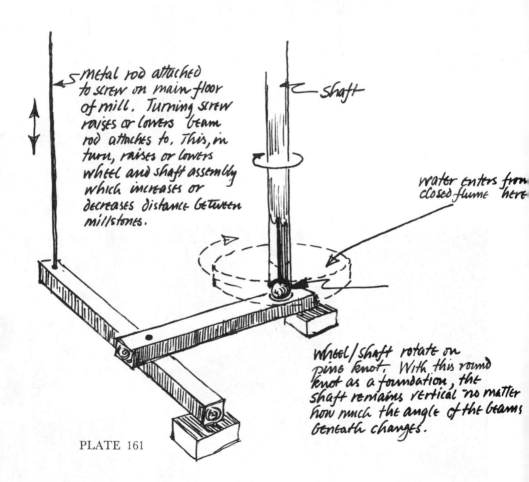

metal rod attached to screw on main floor of mill. Turning screw raises or lowers beam rod attaches to. This, in turn, raises or lowers wheel and shaft assembly which increases or decreases distance between millstones.

shaft

water enters from closed flume here

Wheel/shaft rotate on pine knot. With this round knot as a foundation, the shaft remains vertical no matter how much the angle of the beams beneath changes.

PLATE 161

PLATE 162 Maude Shope also had a little tub mill on her property. It was almost gone by the time we got there, but we managed to get it measured and documented. The following diagrams and photograph show enough details about the Shope mill that you could construct a copy if you wished. The main support beams are all hand-hewn with an axe and adze out of oak and chestnut and fitted together with pegged mortise and tenon joints. The walls are poles, and the roof is covered with hand-split shingles.

PLATES 163–164

In the photo at left, the bottom millstone has slipped down the shaft exposing the wooden collar (arrow) that prevents meal from falling through the bottom rock's central opening. The bottom stone stays stationary mounted solidly in the opening in the floor (see also diagram below while the top stone turns with the shaft. The whole assembly is covered by the circular millstone housing (when operating).

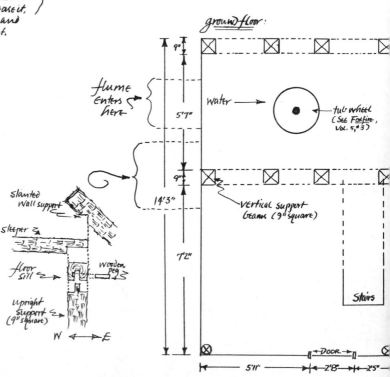

hopper into which grain is poured

millstone housing

Top millstone turns with shaft. Meal packs around sides against housing until only outlet is the chute

floorbeams

floor support

floor sill

Bottom millstone is stationary and does not turn. Only shaft turns inside it.

water enters under pressure

tub wheel

penstock

Entrance to meal chute (only opening available)

turning turnscrew raises attached beam in turn raising wheel & shaft together thus increasing distance between millstones.

block

iron shaft

used water spills out → stream

S ←——→ N

Top millstone is often called the "runner rock" or "running stone." Bottom is called the "bedrock" or "bedstone."

Lard is often put around the wooden spindle to grease it, "crystallize" the wood and keep it from getting hot.

ground floor:

9"

flume enters here

5'7"

water →

tub wheel (See Foxfire, Vol. 5, #3)

9"

Vertical support beams (9" square)

14'3"

Slanted wall support

sleeper

floor sill

wooden peg

upright support (9" square)

7'2"

Stairs

W ←——→ E

DOOR

5'11" — 2'8" — 2'5"

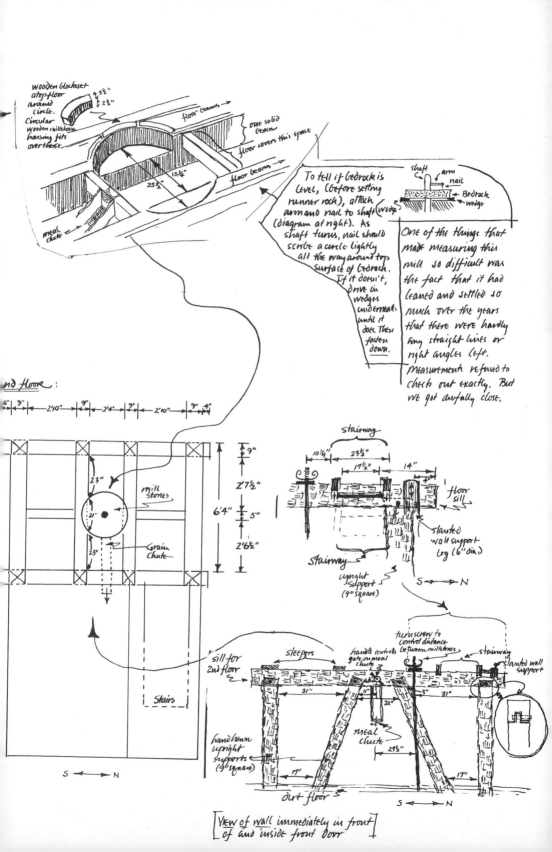

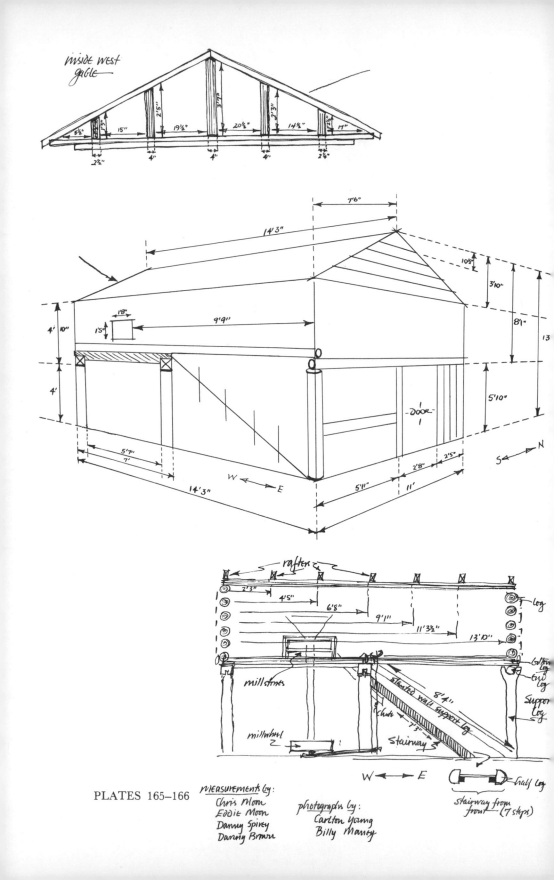

inside west gable

2'5"
3'7"
2'3"
8½"   1⅞"   15"   19½"   20½"   14⅜"   2⅞"   17"
2½"   4"   4"   4"   2¾"

7'6"
14'3"
10½"
3'10"
4' 10"
1'8"
1'5"
9'9"
8'1"
13
4'
5'10"
DOOR
5'7"
7'
2'8"   2'5"
14'3"
W ← → E
5'11"   11"
S ← → N

rafter
2'3"
4'5"
6'8"
9'1"
11'3½"
13'0"
log
millstones
slanted wall support log
8'4"
bottom log
end log
Support log
chute
7'3"
millwheel
Stairway
W ← → E
half log
stairway from front (7 steps)

PLATES 165–166

measurements by:
Chris Moon
Eddie Moon
Danny Spivey
Danny Brown

photographs by:
Carlton Young
Billy Maney

PLATE 167 Ken Kistner measures the wooden housing that fits over the top of the runner rock. Corn to be ground is poured in a hopper which fits in the central hole visible at Ken's left hand.

MAKING A FOOT-POWERED LATHE

"Let's make us one—make th'shavin's fly! I got a deerskin up there in th'barn if you boys'ud cut it up fer me and make strips out of it. We'll nail it together and make us one, huh? It's simple. Real simple."

This was Minyard Connor's response when we asked him how a foot-powered lathe worked; and we were more than glad to oblige him.

The foot-powered lathe is a completely hand-built, muscle-powered machine that has been out of use ever since electric lathes—and other tools that made woodwork easier and faster—became common. After operating the foot-powered lathe myself, I can see why it is rarely used anymore.

The main purpose of this lathe was to make chair rounds, bed posts and table legs. Though it is fairly simple to construct, it takes a lot of patience to work with one for very long. But that is one of the wonders of the mountain people—their patience.

It was after several attempts to set up an interview with Minyard (he was always out logging or fishing, it seemed) that we finally got one in early March. When we first heard of the foot-powered lathe, neither George nor Jimmy nor myself had any idea what it would look like; but when it was finally built and we had all tried it out, we were glad we had carried the interview through to the end.

After we had finished the interview, Mike, Paul, and Frank dropped by Minyard's to see how things looked. Minyard sat on a stump, loosened up, and started telling jokes. That's when I really felt the interview had been a success—I'd made a friend.

GREG STRICKLAND

PLATE 168 The "H"-shaped frame for the lathe is two upright, seven-foot-long 2×4's, and a horizontal beam; and two wooden brackets—a hole on the inside surface of each—for holding the stock to be turned.

PLATE 169 One-inch-wide strips of deerhide are cut as long as the hide will allow and drawn rapidly back and forth across a metal rod (or horseshoe mounted to a wall as shown here) to loosen them up and make them pliable. Here Minyard has handed one strip to Greg to work, George holds a second, and Minyard slices out a third. When enough strips have been cut to make a twelve-foot length, they are tied together. As will be seen, one end is attached to the spring pole overhead, and the other is attached to the foot pedal.

PLATE 170 The frame finished, the foot pedal is now mounted to it. Choose two four-foot 2×4's. Here Minyard sharpens one end of each so they can be driven into the ground. (Note: As in *Plate 171,* they are driven into the ground on a slant, about shoulder width, or 3½ feet, apart.)

PLATE 171 When the braces for the pedal are in place beside the frame, Greg Strickland drills a hole through both with a brace and bit.

PLATE 172 The pedal itself is a two-foot-long 2×4, a hole drilled through it six inches from one end. It is set in place between the two braces, and held by a bolt that goes through it and the two holes Greg drilled in the braces. With the pedal in place, one end of the deerskin rope is wired to the center of the pedal.

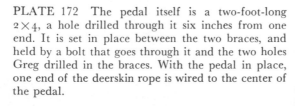

PLATE 174 A piece of stock to be turned for a chair round is sharpened on either end so the brackets can hold it. The spring pole is, in this case, a springy green oak pole mounted horizontally in the barn loft above the lathe. Its base is firmly anchored, and a bale of hay is set under it about four feet from its anchored end to tilt it upward and add to its spring.

PLATE 173 With one end of the hide securely wired to the pedal (as shown) and the other end attached to the spring pole (*Plate 177*), the lathe is ready to use.

PLATE 175 The stock is twisted once in the deerhide, and its ends inserted into the two brackets designed to hold them. Depressing the foot pedal with the stock "fouled" in the deerskin spins the stock so it can be worked.

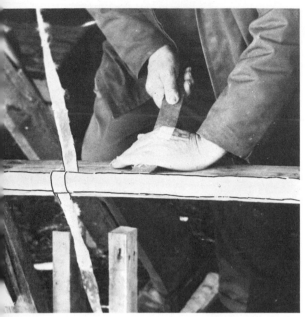

PLATE 176 Each time the pedal is depressed, the pole pulls the pedal back to the return position, spinning the stock in the opposite direction.

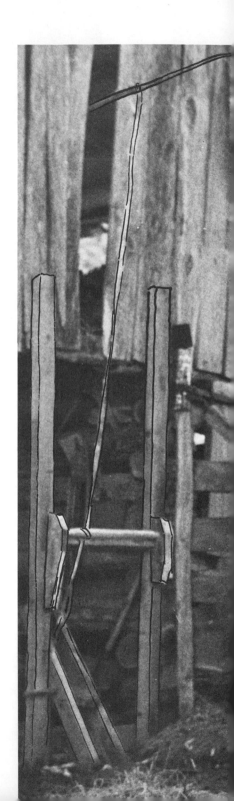

PLATE 177 The whole assembly. Note the end of the spring pole sticking out above the lathe itself.

PLATE 178   Walter Shellnut also uses a foot-powered lathe for the chairs he makes, but his lathe is different from Minyard's in some respects. For one thing, he uses rope instead of deerhide (*Plate 179*). He claims neither he nor his father (who taught him how to use the lathe and make chairs) had any luck with the hide, as it slipped too much.

PLATE 179

PLATE 180 The foot pedal on Walter's lathe is of completely different design, as seen here, but it operates the same. The piles of shavings beneath the lathe bear witness to how much it is used.

PLATE 181 Of special note are the two end pieces that hold the stock being turned. Rather than being mounted permanently on the vertical support beams, as on Minyard's lathe, these are cross-shaped pieces that slide back and forth between two horizontal beams (as shown here and in *Plate 180*) so that stock of varying lengths can be worked. The stock is held on either end by a metal spike driven through each cross-shaped end piece.

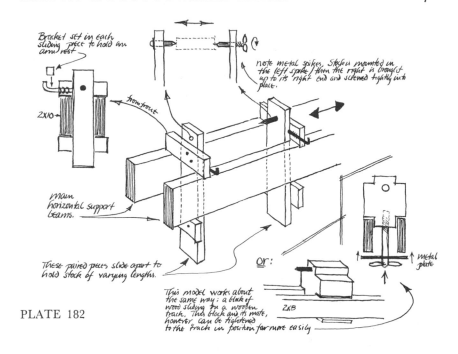

Bracket set in each sliding piece to hold an arm rest

note metal spikes. Stock is mounted in the left spike, then the right is brought up to its right end and screwed tightly into place.

2x10

from front

main horizontal support beams.

These paired pieces slide apart to hold stock of varying lengths.

PLATE 182

_or:_

This model works about the same way; a block of wood sliding in a wooden track. This block and its mate, however, can be tightened to the track in position far more easily

2x8

metal plate

PLATE 183 The hand rest is simply a stick of wood resting in brackets attached to the cross-shaped end pieces. It can be of any length, depending on how far apart the crosspieces are.

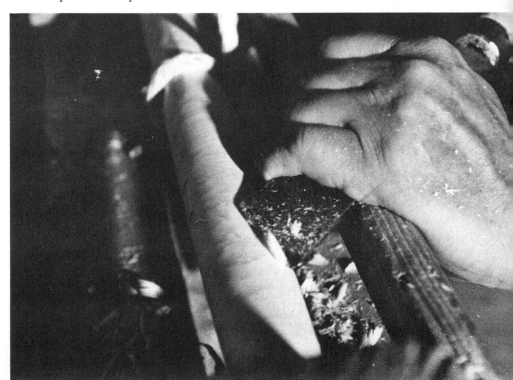

FROM RAISING SHEEP
TO WEAVING CLOTH

RAISING SHEEP

In our fathers' and grandfathers' time, raising sheep was an important factor in weaving, for without wool for yarn, clothing could not be woven. Even though there aren't many people who still weave their own clothes, there are a few left who raise sheep. This chapter was made possible by these few people who took time to talk and share their memories with us.

Through several interviews with five contacts, we acquired a wealth of information on raising and shearing sheep. The people interviewed —Minnie Buchanan, Claude Darnell, Belle Dryman, George Grist, and Gertrude Keener—have either raised sheep sometime during their lifetimes, or have memories of their parents raising sheep.

Minnie Buchanan now has a weaving shop near Highlands, North Carolina, enabling her to bring in an income, as well as to weave for her own personal needs.

Claude Darnell, living in these surrounding mountains, works at the Jay Hambidge Art Foundation. The Foundation is a school that teaches the art of weaving. They raise and shear their own sheep, providing their wool to weave. Claude's job is tending the sheep and managing the grounds.

Belle Dryman, living in North Carolina, does not raise sheep. However, her father did when she was a young girl.

George Grist has been raising sheep for about forty years. As a young boy, George learned how to raise sheep from his father.

Gertrude Keener, a retired art teacher from the Tallulah Falls High School, also had parents who raised sheep. Today you will find Gertrude busy at her loom, weaving for others as well as for herself.

By talking with these people, we learned the ways of the old mountain sheep, how they were raised and cared for, and how they were sheared.

The sheep which were grown years ago for wool were a smaller and hardier strain than the sheep of today. They weighed only about thirty to forty pounds and were no bigger than an average size dog; yet they were stout little creatures that withstood cold, hunger, and disease in the Blue Ridge and Great Smoky Mountains. But they were also shy, timid animals whose only source of protection from wild animals was to flee in fear. If they were attacked by an animal, they would usually give up and let the attacker kill them. Once they were caught and scared, they just gave up without a fight.

For the most part these sheep were white, but a few black sheep were born. George Grist, a sheep producer in Rabun County, said, "They were white. They didn't hardly have any black on'em. Back yonder most of'em had a black sheep or two crop out. They wanted that 'cause they'd weave socks and sweaters out of'em and they wouldn't have to dye it." This is a classic example of utilizing what is available. The farmers like to have a black sheep born every now and then, but sometimes superstitions grow around black sheep. Not according to George Grist, who, when asked if he knew of any superstitions, replied, "I don't know of any superstitions, but you always heard of black sheep in the family."

When the contacts were asked where the first sheep came from, no one knew for sure, but George Grist stated, "I guess if there'd been sheep here, they'd brought'em where they came from. I'd imagine they brought'em here from England. I got some shears from Sheffield, England. I believe that's where the first sheep came from."

It was hard to obtain sheep if you wanted to buy more to increase your flock. Here's what Minnie Buchanan said on obtaining sheep: "Well, you couldn't hardly find'em then. Most folks just kept what they wanted. Then in later years they got to where they kept th'sheep for th'lambs to sell in th'spring. But most everybody back when I was growing up just kept what sheep they had of their own. If they got a bigger flock, they jest had to raise'em. 'Course the sheep didn't cost nothing a head then—about two, two an'a half dollars. They jest didn't have no market sale."

Years ago almost everyone raised sheep. If some family didn't have any sheep, some of their relatives would and they usually shared the surplus wool.

Sheep were relatively easy to raise as they could forage for themselves. Since it was open range here years ago, farmers simply fenced in their gardens, and then turned their cattle, hogs, and sheep loose in the hills to graze. The animals would stay together, and were branded with some identifiable marking; then rounded up when they were needed. As Minnie Buchanan said, "We'd turn our sheep out in the spring and they'd go to the mountains. Maybe they'd come back in the field onst in a while, but not very often in the summer. In the fall, we'd git out and hunt'em up and bring'em through the winter."

When sheep roamed free in the mountains, the sheep producers needed a way to identify their sheep. Minnie Buchanan told us, "We notched their ears and that mark was registered at Franklin, North Carolina, and I guess it's right there yet." When asked if she could remember her father's mark, she wasn't sure, but she thinks it could have been an "overbit." She explained what an overbit looked like: "It's a notch on the top of the ear; if it's on the underside, it's an 'underbit.' A 'crop' is just the end of the ear clipped off."

George Grist said about ear markings, "They'd cut the ears to tell everyone's sheep apart. Lots of time they would split their ears—what they call a 'swallow fork.' They'd split the ear, either the right or the left one, and then cut off the end of the ears and call it a 'swallow fork with a clip'; or they'd notch under the ears, two or three

PLATE 184   Some lambs which Fred Darnell is raising. Notice the notched ears on the sheep at the right.

notches. Everybody around had their own mark and they could tell'em apart that way. Then they turned'em loose in the woods. All summer they'd go a long ways off and stay. They'd come home about once a month for salt. We wouldn't take salt to'em on account of we were afraid they wouldn't come back."

When we asked George how they could be sure the sheep would come home, he replied, "Well, they gotta come home, just like we do. When they want something, they come home. You see, they won't hardly come home unless they feel a need for something. You don't need a fence for'em. If anything gets after'em, they know to come home. They wanna have a place at night to stay—about the same place usually. I heard my daddy say that they'd come back; one morning he'd wake up and they'd all be back. They'd give'em salt and look about'em and in two, three days they'd be gone."

If the sheep weren't home when the owner needed them for some reason, they'd have to be hunted up. When Minnie's father wanted his sheep, he sent his children to hunt them out of the woods: "Us kids'd get out an' sheep hunt in the fall. Sometimes we'd find'em maybe five miles from home. Well, there'd probably be somebody else's sheep with'em, but we'd jest bring'em all in together an' then let them come and get theirs. An' they'd always put a bell on one an' they knowed that there bell."

Of course, not everyone let their sheep run loose in the mountains. Some people, like Belle Dryman's father, kept their sheep fenced in pastures. This eliminated the problems of hunting for the sheep and notching the ears to identify his sheep from the other men's; but then again, fences had to be built and pastures had to be kept in grazing condition. When the sheep were fenced, the best pasture grasses were blue grasses and various types of rye grass for winter grazing. The sheep preferred this softer, more tender grass to the coarse hays or fescue.

Care of the sheep in the summer was relatively easy: just pasture or mountain range, water, and a little salt. The sheep would do fine in the summer with just a little care, but during the winter months things were different. All the contacts agreed on keeping their sheep in a barn during heavy snows and severe cold spells, but the food given to the sheep by their various owners varied a little. Here are the different accounts of winter feeding by the different contacts.

Minnie Buchanan: "It don't take much to feed a sheep. Feed'em corn, hay, corn fodder, blades off cane, 'r jest anythang like that to fill'em up. Lots of people claim that corn would make'em shed their wool but I don't know whether it would."

Belle Dryman: "We had to feed'em fodder 'cause we'uns didn't have no hay back then; nobody did. We had a shelter for'em an' had to feed'n water'em in the winter time."

George Grist: "They'd come home 'round closer to the fields during the winter. Some of'em had sheds for'em. The bad winter months the sheep'd come home, but they'd eat acorns up till Christmas; but if a snow came they would eat ivy [mountain laurel] and that'd kill'em. Back yonder they'd feed'em corn. They wouldn't do good if they didn't eat something green. They like a fine grass more than they do a coarse grass. They like a blue grass or anything wild."

Gertrude Keener: "The sheep were brought into th'barn in a lot. Everybody had what they called a 'sheep house,' an' they always fed'em corn, and a lot of times they had rye. They'd let their sheep graze in th'fields in the winter time and early spring. We'd fasten'em up maybe at night and feed'em corn—shelled corn is one of the best things—and a fodder 'cause we didn't raise hay then."

Claude Darnell: Claude kept his sheep in the barn all winter except for a small pasture, and fed the sheep corn, hay, and cottonseed meal as winter foods.

Rams were needed to continue the existence of the herds. To keep from interbreeding the sheep year after year with the same ram, the neighboring farmers would swap their rams with one another. In doing so, deformed sheep and undesirable characteristics and traits were not common. George Grist said that his father kept one ram for every twenty ewes, and when they had a surplus of rams, "they killed

PLATE 185   An example of the old type of mountain rams which roamed the hillsides many years ago.

an'ate'em. That's about all you could do with'em, except maybe for wethers." Wethers were castrated rams which were slaughtered for mutton when they grew into a desired size. The size depended on how much meat you could use before it spoiled. There was one problem concerning mutton: there was no feasible way to preserve it. Whenever you needed meat to eat, you had to go out and butcher a lamb. It had to be eaten right away due to spoilage, unless it was killed in the winter. Several of the contacts stated that salt would spoil the meat and there was no way to cure or preserve it. "They'd castrate'em and let'em grow until they needed'em. Maybe it'd get two, three, or four years old. Maybe if they wanted one when the sheep came in, in the summer, they'd get one. They'd get an old one. They'd never get a young one 'cause he wouldn't weigh much. You see, they only weighed thirty to forty pounds full grown. It took'em a year or two to get big. They'd let one get big and fat. Maybe they'd weigh sixty or seventy pounds."

At times the rams would fight but usually they would get along. The old mountain rams had large curved horns and sometimes they would lock their horns together and starve to death in the woods before they could unlock their horns.

In the spring along about March the sheep begin to have their offspring. This is what George Grist had to say about lambs and their mothers: "The old type would nurse their young. Now anything that you improve, you run into problems. They take those old mountain sheep and improve'em so they have more wool and mutton, and now they're not as good mothers. Sometimes they don't wanna claim'em and then you gotta make'em nurse. Those old sheep would hold their jug up for'em and push the baby to it and just tell'em, 'you either get it or you die.' And some of these others [improved sheep] just look at their babies and smell'em and paw at'em. And the older type, no matter how cold it gets, they'd clean that baby up and dry it with her mouth. They'd hold their breath right next to'em and keep her baby warm, and some of the newer ones won't do it."

Gertrude Keener, when asked about raising lambs, said, "Sometimes they'd have twins, an' I've heard of'em havin' triplets, but usually when they had triplets one was kinda weak and the mother'd discard it. You'd have t'take it in an' raise it on a bottle. I raised two little lambs on bottles."

Sometimes the ewe would disown her lamb and if she did, it would have to be bottle fed in order to survive. If a mother ewe died, the lamb

PLATES 186–187   Sheep before and after shearing.

would be shut up with another ewe and the ewe would be forced to nurse the orphan lamb. The majority of the contacts at one time or another have raised orphan sheep with a bottle and a lot of loving care. Claude Darnell said, "I raised one all the way one time till it was grown. Then I took it out to the barn. It lived. That beat anything I ever seen. It'd follow me through the house and if I'd get away he'd just bleat."

Sheep will produce wool as long as they are in good health and still have their teeth (the condition of their teeth being one indication of their general health). George Grist explained the life expectancy of sheep and how they cut their teeth: "They go about as long as their teeth last. They grow two teeth a year. They're born with their baby teeth and two teeth a year for four years. When they get eight big teeth in the front, they was four years old. Then they go for about two-three years and those teeth break and give way. Their life is not too long after that. Sheep live maybe eight to ten years."

Shearing took place once every year in the spring, and sometimes again in the early fall if the weather permitted and there was enough wool on the sheep to make it worth while. Minnie Buchanan remembered the methods used by her father: "They sheared'em in the spring, then again about September most of th'time. Some of th'time they would not shear'em but onct a year; but generally they'd shear'em in the spring jest soon as it got warm enough till they could stand it on in the fall before it got too awful cold."

Years ago when sheep were sheared by hand, a good shearer could shear about forty head a day with assistance from someone who would help hold the sheep. The different contacts related different amounts of time required to shear sheep. Belle Dryman's father sheared about one sheep every fifteen–twenty minutes, but Gertrude Keener remembers that shearing by the old method with hand shears took about an hour to shear one sheep. Claude Darnell, another sheep raiser, said sheep could be sheared in three minutes with electric shears, but he could not remember exactly the time required when using hand shears. From these facts I'd imagine the time required to shear a sheep with hand shears depends on the ability of the shearer.

This is the way that Gertrude Keener remembers shearing sheep. "Y'start on th'stomach and shear'em, and y'just peel th'wool back. It just comes off in a big layer. It's like skinning an animal. Off a'th'big ones, you could get a pound or two of wool. That'd be quite a bit. I knowed you'd get at least a pound."

Other contacts figured that you got a little more wool than a pound per sheep—closer to two or two and one-half pounds. It varies from sheep to sheep but averages anywhere around one to three pounds of wool per sheep, compared to today's sheep with six to eight pounds of wool. That is a relatively low figure, but sheep back then were smaller and there wasn't any wool on the tail or legs.

After the sheep were sheared, the wool had to be washed and prepared for carding and spinning. This was done by washing it in warm to hot water with lye soap. The wool was very greasy and the water needed to be fairly hot, but not boiling, because that would ruin the wool. After it was washed, it was customary to place the wool on clean rocks to dry. Once the wool had been washed and dried, it lost about half its weight. Then it was ready to be stored for later use.

The following photographs show the actual process of shearing sheep. We couldn't get any photographs of shearing sheep the old way (no one shears their sheep by hand anymore); but we did take pictures of sheep being sheared by the new electric methods.

Every year professional shearers like Otis Snethen, the man in these photographs, come through this region and shear the sheep for the various sheep raisers. These men are very effective and fast shearers. This saves the sheep owners a lot of time and trouble.

PLATE 188   First the sheep are taken out of the loading chute and held upright by the front legs.

PLATE 189   You then begin to shear the wool off the neck and around the head.

PLATE 190   Shear down from the neck, along the stomach, and down to the hind legs.

PLATE 191 Now begin to shear the wool off one side of the sheep.

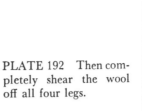

PLATE 192 Then completely shear the wool off all four legs.

PLATE 193 Place the sheep's head between your legs and shear the wool off the back of the neck and shoulders.

PLATE 194 Continue shearing down the sheep's back to his tail.

PLATE 195 Finish shearing the wool off the remaining side and the sheep is then completely sheared.

PLATE 196 Take the remaining wool and tie it in a bundle to be stored until washed.

PLATE 197 Harvey Connor holds an original pair of hand shears made in Sheffield, England.

When the contacts were asked if their forefathers ever used sheep dogs, they unanimously agreed that sheep dogs weren't too common up in the mountains. The sheep either came home on their own or you hunted them out of the hills on foot. When we asked the following contacts if their fathers had sheep dogs, they replied:

Minnie Buchanan: "He just had us young'uns, two-legged dogs. I've heard of people with sheep dogs, but Dad never did have nothin' like that. Us kids done th'takin' care of th'sheep."

Belle Dryman: "No, we didn't have no sheep dogs. 'Course we only had a few [sheep]. People generally didn't have sheep dogs."

George Grist: "No, I don't think so. Th'sheep just come home on their own accord."

Here are some statements from the various contacts on wild animals which bothered their sheep:

Minnie Buchanan: "Once in a while there was an old shepherd dog that'd kill'em. My daddy had a dog that was half shepherd. I thought it was an awful fine dog. He got off with some more dogs and got after some sheep and he [her father] didn't wait till he killed any. He just took him [the dog] out and killed'im. 'Cause if they ever killed a sheep they say you can't break'em. That's what they said—you can't break'em."

Claude Darnell: "We lost sixteen one time. Just to the neighbors' dogs. The dogs got after'em one time in the bottom. Just ran'em in the creek and drowned'em. Didn't try t'eat none of'em."

Belle Dryman: "Well now, the dogs used t'kill'em and I used t'call them sheep-killin' dogs."

George Grist: "The wildcats would get'em. Wildcats were the worst but you used to have lots of wild dogs and things like that which would keep the wildcats run back. When the sheep got too far back, then th'wildcats got'em. The sheep will move back when th'cats bother'em. They got a whole lotta sense about things like that. If anything bothers'em, they come back home and they won't go to anybody else's house—jest their own wherever they're raised."

Gertrude Keener: "Bobcats is bad on killin' th'lambs. Dogs is th'worst things. Wild dogs or somebody's pet dogs'll kill two'r'three at night. I guess they would eat'em, but they tasted th'blood an'they just wanted t'kill'em. They were sheep killers, and a lot a'times one dog would kill two'r'three—a bunch a'sheep in one night."

The sheep which ran free in the mountains were relatively disease free. The only external parasites were ticks. The wool was so thick and greasy that only a tick could bother the sheep. Some of the sicknesses of sheep were described as follows.

Minnie Buchanan: "They might get what they call the 'rots'—cold in their head. They'd get over it when spring came. We never did doctor no sheep. Sheep had to take care of theirselves."

Claude Darnell: "They get the worms and to cure'em, feed cotton meal. It's got medicine in it t'kill th'worms."

George Grist: "They didn't have many diseases back then. Once in a while they'd get th'milk sick. This is the only country in the world that has milk sick. When the sheep got it, they'd die. Not all of'em would get it, but some would and died." [Little is known about the milk sickness. No one knows exactly where it comes from, but most think it is caused by a plant that sheep and cows sometimes find in dark coves and eat. An epidemic of milk sickness may occur one year and then disappear for a period of seven or eight years before recurring.]

The men and women who raised sheep many years ago were a sturdy, independent type of people. They raised sheep because they had to. They couldn't run out to the nearest store and buy clothing or material. This emphasized how important sheep raising was. Without wool, clothing, blankets, and woven goods could not be made. This type of independence is what made the people in this region so unique.

GARY WARFIELD (with a lot of help from his friends)

CARDING AND SPINNING

For many years the mountain people made their own clothing with hand-spun thread. Before the wool can be spun, it must be washed and carded. Most of the people we interviewed recommended washing the wool twice, both times in detergent and warm water, and rinsing in cold water. If washed too much, the oil will be washed out and the wool cannot be spun.

Carding is the process of breaking up the wool and preparing it to be spun. There are two sets of cards: the "breaking cards," which begin to separate the fibers; and the "fine cards," which comb the wool into rolls for spinning. A corn shuck or paper is used for the core of the bobbin and the wool is spun on it. When the wool has been spun, the full bobbin is simply slipped off the spinning wheel's spindle and replaced with an empty one.

When we asked Aunt Arie if she liked to card and spin, she said, "Ah, yes! I loved it. I'd be up a'settin' an'a'cardin' an'a'spinnin' till one'r'two o'clock in th'mornin'. They'd holler at me, 'Get in that bed!' Spinnin' makes a racket. Oh, Lord, I just loved t'spin. Get that thread up there. Have y'ever seen anybody spin? It's th'prettiest work, ain't it? Turn that wheel, run that thread up. I always had t'run it on a shuck. Put a shuck on th'spindle. Oh, I wish I could do that now. I loved t'do that."

The following pictures and captions show the steps involved in preparing the wool for weaving by carding and spinning it.

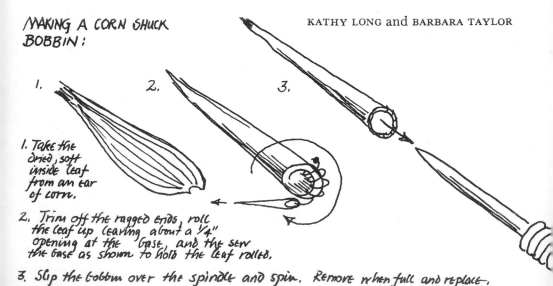

MAKING A CORN SHUCK BOBBIN:

KATHY LONG and BARBARA TAYLOR

1.

2.

3.

1. Take the dried, soft inside leaf from an ear of corn.

2. Trim off the ragged ends, roll the leaf up leaving about a 1/4" opening at the base, and then sew the base as shown to hold the leaf rolled.

3. Slip the bobbin over the spindle and spin. Remove when full and replace.

PLATE 198

THE BASIC MOTIONS:

A.

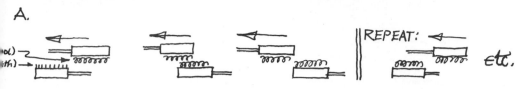

This is the basic carding motion. In this step, the bottom card is held stationary, and the top card is drawn across it (pulling toward the body). Use a good bit of pressure to straighten the fibers.

B.

This motion redistributes the wool on the teeth of the cards either before repeating a series of step A's, or as the first motion in the creation of a bat. Both handles point towards the body, and the top card is shoved firmly across the bottom card once.

C.

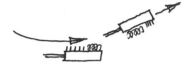

This motion transfers all the wool onto the top card. Both handles point towards the body, and the top card is drawn firmly across the bottom once.

D.

This motion, usually used as the first step in the creation of a roll, transfers ⅓ of the wool (just enough for one roll) in the full top card to the empty bottom card.

E.

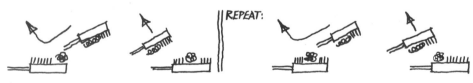

This motion, repeated 2-3 times, is the next, after D, in the creation of a roll. The handles of both are towards the body, the bottom card is held stationary, and the handle edge of the top card strokes the roll on the bottom card in short, choppy, bouncing motions that pull the roll backwards and help consolidate it.

F.

This motion is used to pack the roll more tightly. Teeth up, the back of the top card rolls backwards over and presses firmly down upon the roll, pulling it backwards. The motion is repeated 3-4 times. Just prior to each repetition, the roll is picked up and replaced at the back of the bottom card.

PLATE 199

PLATES 200–201   The first goal in carding is to prepare a number of "bats," for which a set of rough-toothed "breaking cards" is used. Margaret Norton first loads the top card with raw wool.

PLATE 202   When the top one is filled with raw wool, Margaret draws it over the bottom one, using substantial pressure, ten to twelve times (motion A, *Plate 199*). Then she gets the wool back onto the top card (motion C) with one firm stroke, and repeats the combing. By then the wool is usually well broken and fluffy. If not, she repeats a third time.

PLATE 203   When the wool is sufficiently broken, Margaret then makes the actual bat by one firm forward stroke (motion B, left) and two light backward strokes (motion C).

PLATE 204   The bat ends up on the top card and is peeled off and set aside. Usually Margaret makes bats all one day and rolls all the next.

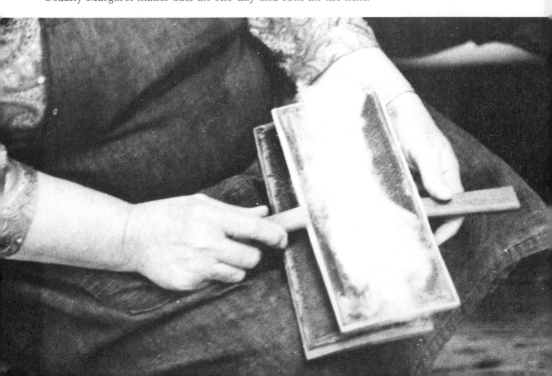

PLATES 205–207 In making rolls for spinning, Margaret uses a set of fine-toothed "roll cards." She takes one bat, pulls it apart, distributes it over the top card (*Plate 205*) as before, and combs the wool several times (*Plates 206–207*) as before (motions A and C).

PLATE 208   When the wool is completely combed and is soft and silky (*Plate 207*), Margaret begins the actual process of making the rolls. First, with one smooth stroke of motion C, she transfers all the wool onto the top card. Then, using motion D, she moves one-third of the wool from the top card onto the leading edge of the bottom, as seen here. There should be enough wool on the top card (i.e., in each bat) to make three rolls.

PLATE 210 . . . Margaret picks up the roll and places it on the leading edge of the bottom card.

PLATE 209   Then, using several strokes of motion E, she gently nudges the roll backwards. This helps to gather the fibers and consolidate the wool into an actual "roll." When the roll is at the back of the bottom card . . .

Plate 211   Then, using the back of the top card and motion F, she presses and pulls the roll backwards . . .

PLATE 212   . . . until it reaches the back of the card. She repeats this three or four times to make sure the roll will hold together.

PLATE 213   This done, she picks up the finished roll and places it with the others—ready to be spun into thread.

Spinning

If you are trying to spin, and the band jumps out of the track cut in the wheel, one of two things can be done. First, check to make sure the band is in the correct groove of the spindle (it should be on a *straight* line between the spindle and wheel's track). Second, tighten the tension on the band by twisting the wooden screw at the base of the head post. If neither works, your wheel may well be warped, making it impossible to spin.

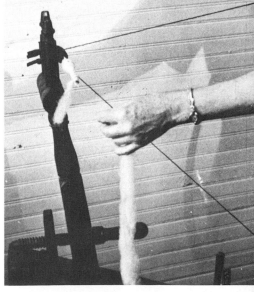

PLATES 214–215   Dean Beasley shows us how to spin using one of Margaret's rolls. Her corn shuck bobbin (*Plate 198*) was already in place on the spindle as she had been spinning (*Plate 214*). She simply took the end of one roll and pressed it against the tag end of the roll she had been spinning (*Plate 215*), and then . . .

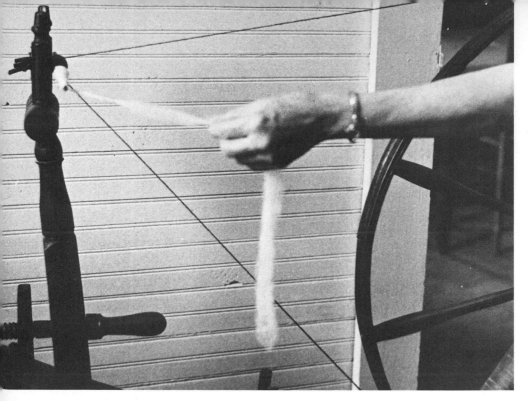

PLATE 216 . . . holding the ends together, she slowly turns the wheel and draws back gently with her left hand, being sure to keep the thread spinning on the very tip of the spindle by . . .

PLATE 217 . . . keeping her hand out to the left of the spindle's tip rather than on a line directly behind it.

PLATE 218   Keeping the wheel turning, she draws the thread back until it is about three feet long.

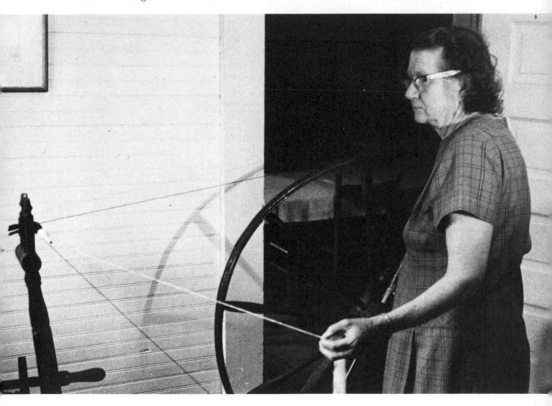

PLATE 219   When the thread is about three feet long, Dean drops it, grasps it again at the spindle's tip, and, turning the wheel, pinches the thread tightly between her thumbnail and forefinger and runs down the entire three-foot length once to help smooth out rough spots. Then, holding tension on the thread, she moves her hand in an arc until it is in a line directly behind the spindle. This time as she turns the wheel, the thread winds onto the bobbin. She then repeats the process, twisting the remainder of the roll into thread, adding another roll to the end of the last, and so on until the bobbin is full.

MAKING A SPINNING WHEEL

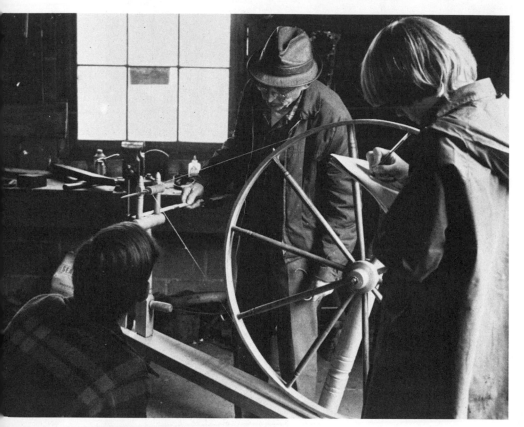

PLATES 220–222   Harley Thomas is one of the finest craftsmen still active in our area. (For our log cabin research, Harley showed us, with an axe, how to cut the almost impossibly intricate dovetail notch.) The spinning wheel shown in the photographs is one of his latest creations—the sort of thing he does best. Years ago, he and the other craftsmen who made wheels would make the rims for the wheels out of one, continuous, straight, heavy (¼″ thick) green white oak split. They would taper each of the ends (as shown in the diagram on p. 205), draw the split into a circle, attach the ends together with pegs or short nails, and then set the wheel up in the attic pressed flat in a mold so it wouldn't warp out of round while curing.

The following photographs show Harley pointing out various features of the wheel he made for us: wheel, hub, bench and head post of white pine; spokes of cherry; front leg of white poplar; and back legs of maple. Traditionally, almost any kind of hardwood was used. Rounds were turned on either foot- or water-powered lathes. Other pieces were carved or hewn.

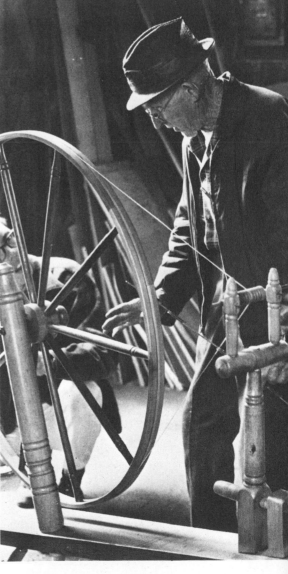

PLATE 223 Wheel ✕1 from the Jay Hambidge Art Foundation. Note the two upright pegs on the bench used for holding rolls while spinning.

PLATE 224 Wheel ✕2 from the Hambidge Foundation. The dark shape behind the wheel is skeins of dyed, hand-spun wool waiting to be woven into cloth.

PLATE 225   Wheel #3 from the Hambidge Foundation.

PLATE 226   Wheel #4 from the Hambidge Foundation.

PLATE 227 Wheel #5 from the Hambidge Foundation.

PLATES 228–229 These two photographs illustrate some of the tremendous variation between the five wheels measured at the Hambidge Foundation. In *Plate 228*, note the difference between the height of the front of the benches, the front widths of the benchs, the posts, and the head assemblies. In *Plate 229*, note the differences in the tops of the wheel posts and in their angles.

PLATE 230 Mrs. Thomas Barnes (whose husband Thomas made the ox yoke described earlier in this volume) stands behind the wheel she used at home. It was made of white oak by her husband's father, Allen Barnes, at the turn of the century. The rounds were all turned on a water-powered lathe. The wheel is now part of the *Foxfire* collection.

PLATE 231 The wheel used by Gertrude Keener's mother, and later by Gertrude, who says she spun enough wool on it one year to fill her living room and bedroom. It is shown here sitting on her front porch. The head and spindle are temporarily missing. (See chart.)

PLATE 232 Esco Pitts spent a large portion of his life working as a supervisor on the farm of the Rabun Gap-Nacoochee School in the days when all the farm work was done by mules. Now he spends much of his time in the wood shop behind his house. He is shown here with the wheel he made for the *Foxfire* museum. See measurements on the chart on page 204.

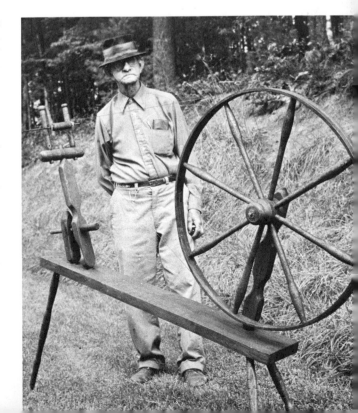

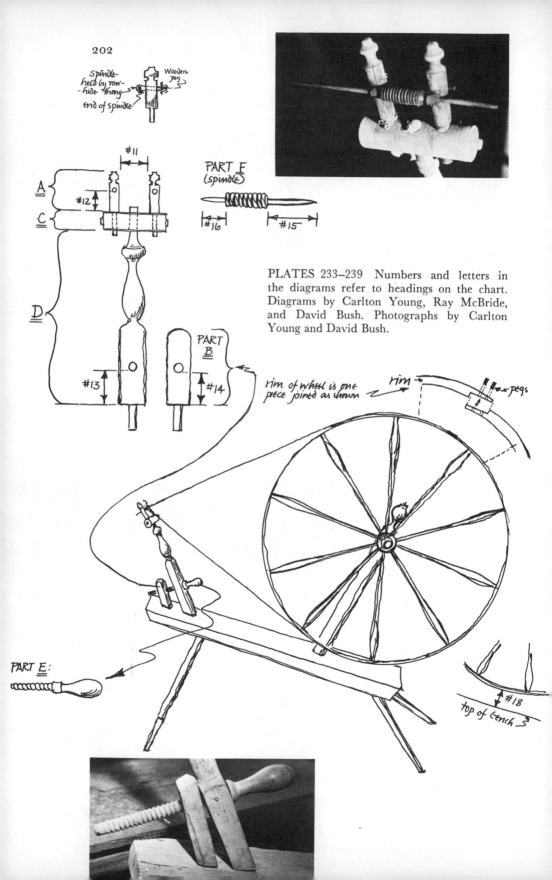

spindle held by raw-hide thong

Wooden peg

end of spindle

#11

A

#12

C

PART F (spindle)

#16   #15

D

PART B

#13   #14

PLATES 233–239 Numbers and letters in the diagrams refer to headings on the chart. Diagrams by Carlton Young, Ray McBride, and David Bush. Photographs by Carlton Young and David Bush.

rim of wheel is one piece joined as shown

rim

pegs

PART E:

#18

top of bench

note variations
between head
assemblys and
posts

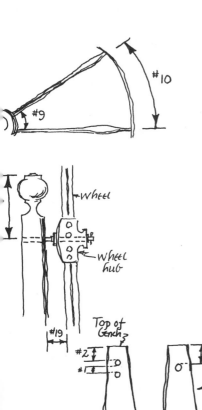

#10

#9

Wheel

Wheel
hub

#19

Top of
Bench

#2
#1

#3
#4

#8

Bottom of
Bench (holes
are for legs)

#5 #6
#7

	WHEEL		SPOKES		WHEEL POST		HUB		BENCH						LEGS				A(1&2)		B	
	Diameter	Circumference	Number / Diameter	Length	Length	Diameter	Width	Diameter	Back width	Front width	Height of back	Height of front	Overall length	Thickness	Length front leg	Length back legs	Distance apart at base	Average diameter	Height	Diameter	Height	Width
rley omas	36"	9'6"	10 / ⅝"	15¾"	25½"	3"	4¼"	3¾"	7"	4½"	11"	22"	41⅝"	1¾"	25"	14"	11"	1⅜"	5½"	¾"	4¾"	2"
co tts	31½"	9'4⅜"	8 / ⅝"	13¾"	21½"	1½"	4¼"	3¼"	7¼"	5"	11¼"	25"	48¾"	1½"	28¼"	13½"	10"	1¼"	7½"	¾"	8½"	2"
omas rnes	40"	10'7¼"	10 / ¾"	17¾"	29½"	2½"	4¼"	4"	7½"	5½"	9½"	26"	43"	1¾"	24¼"	15"	20¾"	1½"	5¼"	1"	5"	1½"
rtrude ener	40"	10'8"	10 / 1¼"	18⅛"	28½"	2½"	5"	3¾"	7⅞"	5¼"	11"	23"	47½"	2⅜"	22⅛"	14¼"	13"	1⅝"	*	*	9⅜"	2"
mbidge t undation . I	35"	9'4½"	10 / ⅜"	15½"	26"	2½"	5"	4"	7"	4½"	11"	26¼"	42½"	2"	26"	14½"	11"	1⅝"	5"	1"	5¼"	2⅛"
mbidge t undation . II	39½"	10'6"	10 / 1¼"	17¾"	29⅜"	2½"	4½"	3⅝"	7⅞"	5½"	9½"	25¼"	43⅛"	2⅛"	25½"	15"	21½"	1⅜"	5¼"	1"	4¾"	1½"
mbidge t undation . III	41½"	11'¾"	10 / 1"	18¾"	27"	3⅛"	4½"	3¾"	7⅞"	2⅜"	11⅞"	31"	42⅞"	2½"	30⅜"	15"	16"	1⅝"	3⅜"	¾"	6"	2¼"
mbidge t undation . IV	40"	10'9"	10 / 1¼"	18"	26"	2½"	4½"	3¾"	7⅜"	5⅛"	9"	25¾"	42⅛"	2"	26"	16⅛"	21½"	1¼"	4¾"	¾"	4¼"	1¾"
mbidge t undation . V	43"	11'5"	10 / ⅞"	19⅜"	33"	2⅝"	5¼"	3½"	6½"	5"	11¾"	21¼"	49⅛"	2 3/16"	25½"	13"	12⅞"	1½"	6¼"	1"	5½"	2⅛"

MAKING SKEINS

Though some people dyed the wool before spinning it, many went ahead and spun it in its natural color. When they had enough full bobbins to make a warp and weave, they then had a choice of either leaving it in its natural colors of white or brown, and winding it directly from the bobbins onto spools for making the warp; or they could make skeins for easy dyeing, by means of the "reeler." For dyeing, the skeins were simply hung suspended by sticks into the hot dye and turned and dipped frequently until they were the desired shade.

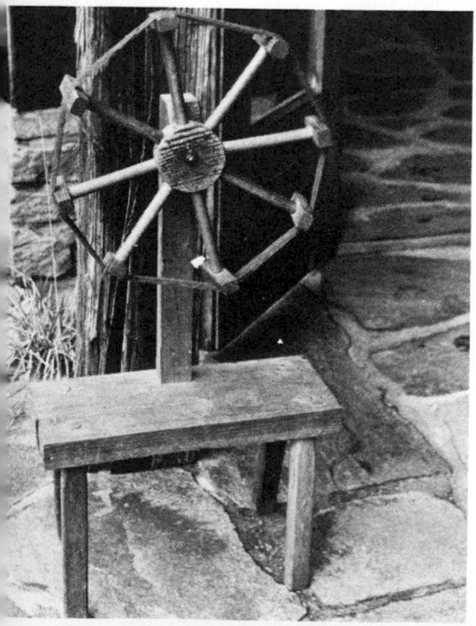

PLATE 240 Shown here is one type of reeler that is relatively easy to make. It can be put together either with nails or with wooden pegs. One-inch holes are drilled through the bench at a slant, and the ends of the legs are tapered to the holes with a drawknife. Almost any type of wood is suitable.

	D		E				F		KEYED MEASUREMENTS																		
Diameter	Length	Diameter or width	Length of handle	Length of screw	Width of handle	Width of screw	Total length	Length of wooden part	1	2	3	4	5	6	7	8	9	10	11	12	13	14	15	16	17	18	19
1½"	14½"	2"	3"	9"	1¼"	1"	12"	3½"	1½"	3"	7¼"	⅜"	2½"	1⅛"	2¾"	8¾"	⅝"	10½"	3⅝"	3¾"	3½"	3"	6¾"	1⅝"	6"	1½"	1"
1¾"	18½"	2¼"	3½"	12"	1¼"	¾"	11½"	3¾"	2½"	5½"	6¼"	1½"	2¼"	1½"	3¾"	1½"	¾"	11"	4"	3¾"	6"	5"	6"	2"	3¼"	2¼"	1¼"
2"	15½"	2"	4⅜"	7¼"	1¾"	1"	11¼"	2"	2¼"	2½"	13"	¾"	2¾"	¼"	½"	7¾"	¾"	11"	2¼"	2⅜"	3¾"	2¼"	7¾"	1⅜"	7"	1½"	1½"
*	16½"	2¼"	5⅜"	5⅜"	1½"	⅝"	*	*	1½"	4¼"	16¼"	1¼"	3"	1"	1⅝"	4"	¾"	11¾"	4¾"	*	4¾"	4"	*	*	5⅝"	1½"	1½"
1¾"	16½"	1¾"	4½"	6½"	1¼"	¾"	13"	2½"	1⅜"	3¼"	10⅝"	1"	2½"	½"	½"	7¼"	⅝"	10"	2"	1¾"	2¾"	2"	7⅝"	3¼"	6"	2¾"	1½"
2"	14½"	2⅛"	4½"	6¾"	1½"	1"	12¼"	2½"	1½"	3"	13⅝"	⅞"	4¼"	½"	¾"	7½"	⅝"	10¾"	2⅜"	2"	3⅜"	2½"	6"	3¾"	5½"	1¾"	1⅜"
2"	16¼"	2⅛"	4¾"	5¼"	1¾"	1"	13½"	2½"	1½"	2½"	11⅝"	1⅛"	1⅜"	⅞"	1½"	11¼"	⅜"	12⅜"	2½"	2¾"	3⅝"	2⅜"	8¼"	3¼"	5¼"	1¼"	½"
2"	14"	2⅛"	3¼"	7⅜"	1⅝"	1"	13½"	2⅛"	1½"	2⅜"	12⅝"	¾"	4¼"	1¼"	¼"	8⅜"	⅜"	11¼"	2⅜"	2"	3⅝"	2"	8⅜"	2⅜"	4½"	¾"	1⅛"
1⅝"	17¾"	2⅛"	4⅜"	8¼"	1⅝"	⅞"	13⅜"	2⅛"	1"	3⅝"	12⅛"	1"	2"	¼"	2⅜"	2⅛"	½"	13⅛"	3⅜"	2⅜"	4⅝"	3½"	9"	2⅝"	7¾"	2"	1½"

REELER

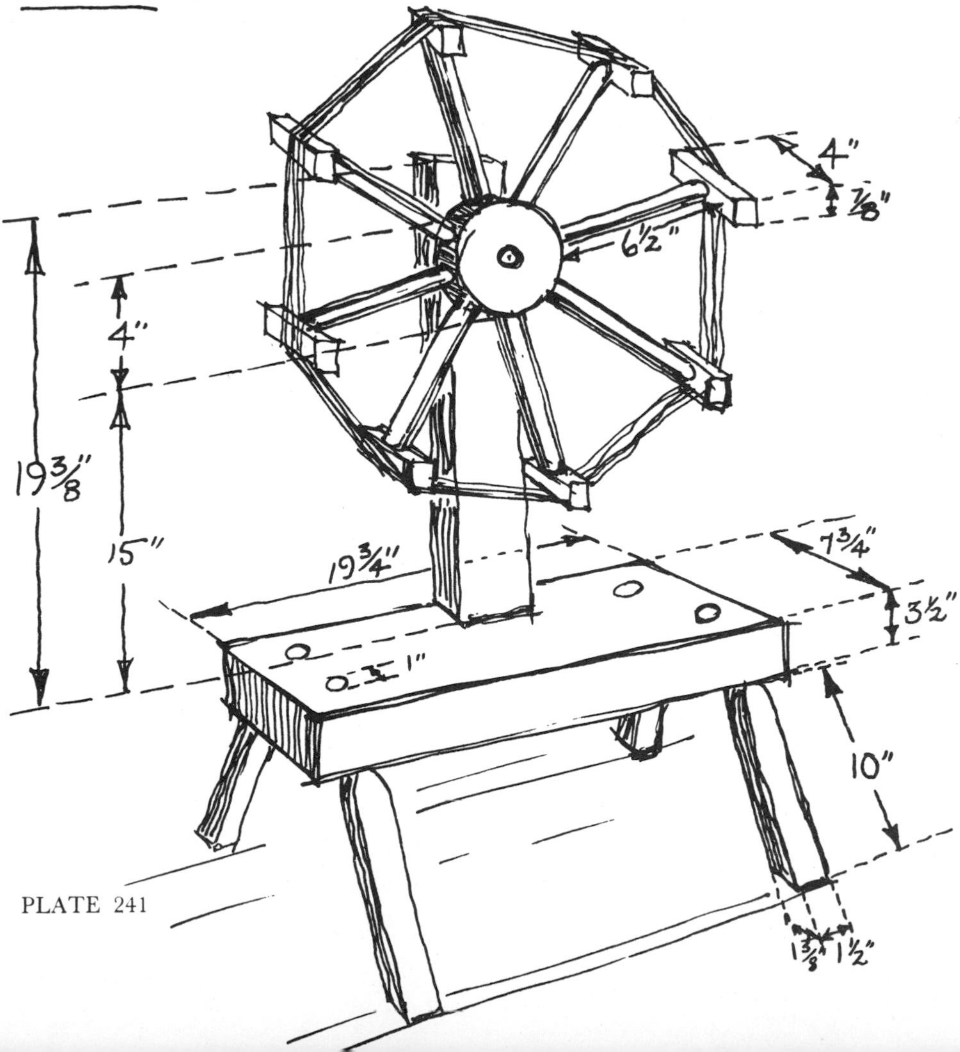

PLATE 241

PLATE 242 When Dean has the bobbins completed and ready to be dyed, she winds them off, one at a time, into skeins. Each full bobbin makes one skein.

PLATE 243 When the skein is complete, it is tied in several places, hung from a peg in the weaving shed, and another skein made. Then all the skeins together are dyed prior to weaving them into cloth.

DYEING WITH WILD PLANTS

Back many years ago when store-bought dyes were scarce, often only the natural shades of wool were used for material. However, when people did start dyeing wool different colors, usually their only sources for dyes were plants, which were boiled down in iron pots. Today, copper vats serve this purpose although none of our contacts used them. When the plants were boiled down, the material or thread was added to be dyed.

People often mixed mordants with the dye to set or fix colors and keep them from fading. Vinegar and salt were used quite frequently as mordants when dyeing with plants. Copperas, a green sulfate of iron, and alum, a white mineral salt, were also successful mordants for dyeing cloth. Acetic acid was used as a mordant to color red and potassium bichromate to color yellow. Most of our contacts didn't use a mordant when dyeing with walnut hulls, however, as the brown produced by the hulls rarely faded.

PLATE 244   Dyed skeins of wool ready to be woven on the front porch of the Jay Hambidge Art Foundation.

To keep the wool from getting full of roots and stems, some of our contacts boiled the plants to produce the dye, strained the foreign matter out of the liquid, and then boiled the wool in the dye. Other contacts boiled the plants in a bag together with the wool to prevent them getting entangled with the wool. Still, many of our contacts boiled both plants and materials together.

When the cloth is boiled, it should be dyed a shade darker than the color you want, since the shade will lighten as the wool dries. The amount (strength) of dye used depends on how dark a shade you want.

If you're really interested in dyeing with natural plant dyes, try it. There are plenty of books that explain the detailed procedures for dyeing with plants. A fascinating book on this is *Natural Dyes in the United States* (Rita J. Adrosko, Associate Curator, Division of Textiles, Museum of History and Technology, Smithsonian Institution Press, available at $3.25 from Superintendent of Documents, U. S. Government Printing Office, Washington, D.C. 20402). But it's almost more fun to experiment and surprise yourself. Minnie Buchanan described a woman who experimented with different dyes:

"Now there's a woman been aworkin' here a little with me for th'last month. She worked up t'last Friday just learnin' t'weave. She'd been studyin' dyein', too. She found a recipe somewhere t'dye with coffee an'tea leaves. She got her some white wool an'dyed it an'got a nice gold color. She got it spun right up here an'wove her a mat out of it last Friday. Then she tol' me she'd tried some with dandelion blooms an' she said it didn't turn out as well as she thought it ought to. She did get a pale yeller out of it. Then she tried some with clover leaves an' said she got just a pale pink with it. She set it with vinegar."

From eleven contacts—people like Lula Norton, Blanche Harkins, Edith Darnell, and Beulah Perry—we were able to amass a collection of recipes they used for dyeing cloth. Again, however, the real fun is in experimenting and surprising yourself with the colors you get. Good luck!

KAREN COX

BROWN-BLACK

Walnut hulls, roots, and bark were commonly used as a natural dye to produce shades of brown and black. The hulls were used for dye when the walnuts fell off the trees in the fall of the year. Darker shades of brown or even black were obtained by leaving the hulls, roots, or bark in the boiling water a longer period of time.

Edith Darnell: Use the outside hull of black walnuts. Add hulls with the material to boiling water. "They're damp an' when they get wet, that makes th'prettiest brown. Now they might put th'hulls in some kind of a bag in th'bottom while it boiled. 'Cause I know Mommy used t'dye quilt linin's an'all with it. I don't guess it'd take too long. I guess she'd boil'em till th'dyes got in'em."

Mrs. Darnell said you'd need approximately a peck of walnut hulls to dye a quilt lining. The hulls can only be used once as a dye. Her mother added salt as a mordant to set the dye, just before the material got through boiling.

She also said you could dye with the walnut tree roots. First, you heat the roots and then peel off the bark. Next, add salt or vinegar to the dye as the mordant. Then boil the roots with the cloth. It colors a dark brown.

Belle Dryman's mother only dyed with the brown dye from walnut hulls; otherwise, she used plain white wool or dark wool from the black sheep. Belle told us people usually used white wool for blankets and colored wool for clothes. These are the directions she gave for dyeing: Wash the wool directly from the sheep. Do not card or spin before dyeing. Fill a large iron pot with a layer of wool (about two inches in height) and then a layer of walnut hulls. Continue in this fashion until pot is full. Fill pot with water and boil it until desired color is reached. No mordant is necessary.

To make a dark brown, Aunt Arie said to use the walnut bark off the roots as soon as you dig them. Alternate a layer of wool and a layer of bark to fill up the pot. Then fill the pot with water and boil. She said a mordant is unnecessary to make the walnut dye set—the dye will not fade. For a darker brown, add extra bark.

Mary Carpenter's procedure for a brown dye: gather walnut hulls in the fall when the hull starts drying up. Boil the hulls in an iron pot; then remove hulls and strain the juice. Add mordant (one pint of vinegar or one pint of salt) and stir until fully blended. Add material and let it boil. Lift material out of the water regularly. Rinse wool out until water is clear.

Lula Norton's method was to boil walnut hulls until mushy. No mordant is required. Strain the dye and put material in and let it simmer. The colors are shades from tan to brown. To color a rose beige, add madder root (a plant that grows around the mountains).

Minnie Buchanan's variation was to tie two gallons of walnut hulls in a cloth sack. Put the sack of hulls in an iron pot and add water. Put wool in and boil an hour. This will dye more than four skeins a nice brown color.

Another way to acquire a dark brown is to use both walnut hulls and roots together. Fill a ten-gallon pot half full of chopped walnut roots and add one gallon of walnut hulls. Add either one teacup of salt or vinegar as a mordant. Boil. Lift out roots and hulls and put in the thread. Boil wool in dye for at least an hour. Add more roots and hulls for a darker brown.

To make a dye between a rust and brown color, Mary Carpenter told us to trim the bark off a maple tree. Mix copperas with the bark in an iron pot. Boil this solution and add thread or material. Take out when it is the right shade; wash and rinse it.

Use witch-hazel (tree) bark for black. Boil it and add material.

For light tan to yellow color, boil broom sage (broomsedge) and add to material.

ORANGE-YELLOW

Gertrude Keener: Use the gray moss from an oak or apple tree. Add water to the moss in a kettle and boil for one hour. Use more moss for a stronger dye. Sift out the foreign matter. Put thread or material in. Add five cupfuls of salt as a mordant per two gallons of moss. Color varies from an orange or yellow to a light brown. Mrs. Keener commented, "It would be nice t'keep yer moss in a bag. Th'lady that taught me t'do all these dyes had us t'put th'wool right down in th'moss, all in with th'roots."

Mrs. Keener also told us that wild broomstraw would make an orange or yellow dye. Fill a ten-gallon pot with broomstraw. Boil the broomstraw and cloth together. Add salt as a mordant. Broomstraw colors both wool and cotton.

Margaret Norton: Use dye flower (dye weed)—blooms in late summer in untended fields. Gather the flowers when in full bloom. Boil in water from ten to fifteen minutes, long enough to make it a shade darker than your desired color. Strain it. It makes a yellow color.

Lula Norton also used coreopsis flower (a plant of the same family as the aster with yellow, red-and-yellow, or reddish flowers shaped like daisies) for a yellow color. She boiled the blossoms.

She also gave us this information on black bark making a yellow dye: "Th'outside of black hickory bark was made for yellows. Just go out and beat it off th'trees. Boil it up and it makes beautiful yellows." For mordants, alum for one shade of yellow and potassium bichromate for another. "We put th'bark in flour bags. They hold quite a bit." By putting the bark in a bag, the solution doesn't have to be strained before dyeing the material. When asked the length of time to boil the bark: "There's no way of measuring your time. The bark has to be boiled until you get the desired color. People used t'do a lot of things by th'moon. They thought by getting it on a certain time of the moon, they made more coloring or juice."

Yellow root can be boiled down to make a yellow and then it fades out to a soft green.

Get hickory bark when the sap is up so it will peel out better. Boil it down to make beautiful shades of yellow.

Oak bark also makes a yellow. Boil it until you acquire a thick "ooze" and then add material.

BLUE

Lula Norton: Use indigo root (colors a blue). "I know that when my grandmother was making her indigo, she had what they called a 'dye pot.' They had to let this indigo set so long. I used a kind of lye to make my indigo. They used some kind of a 'brand' and mixed it up and let it ferment several days before they used it. [The brand is used to make it ferment.]

"I've understood that they had to put it in barrels of water and let it sit so long and ferment. The settling to the bottom of the barrel was what they used for the dye [a clay-like substance]. Now I bought it in the powdered form. I had a chemical to go with a powder. You don't boil it; you just dip it in the hot dye until you get the indigo."

Mr. and Mrs. Tom McDowell: Use maple bark. The color is obtained mainly from the inside bark, but both inside and outside bark are used. Boil it in a kettle. Remove bark from the dye; add copperas to set the dye and let it boil about a day. This colors a blue.

Blue can also be obtained from galls (insects form these on the stems of a ragweed plant, or any other plant). Boil the galls and add material.

RED

Lula Norton: Use madder. Grind the root up into powder and boil it with material. Colors from shades of rose pink to red are obtained from madder. "When I was at Berea, Kentucky once, I heard of a girl who had inherited her grandmother's madder bed."

Gertrude Keener: Use pokeberries (one gallon of berries to a ten-gallon pot). Boil them and add your material. This colors from a red to a maroon. Blackberries, grapes, or any other berries will yield various other shades of red.

Use red clay (one gallon of clay to a ten-gallon pot). Put clay in a cloth bag and let it boil. Remove clay and add material. Possibly use a cup of salt as a mordant. Clay colors a deep orangeish-red.

PURPLE

Use pokeberry roots. Chop up the roots and boil them. Add material to get a deep purple color.

GREEN

Use green oak leaves. Boil leaves with material for one to one and one-half hours. Add salt as a mordant.

Mrs. Norton's variation for green is to dye it yellow first. Then dye cloth with indigo (blue). "Dye the yellow *first* because the blue will take th'color out."

SHUTTLES, ETC.

PLATE 245 The SWISS was not widely used traditionally, but it does save work and is common today. The sliding wooden screw (arrow) clamps the expandable swiss in position in either its expanded (shown here) or contracted position. A skein is slipped over a contracted swiss, and then the swiss is expanded.

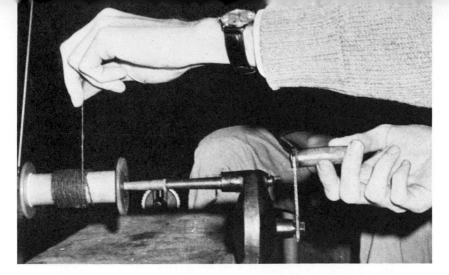

PLATE 246   Now a spool is mounted on the SPOOLER directly below the swiss, and thread from the skein fed onto the spool. As the spooler's crank is turned, the swiss turns also, feeding thread into the spool until it is full, at which point it is replaced by another. Spools can also be filled from broaches (filled bobbins off the spinning wheel) if desired. The swiss would not be used in this case, however.

PLATE 247   Filled spools can be mounted on a SPOOL RACK. The number of spools set into the rack depends on the number of threads the weaver wishes to feed into the warper.

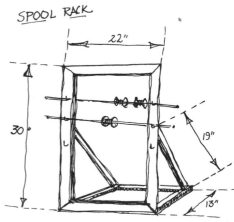

PLATE 248

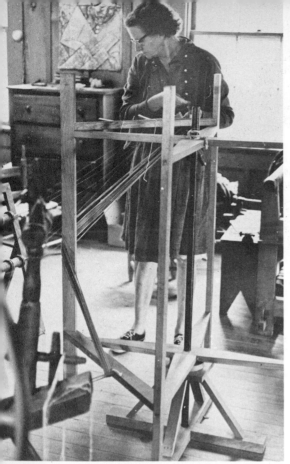

PLATE 249 Dean uses a WARPER like the one shown here rather than use the more traditional warper described later. One revolution of the warper (bottom peg to top peg) equals three yards. When Dean weaves a three-yard piece the width of a stole (230 threads), she mounts ten spools in the spool rack, and goes from top pegs to bottom pegs twenty-three times. As each spool runs out, she mounts a full spool in its place, ties the thread ends together, and continues.

PLATE 250 When the warp is in place, the weaver loads the bobbins for the shuttles. Often a BOBBIN WINDER is used for this, as seen here. Bobbins can be loaded either directly from a skein mounted on a swiss, or from undyed thread still on broaches.

PLATE 251 SHUTTLES come in many different styles and sizes. Their function is the same, however— to carry the thread across the warp, thus creating the weft.

PLATE 252 Claude Darnell made much of the equipment for the Jay Hambidge Art Foundation, including the shuttles. He fashioned them out of close-grained hardwoods (mostly dogwood, but walnut and cedar are also acceptable), all of which had been cured. He avoided green wood as it might split and snag the threads. The shape was fashioned with a drawing knife and the holes cut with an auger and coping saw.

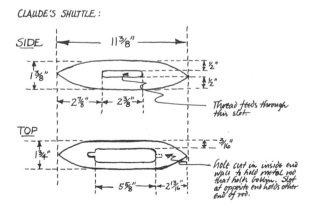

PLATE 253

THE GERTRUDE KEENER LOOM

The loom shown on these pages was Gertrude Keener's great-grandmother's loom. Gertrude estimates it to be at least 150 years old. Recently she took the pieces down from the barn loft so we could measure them, and then she put it together for us so we could see how it worked. It was a nostalgic moment, for material she wove on this loom paid her way through school.

WEAVING

The procedures of setting up a loom and weaving on it are hard to explain. Rather than delve into the different types of looms and intricate patterns, this section describes the use of a four-harness loom using the same colors of thread for the warp and weft, and using a simple 4-3-2-1 threading for a plain weave. Although a less complicated method of weaving, this is the traditional way it was done many years ago.

To fully understand how to weave the more difficult patterns (pages 246–55) refer to *The Shuttle-Craft Book of American Hand-weaving* (see Book List, page 246). It shows the pattern drafts for these patterns as well as several hundred others.

Photographs for this section were taken by Ray McBride, Chuck Ferriss, David Young, Gary Warfield, Carlton Young, and Eddie Moon.

The contacts who contributed information are Marinda Brown, Kate Hopper, Dean Beasley, and Jule Anderson.

PLATE 254 This photograph shows the entire loom assembled. The room was so small that we couldn't photograph the assembled loom with our widest camera lens. So we had to try to fit several photos together. There is some distortion, but we hope you can figure it out. Details of the various pieces follow.

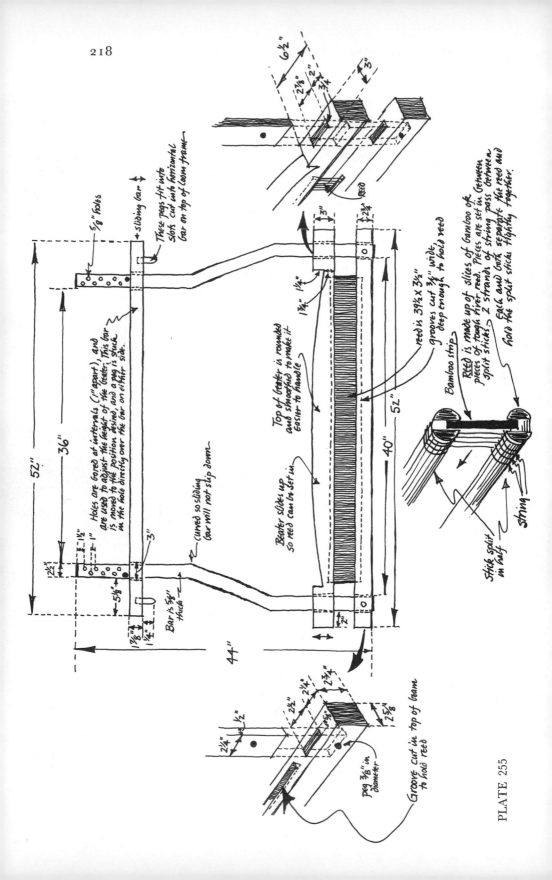

5/8" holes

← sliding bar →

These pegs fit into slots cut into horizontal bar on top of loom frame

Holes are bored at intervals (1"apart), and are used to adjust the height of the beater. This bar is moved to the position desired, and a peg is stuck in the hole directly over the bar on either side.

52"

36"

3/4" 1/2"
1" 1 1/2"

12 1/2"

5/8"

1 3/8"
1 1/4"

Bar is 5/8" thick

3"

curved so sliding bar will not slip down

44"

6 1/2"

2 7/8" 2"
3 1/4"

3"

reed

Beater slides up so reed can be set in

Top of beater is rounded and smoothed to make it easier to handle

3"

2 3/4"

1 3/4" 1 1/2"

reed is 39 1/2 x 3 1/2"

grooves cut 3/4" wide, deep enough to hold reed

52"

40"

2"

Bamboo strip

Reed is made up of slices of bamboo or pieces of tough river reed. Pieces are set in between split sticks. 2 strands of string pass between each and both separate the reed and hold the split sticks tightly together.

string

Stick split in half

1/2"
2 1/4"
2 1/2"
2 1/4"
2 3/4"
2 5/8"

Groove cut in top of beam to hold reed

peg 3/8" in diameter

PLATE 255

PLATE 256 Photo of beater frame without reed in place.

PLATE 257 Reed in place. Heddles in background.

PLATE 258 Beater raised to show groove cut to hold reed.

PLATE 259 Splits holding bamboo strips can be wrapped with a cloth for extra protection as shown.

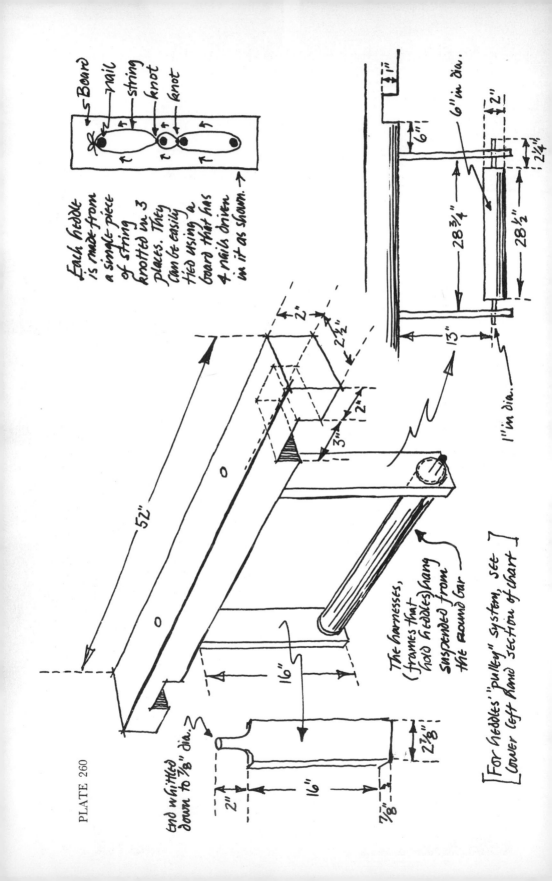

PLATE 260

Each heddle is made from a single piece of string knotted in 3 places. They can be easily tied using a board that has 4 nails driven in it as shown. →

Board
nail
string
knot
knot

6" in dia.

1"

6"

28¾"

2"

2¼"

28½"

1" in dia.

15"

52"

2"

2½"

2"

3"

The harnesses, (frames that hold heddles) hang suspended from the round bar

16"

2⅞"

16"

2"

⅞"

end whittled down to ⅞" dia.

[For heddles "pulley" system, see lower left hand section of chart]

PLATES 261–262   These two photographs show how the frame that holds the heddles (the fifty-two-inch bar) fits down over the top of the loom frame. It is not held in place by anything other than notches.

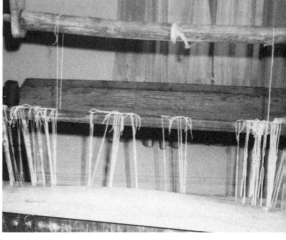

PLATE 263   The frame itself. See diagram (260) for measurements.

PLATE 265   One heddle in place on a harness. Thread (warp thread) passes through the central eye.

PLATE 264   A harness with heddles in place. For proper stringing, see diagram (260).

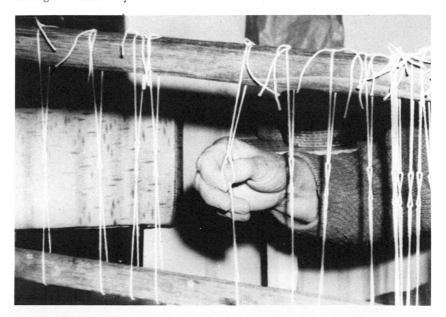

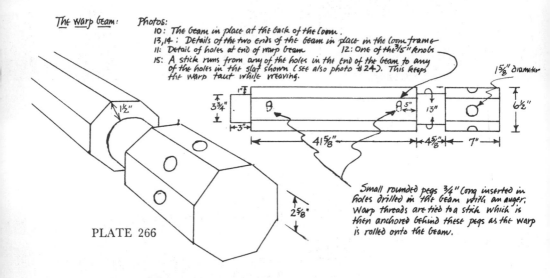

The warp beam: Photos:
10: The beam in place at the back of the loom.
13,14 : Details of the two ends of the beam in place in the loom frame
11: Detail of holes at end of warp beam   12: One of the 3/15" knobs
15: A stick runs from any of the holes in the end of the beam to any of the holes in the slat shown (see also photo #24). This keeps the warp taut while weaving.

1 5/8" diameter

1 1/2"
3 3/4"
1"
3"
41 5/8"
5"
13"
4 5/8"
7"
6 1/2"

2 5/8"

Small rounded pegs 3/4" long inserted in holes drilled in the beam with an auger. Warp threads are tied to a stick which is then anchored behind these pegs as the warp is rolled onto the beam.

PLATE 266

PLATE 267   The beam in place at the back of the loom.

PLATE 268   Details of holes at end of warp beam.

PLATE 269   One of the $\frac{3}{5}''$ knobs.

PLATES 270–271   Details of the two ends of the beam in place in the loom frame.

PLATE 272   A stick runs from any of the holes in the end of the beam to any of the holes in the slat shown (see also *Plate 286*). This keeps the warp taut while weaving.

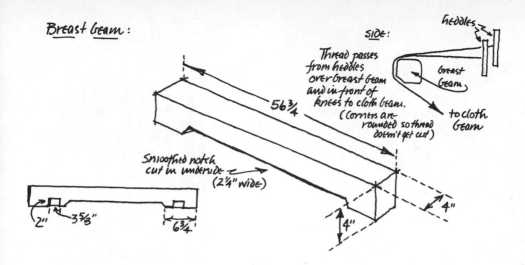

Breast Beam:

SIDE:

heddles

Thread passes from heddles over Breast Beam and in front of knees to cloth beam. (Corners are rounded so thread doesn't get cut)

Breast Beam

to cloth Beam

56¾

Smoothed notch cut in underside (2¼" wide)

2" 3⅝" 6¾

4"

4"

PLATE 273

PLATE 274 Breast beam from bottom with cloth beam in background.

PLATE 275 Notches cut in underside of beam fit top of loom frame.

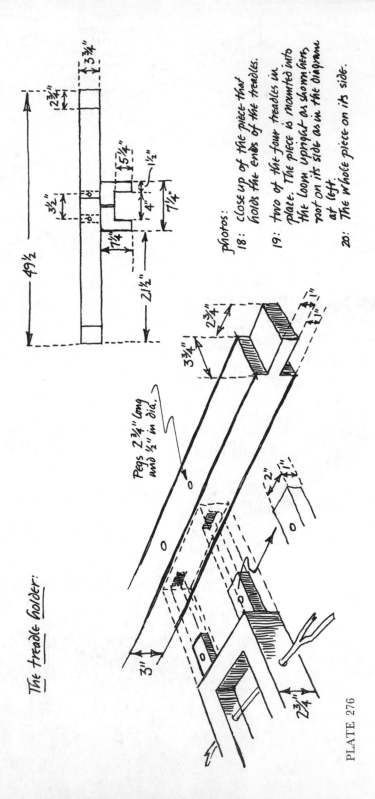

The treadle holder:

Pegs 2¾" long and ½" in dia.

3 ¾"

2¾"

1½"

5¼"

3½"

4"

7¼"

7¼"

49½

21½"

2¾"

3¾"

1"

1"

2"

1"

3"

2¾"

Photos:

18: Close up of the piece that holds the ends of the treadles.

19: Two of the four treadles in place. The piece is mounted into the loom upright as shown here, not on its side as in the diagram at left.

20: The whole piece on its side.

PLATE 276

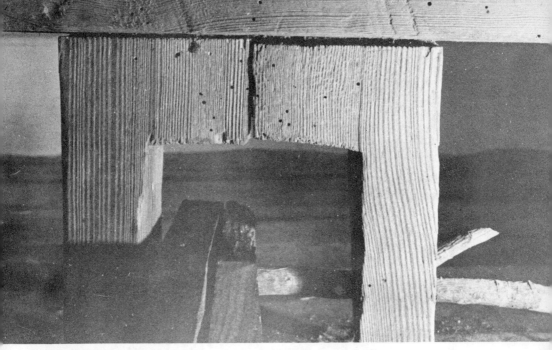

PLATE 277   Closeup of the piece that holds the ends of the treadles.

PLATE 278   Two of the four treadles in place. The piece is mounted into the loom upright as shown here, not on its side as in the diagram (276).

PLATE 279   The whole piece on its side.

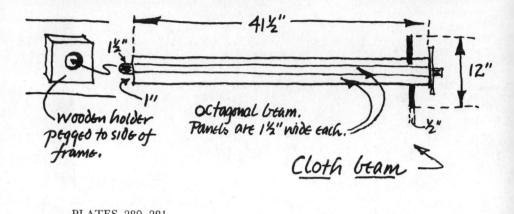

41½"

1½"

1"

Wooden holder
pegged to side of
frame.

Octagonal beam.
Panels are 1½" wide each.

Cloth beam

12"

½"

PLATES 280–281

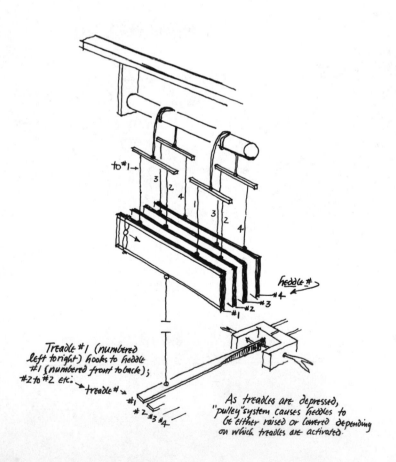

to #1→

3
2
4

1

3 2

4

heddle #→

#4

#3

#2

#1

Treadle #1 (numbered
left to right) hooks to heddle
#1 (numbered front to back);
#2 to #2 etc.→ treadle #→
#1
#2 #3 #4

As treadles are depressed,
"pulley" system causes heddles to
be either raised or lowered depending
on which treadles are activated.

PLATE 282   This end of cloth beam is hewn into a knob to fit into hole in loom frame.

PLATE 283   Opposite end of beam showing metal cog.

PLATE 284   Cog end in place. See also *Plate 289*.

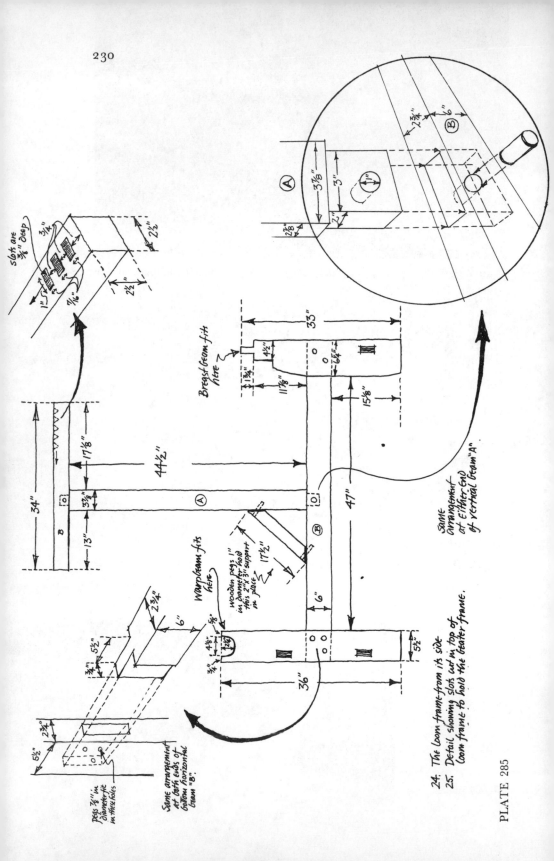

24. The loom frame from its side.
25. Detail showing slots cut in top of loom frame to hold the beater frame.

PLATE 285

PLATE 286   The loom frame from its side.

PLATE 287   Detail showing slots cut in top of loom frame to hold the beater frame.

PLATE 288   Detail showing how side beam fits into loom leg. Note mortise and tenon joint with pegs.

PLATE 289   Brace (clutch) mounted to side (inside) of frame to articulate with cogs and hold cloth beam steady and in place so threads are kept taut.

MAKING A WARP

The first thing you have to do is to make a warp. For this you need your thread and a warper, or warping frame. Marinda Brown made a warp for us to show us how she does it, and used it to make striped belts.

Before you can actually make the warp you have to figure out how long it will be, and how many threads it will have. To determine the length, add one yard to the number of yards of cloth desired, plus another two inches for every yard desired. The extra yard makes up for the warp on the loom which can't be used because of the threading; it can't be drawn through far enough to weave. The extra two inches per yard compensates for warp taken up as it is woven—the threads in cloth don't lie perfectly flat. You can also add a little extra for fringe and/or hems. Bear in mind the longer the warp, the harder it is to put on the loom.

The number of threads used depends on four things, which in turn depend on each other—the size of the thread, how tight you want

PLATE 290

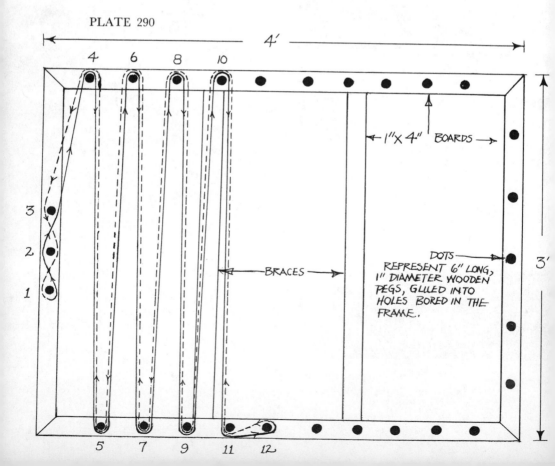

PLATE 291 Mrs. Brown puts on a warp. There are several different colors of thread being used as Mrs. Brown wants a striped warp. Some advance calculation is required to figure out where the stripes should come and how many threads wide they should be. They are put into place on the frame in order. Mrs. Brown: "There is a yard between each one of these pegs. Say you want to put on ten yards (want a warp ten yards long). You measure off ten yards; then you start at this end of your frame [point ✳1 on *Plate 296*] and tie a little knot in your thread and wind as far as ten yards will go."

your weave, the number of dents per inch in the reed, and how wide the cloth is to be. The following directions are based on one thread per dent in the reed. Count the number of dents per inch in the reed of your loom. Multiply this number by the desired width in inches of your cloth, plus two inches. The added two inches compensate for the fact that the weft draws the edges of the warp in, creating the selvage, and makes the cloth somewhat narrower than the threaded warp.

Measure off the desired warp length on one thread. Following the pattern in the diagram (*Plate 290*), tie one end to peg ✳1, and string following the solid line until you reach the end of the measured length. Then follow the dotted line in the opposite direction back to peg ✳1.

String your warp in this fashion, counting carefully—every "round trip" from peg ✳1 back to peg ✳1 equals two warp threads—until you have the desired number of threads on (*Plate 291*). If the warper fills up before you're done, take it off the warper (explained in *Plates 292–293*) and repeat the process until you have enough threads. When you are through stringing the warp, tie a string or ribbon loosely around the cross between pegs ✳2 and ✳3. These crosses keep the warp threads in order, but both would come completely out if you failed to tie them.

Slip the end of the warp off the last peg used, and make it into a chain so the threads will not tangle and sets chain(s) aside. See diagram in *Plate 295*.

PLATE 292 Mrs. Brown ties a ribbon around the cross made by the warp threads between pegs 1 and 2. This step is necessary to prevent the threads from getting mixed up and out of order when they are taken off the frame. (Note the different colors of threads in place in the same position they will hold when the warp is put on the loom.)

PLATE 293 Both crosses are tied and the threads are ready to be taken off the frame.

PLATE 294 Minnie Buchanan's hand-made warping frame—a little different, but it works on the same principle as Mrs. Brown's.

X = points where threads are grasped

⟶ = left arm

---⟶ = right arm

① ② ③

Repeat 1 and 2, using the new loop just created. Continue to end of warp.

PLATE 295

THREADING THE LOOM

A loom can be threaded from the front or from the back. We will describe how to thread it from the back, using a simple 4-3-2-1 pattern through the heddles in the harnesses. The threading itself is not done initially with the long warp, but with an equal number of short threads called thrums, which are tied to the apron of the warp beam. Cut about a yard long, as many threads as you have in your warp. Take the desired width of your cloth plus two inches, and center this width on the apron of the warp beam. Starting at the right edge of this width (standing at the back of the loom, facing the front) tie a small group of thrums, say twelve, to the apron. Continue tying on groups of thrums, spacing them evenly over the measured width on the apron, until they are all tied on. See diagram (*Plate 296*) for a good knot to use.

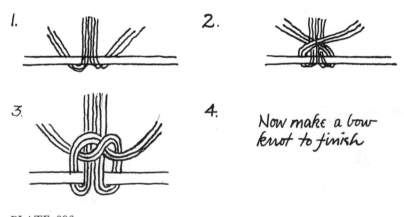

1.   2.   3.   4.   Now make a bow knot to finish

PLATE 296

Now you are ready to thread, or draw in, the thrums through the heddles in the harnesses. The harnesses are numbered from one through four (in a four-harness loom) beginning at the front of the loom. See harness diagram (*Plate 297*). The pattern shown is a simple 4-3-2-1 pattern. One quarter of the warp threads will go through the heddles in each harness, so we suggest taking out of each harness all but the number of heddles which are to be used.

The top diagram in *Plate 297* shows the order of the harnesses in the loom. The other diagram is a draft for the 4-3-2-1 pattern. The horizontal-numbered rows represent the different harnesses, and the blackened boxes represent threaded heddles.

Harness Numbering:

front of loom

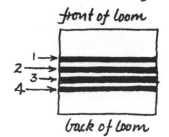

Black bars represent the harnesses, numbered from 1-4, beginning at the front.

back of loom

Pattern draft for 4-3-2-1 threading:

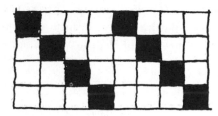

1   numbers correspond to numbering of harnesses.
2   Each blackened box represents
3   a heddle through which a
4   thread passes.

PLATE 297

PLATE 298   Marinda Brown uses a hook to pull threads through heddles.

Using your fingers or a long hook, as in *Plate 298* thread the thrum farthest to the right through the eye in the first heddle on the right in harness ⅓4, (the one closest to you). Working toward your left, thread the second thrum through the first heddle on the right in harness ⅓3, keeping this thrum to the *left* of the threaded heddle in harness ⅓4. Thread the third thrum through the first heddle on the right in harness ⅓2, keeping it to the left of the other threaded heddles. Thread the fourth thrum through the first heddle on the right in harness ⅓1, again keeping it to the left of the threaded heddles. String the fifth thrum through the second heddle to the right in harness ⅓4, beginning the pattern over—continue until you have threaded all the thrums. It is a good idea to keep checking your threading as you go along, to make sure it is correct. It is hard to correct later. Pull all the thrums as far as they will go toward the front of the loom.

SLEYING

Center on the reed the desired width of your cloth plus two inches. Sitting at the front of your loom, using the hook again, take the first thrum on your left, and draw it through the leftmost dent to be used in the reed. Continue pulling all the thrums through the dents, one at a time, one in each dent, in the order threaded from the left to the right. You may do this from right to left; it's a matter of preference. It is important that this is done correctly, or your warp will look uneven in the woven cloth. Once they are all pulled through the reed, pull the thrums toward the front of the loom so they will not slip back.

Now you are ready to tie your warp to the thrums. First push the beater all the way forward, away from you. Without unchaining your warp, cut the loops which were strung around peg ⅓1, just above the two tied crosses—don't let the ties slip out (*Plate 300*). Sit or stand at the front of the loom. Keeping your warp ends in order—this is very important—tie the first warp thread on the left to the first thrum on the left (*Plate 301*). Do the same with the second warp thread and second thrum, and continue working toward the right until the whole warp is tied onto the thrums. You may also work from right to left, as it is a matter of preference. If you have more than one warp chain, handle it (them) in the same manner as the first one. Make *sure* all your warp threads and thrums are in the right order. The knots should be as small as possible, with short waste ends of equal length for each knot.

PLATE 299 Minnie Buchanan's loom, thrums all threaded through the dent and in place, waiting for a warp to be tied on.

PLATE 300 Marinda Brown cuts the cross that was formed around peg ⚹1 on the warping frame.

PLATE 301 The ends of these warp threads are now tied to the threaded thrums.

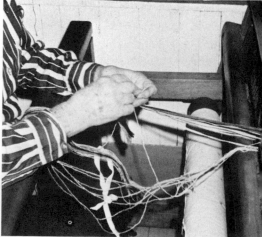

PLATE 302 When the warp threads are all tied to the thrums, the "beaming" begins. First, all the knots must be pulled through the reed and the heddles.

BEAMING

Now you are ready to roll the warp on, a procedure also called beaming. It will go through the reed and the heddles, and roll around the warp beam (*Plate 302*). You will need another person to roll the warp beam, plus several slim, smooth sticks longer than the width of the warp. Carefully untie the ribbons around the crosses on the warp chain. Standing at the front of the loom with the other person at the back, unchain a couple of feet of the warp. Holding it taut straight back from the loom, have the warp beam rolled slowly, and give gently as it is rolled on. Be very careful as the knots go through the reed and heddles. Stop the rolling and unchain more warp; have it rolled on again. One or two sticks should be placed lengthwise between the beam and the warp being rolled on, for every revolution of the beam (*Plate 305*). (The sticks keep the warp from tangling on the beam, and keep the strands on the edge from rolling on tighter than the rest.) Continue in this way until the end of the warp is about even with the breast beam.

Unroll the cloth beam and bring the apron over the breast beam. Center a width on the cloth beam apron a little wider than the width centered on the reed. Cut the loops at this end of the warp. Beginning at the left, tie the warp onto the apron (*Plate 303*) in small groups of threads (as you tied the thrums onto the warp beam apron, using the same knot). Spread the groups of threads out so they are evenly spaced on the centered width on the apron. Make sure all the threads are in the right order, as they were threaded, and keep them evenly taut (*Plate 304*). You may begin tying from the other side or from the center, if that is easier.

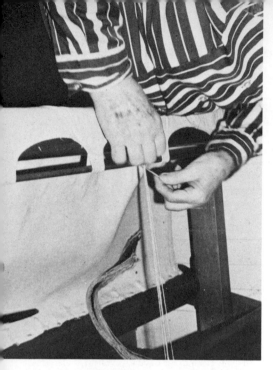

PLATE 304 Make sure the threads are tied on with an equal amount of tension.

PLATE 303 Then the warp is rolled all the way through, and its leading end tied, one thread at a time, to the cloth apron.

PLATE 305 Most weavers place sticks between the layers of warp as it is rolled onto the warp beam to keep the threads from becoming tangled.

PLATE 306 A beautifully threaded and rolled warp executed by Kate Hopper.

WEAVING

You are almost ready to weave. Roll the cloth beam back so the end of the apron is just over the breast beam, and roll the warp beam until the whole warp is taut. Fill your shuttles with thread for your weft. You must first throw five or ten shots for a header, or heading, which will even out the warp and bring it to proper width. Weaving involves three fairly easy motions—throwing the shuttle (*Plate 307*), treadling, and pulling back the beater, or batten. We'll give you the treadling pattern which will make a plain weave with the given threading. The treadles are numbered one to four, from the left to the right on a four-harness loom (*see Plate 281*). The treadles are tied to the harnesses; the treadling pattern plus the threading pattern determine the type of weave.

Your treadling pattern is one and three, two and four, one and three, two and four, etc. Push down treadles ⋕1 and ⋕3. Hold one end of the thread in the shuttle at one side of the warp; with the other hand throw the shuttle through the opening between the two layers of warp. Do not pull the weft too tight. Pull the beater back gently (push it forward to its original position each time you use it), change to treadles ⋕2 and ⋕4, which in turn changes your shed. Use the beater again, and throw your shuttle through the other way. Use the beater, change to treadles ⋕1 and ⋕3, use the beater, throw the shuttle the other way. Continue this pattern, using treadle, beater, shuttle, beater, treadle, etc. until the header is even and smooth. Once you have an inch or two woven, you may use the beater with greater force.

You're finally ready to weave whatever you like. Weave an inch or so for a hem, or leave a space for fringe. Continue weaving as you would the header; you'll notice that as you weave, the cloth takes up your shuttling space. Release the warp beam, as much as necessary, lock it again, and roll the cloth beam as far back as you can and still weave. Make sure the warp is taut before you go on weaving. When you leave your loom for any time, always loosen the warp beam so the warp won't weaken and stretch. When your cloth reaches the desired length, weave another inch or so for a hem and weave another header, or skip a place for fringe, then weave a header.

To remove the cloth, loosen the warp beam, push the beater forward, pull the cloth toward the breast beam, and cut the cloth just above the header. Make sure the rest of the warp does not slip through the reed. Completely unroll the cloth beam, and cut just below the first header. Tie your loose warp ends (now thrums!) so they will not slip through the reed. (You can tie another warp to these thrums and start all over.) Finish off your cloth by cutting off the header and hemming, or tying the fringe so the cloth won't ravel. Finished material is usually washed, then stretched, while wet, on a frame to dry (*Plate 309*). The dots represent nails on which the material is speared while drying.

PLATE 307   Dean, after tying the warp to the cloth apron, throws several shots to get started.

PLATE 308 Many say you can instantly tell how good a weaver is by looking at the edges of the finished cloth. A careless weaver will invariably produce sloppy, ragged edges. Dean produces flawless edges by first throwing the shuttle through the warp, then putting the shuttle down and pulling the remainder of the "shot" gently through the warp by hand and checking to make sure the tension is exactly right so that each shot neither pulls too hard on the warp threads, nor leaves a loop dangling out from the edge; and only *then* pulling the beater back.

PLATE 309

Finished material is usually washed, and then stretched, while wet, on a frame like the one shown to dry. The dots represent nails on which the material is speared while drying.

3'

(as long as you wish (usually 8'-15'))

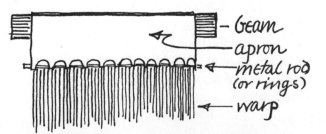

— beam
— apron
— metal rod (or rings)
— warp

PLATE 310

GLOSSARY

Aprons—the strips of heavy canvas attached to the cloth beam and the warp beam. The loose flap of the apron holds the metal rod to which the warp threads are attached. See diagram in *Plate 310*.

Beam (verb)—to roll a warp onto the warp beam; pulling it from the front of the loom through the reed and heddles, around the warp beam, by means of turning the warp beam.

Beater (or batten)—a swinging frame set crosswise of the loom. It carries the "reed" or "sley." The beater, falling forward against the edge of the web, delivers most of the beat by its own weight. As each new weft thread is thrown, the beater is pulled back to press it into place.

Breast beam—from beam of loom over which the material passes.

Chain—the warp is made into a chain as it is taken off the warping frame. See chain diagram (*Plate 295*).

Choker—tie thread about one-half yard from the cross. It keeps thread same tension while tying on to tabby thread or drawing in.

Cloth beam—the beam onto which the finished cloth is rolled.

Cloth beam apron—see *Aprons*.

Cross—formed where warp ends cross in alternate succession around pegs on a warper. Its purpose is to keep the threads straight.

Dent—the space between the vertical bars of the reed. The threads pass through these spaces.

Draw-in—see *Thread*.

Draft—a drawn pattern which shows how to thread a loom in a particular way. Each different threading can be depicted by a draft.

Filler—see *Weft*.

Harness—the shedding mechanism consists of two or more harnesses (or heddle frames) carrying "heddles," operated to rise and sink by means of foot treadles or hand levers.

Header—one inch of scrap weft to begin piece of material.

Heddles—the wires or strings mounted in the harnesses. Each heddle has one eye in its center through which a thread passes.

Loom—machine for weaving cloth.

Reed—a comb (the teeth of which are made of metal, reed, or bamboo) which is mounted in the beater and serves to space the warp threads.

Selvage—the very edges of woven cloth, where the warp threads are drawn closer together than in the rest of the cloth.

Shed—the pattern of the warp threads in the opening made between the two layers of warp, made when part of the treadles are pushed down. The shuttle is then passed through this opening.

Shot—the action of throwing the shuttle between the two layers of warp thread created by using the treadles.

Shuttle—carries thread from one side of the web to the other.

Sley—to draw the thrums or warp through the dents in the reed.

Tabby—the threads left on loom to tie the new warp to.

Thread (draw-in)—to bring the thrums, or warp, through the heddles in a certain pattern.

Thrums—short threads around a yard long which are tied to the apron of the warp beam, and used to thread the loom. They are much easier to thread than the warp itself would be.

Treadle (verb)—to manipulate the heddles of the loom.

Treadle (noun)—foot pedals under loom which cause the harnesses to go up and down.

Warp—the threads running parallel to the sides of the loom, and crossed by the weft. The warp is rolled onto the warp beam, threaded through the heddles and reed, and tied onto the apron of the cloth beam.

Warp apron—see *Aprons*.

Warp beam—the beam around which the unwoven warp is wound.

Warper—a square or rectangular frame with pegs on it arranged in a regular pattern, or similarly arranged pegs fitted into a wall. A warper is used to measure off a warp to thread onto a loom. When used correctly, all the threads stay in the same order they are put on the warper.

Weft—the threads which are woven across the warp, perpendicular to the sides of the loom. The weft (or woof) spins off a bobbin in the shuttle as one weaves. The weft is also called the filler.

BOOK LIST

Here are the names of a few books and pamphlets our contacts had. You might be able to order them if you would like to.

1. *Foot Power Loom Weaving*, Edward F. Worst, Bruce Publishing Co., Milwaukee, Wisconsin. Copyright 1947.
2. *Opening a Door to Two Harness Techniques,* Irene Francisco, Lily Mills Co., Shelby, N.C. Copyright 1960.

3. *The Shuttle-Craft Book of American Hand-weaving,* Mary Meigs Atwater, the Macmillan Co., New York. Copyright 1961.
4. "Practical Weaving Suggestions," Lily Mills Co., Shelby, N.C. (no date given).

T'ME, WEAVIN'S LIKE LIFE

In trying to learn about the actual process of weaving, we were especially interested in the personal feelings of the weaver.

As we began talking to these people, we found that weaving was more than just a job or a way to make a living. It took away the loneliness of an endless day. We realized this when Mrs. Darnell said, "When no one's aroun', you can be a hummin' an' a singin' while you're sitting there weavin' that pattern."

Weaving also proved to be a challenge when Mrs. Brown asked us, "Have any of you ever taken music? Well, you see a piece o' music an' you want t'sit down an' try it out an' see what it's like. Well, I'm that way with my weavin'. If I see a pattern draft, I wanna sit down an' try it out."

After talking to Gertrude Keener, we found that weaving is something very special and meaningful to her. "When you watch your pattern grow, t'me it's like life—more like living. It's more like building character than anything else I can describe it with. It's like teachin' a child from th'beginning to grow. As your pattern grows 'r as your cloth grows, it's just like a child growin' up. You weave your life into somethin' beautiful. That's the way I see it."

We realized the deep meaning and love they had for their work. The women we talked to have something rare and valuable to carry with them throughout life—stories to tell, a deeper insight into people, more patience and endurance, and, most important of all, the knowledge to pass down an art that is dying.

BETSE WHILDEN and KAREN COX

Mrs. Harry Brown is undoubtedly one of the most fascinating weavers we interviewed. She is constantly at work weaving rugs, belts, mats, stoles, ponchos, pocket books, and other pieces of beautifully done work. She is an expert in accuracy and skill with her craft. She always weaves for more people than she has time for, but still manages to do it with a smiling face and happy attitude.

PLATE 311 "Octie Bates wove this slip. Y'see how big it is. I wore it ever since it's made—forty, sixty years ago. How 'bout that—they lastin' so long? Don't look like it would, does it? It's homemade. It'll last so much longer than anything y'buy"— Aunt Arie.

PLATE 312 Suzy helps Belle Dryman hold up a handspun, handwoven blanket outside her home. The blanket was woven in two separate pieces and sewn together since the loom was not big enough to hold the entire width. Colored stripes, as below, are achieved by simply placing colored threads in the warp in place of white ones before actually beginning to weave.

PLATE 313 Whig rose pattern woven by Marinda Brown.

Mrs. Brown's history of her career in weaving is a long but interesting one. "Harry's mother, 'Mother Brown,' taught me t'weave. I helped her thread up th'loom. She made some coverlets for all of her children. I went with her down to Mrs. Zac Dillard's, Barnard Dillard's parents. She had a warping frame. Oh, it wus a great big thing. She kept it outside an' it went just about all th'way across th'house. Mother Brown put on about a hundred yards of warp. An' I helped her carry that thread back an' forth. It seemed like we walked miles an' miles in getting it on. That's how older people that lived a long time back warped their thread. It wus a lot stronger than thread we get hold of today that we weave with. It has made me wonder in working with th'fine threads that I do, how they ever managed t'get it on. That's th'hardest part about it.

"I do remember helping her thread up th'loom. Sometime after she made these coverlets, she brought her loom here an' put it on our porch that went all th'way aroun' th'house. An' she let me set th'loom up on th'porch an' she did some weaving on th'porch. Then she let me keep th'loom an' weave rugs. I made quite a few rugs with worn clothing that I worked up th'strings myself.

"Mother Brown died in 'thirty-nine. She had parts o' that loom borrowed from people all over th'community. When she died, we returned those parts an' there wadn't anything left much. We took th'loom down an' set it out an' o' course it just went t'bad.

PLATE 314 The material on the left is the cup and saucer or wheel of fortune pattern. On the right is the honeysuckle, both woven by Marinda Brown.

PLATE 315 Ada Kelly and Mary Rhodes hold the rose and vine bedspread woven by Ada.

"Then I didn't do anything but weave rugs fer 'bout four 'r five years after I got my own loom. After they started th'rug plant I got lots o' their waste yarns. I salvaged them from th'dump people. I'd find boxes of yarn in some of our gullies. So after I got hold o' that I just branched out an' started doing other things.

"I think about th'first thing I did after I made rugs, I wove a stole. I had taken about a week's course at Gatlinburg an' this lady showed us how t'make stoles. She had a draft that she had made up herself that gave th'steps in it. I debated on that fer a good many weeks before I ever undertook it. Finally I did get around an' I ordered th'thread that she recommended t'use. An' I went t'work on th'stoles an' it wasn't hard to do.

"We had four small gran'daughters, an' I made them each a skirt. They had made skirts over at Calmia when I got my loom. An' I just thought they were so pretty. They'd make th'plain weave an' then they'd put bands aroun' th'bottom. I got my idea from them an' then I worked out my colors an' my designs an' made those girls a skirt each. I did that after I did my stole an' found out I *could* work th'finer threads.

"It took me quite a long time t'learn how t'thread it up an' change my different pattern drafts. Then finally they had a book over at th'Craft Shop that I borrowed and later bought myself. From that I just worked an' learned to do a lot o' different patterns, but for a long time I just practiced.

"Have any of you ever taken music? Well, you see a piece o' music an' you want t'sit down an' try it out and an' see what it's like. Well, I'm that way with my weavin'. If I see a pattern draft, I wanna sit down an' try it out."

After seeing all the many different kinds of things Mrs. Brown had woven, we were curious as to what was the most difficult for her to do. She said, "I guess maybe 'bout th'hardest work t'do is t'make ponchos and stoles with wool thread—it's fine thread an' sometimes you get a hold of some of it that isn't very strong. Sometimes I don't get m'warp on as good as I'd like. It took me a long time t'learn how t'weave with wool. I've made some pieces that I've had t'just tear up completely."

Mrs. Brown has enjoyed weaving a little bit of everything. She felt proudest after she had woven a coverlet because it was such a difficult project to undertake. "The first coverlet I did I got ahold o'some thread at th'plant that worked up real pretty. My husband had made two of th'gran'daughters a three-quartered size bed out of some walnut trees he had taken off th'place. He made those beds an' after he got them fixed up, I thought, 'Now how nice it'd be t'make a coverlet for each one.' So I threaded it up t'that whig rose pattern because it's somethin' I wanted t'work out an' it's my favorite pattern. It really worked out right pretty. I made it so I could put three panels together if I wanted to. One o' th'panels I got my design all messed up an' I didn't have enough thread t'go back an' do it over an' make another one like it. So I fixed up one that they could use on th'bed an' then th'other one I fixed so they could use it on th'couch. They were done in light blue an' white and it worked out all right. That showed me that I could do it. So I had quite a bit of practice when I got ready to do a good one."

Weaving was Mrs. Brown's answer for something to occupy her time. She never had to weave for money, but in the past year or two she has sold almost all of her work. Her story explains this: "I didn't expect t'make anything off of it. I would work in th'community and I worked in th'church and in Sunday School for a long period of time. Then after our boys left home my husband wus busy all th'time an' he didn't have time t'take me here an' there. I never did learn how t'drive, so I depended on our boys t'take me where I had t'go. After they left home I realized, 'Well, I don't have anything t'do.'

"I walked many a time to th'school house to a club meeting'r a missionary meeting, but later I found that I couldn't walk like I used to an' I ended up staying at home all the time.

"I tried knittin' an' I tried embroiderin', but m'eyes were troublin' me when I did close work like that. So I just kept looking aroun' for something t'do. When I took my rags over to Calmia, I started weavin' rugs. It wus just really fascinating how you could take your colors an' blend them in.

"One day while I was weavin' some customer came in an' wanted t'know if they had any rag rugs for sale. Mrs. Hopper tol' 'em, 'No, we don't do very much o' that.' I had an idea right there—why don't I let that be my hobby?

"I talked with Mrs. Van Gorder about it. She wus another inspiration. She wus th'music teacher at th'time in th'school. She had a loom in her cottage that she worked on at night. Our son took music and in order t'keep him interested, I took music awhile. I would take a lesson when he would take a lesson an' she would have her loom set up an' things that she'd done on it. I just raved over it—I thought it wus so pretty. I just kept gettin' an inspiration every time I'd see a piece of woven work. She encouraged me t'go ahead an' buy a loom. She advised me for a long time not t'do anything but rugs.

"An' I managed in some way t'dispose of m'rugs. Some I would give away an' some I would just sell for almost nothin'. After a while I got started where I could sell enough t'buy my thread an' my materials. I wove out o' things that were given to me at first so I could afford t'give'em away if I wanted to. I gave away just about till I supplied ever'body with somethin' that I had done.

"Soon I got t'sellin' a little here an' a little there. An' I got advertised by word of mouth. Somebody would see something placed in a home an' they'd come get an order in. There were lots o' friends that were interested in what I wus doin'. It just kind of grew.

"Then th'fellow that writes these articles for the *Constitution* came an' interviewed us both [Harry and Marinda]. We call this our 'old age hobby.' He gave us a writeup in th'*Constitution* an' that just swamped us. About that same time Suzy came along an' she helped us a whole lot with the Craft Organization that we had in th'county. An' just by degrees we kind of worked up. Now we have t'work hard t'supply th'demand."

Mrs. Brown's craft has brought her some close friends who share her interest. "It's unbelievable how many people you meet. Take for instance in our harvest sales, people will come along an' see that you've done weavin' an' they'll strike up a conversation with you an' tell you that they are interested in that an' they have done some. Then they tell you so many interesting things—the people traveling like that to foreign countries that know a lot about weavin' an' what th'people have done. It surprises you how many people are interested in that kind o' work. I thought when I started this business that this had just about died down. I never had th'opportunity t'meet people that were interested in that type of work.

"An' we've had quite a bit of correspondence with people since this article came out in th'*Constitution*. People'd write an' say, 'My mother'r my grandmother used t'weave so an' so, can you do that?' There were lots o' interesting letters."

Weaving seems to be on a give-and-take basis for Mrs. Brown. "It takes a lot of patience. Things that I would start t'do I'd want t'do too quick an' not turn out a good job. Now I take my time in weavin'. It just don't pay t'weave a piece o' material an' throw it away, I found out. Weavin's just so satisfying. If you're interested in what you're doing, you can just sit down an' forget everything. I've woven when I wus disturbed. Last week I didn't feel too good. I wus tired but I wus doing something that I wanted t'get done. I kept right at it when I really didn't feel like it an' m'mind wouldn't stay on it. I'd have t'go back an' take some out. I'd put in some that didn't do right. I noticed yer feelings have something t'do with it. Like th'way y'work yer beater. Sometimes you give it a harder jerk than y'do other times. An' it makes your weaving a little closer together. It'll tell on you all th'way through."

Mrs. Brown has changed considerably since she started weaving. Her entire personality has been opened up. She proved this by saying: "It's just broadened my vision of living all together. I feel like I have more t'talk about. Sometimes I'm afraid I bore people by talking about my craft, but I'm still interested in any kind of craft that other people do. That has broadened my sense of other people's interests. I used t'be real shy before I started weavin'."

Living on Betty's Creek is an excellent weaver and delightful person named Edith Darnell. Her loom sits in the family room of her home where it is put to use a great deal of her time. Other than weaving a little for each of her eight daughters, she manages to weave for almost anyone who likes her work. She was first introduced to weaving about

PLATE 316   Edith Darnell sits at her loom weaving the snail trail pattern, a finished sample hangs over the loom.

twelve years ago: "The Jay Hambidge Art Foundation didn't have no-body one day t'help weave. I wus on a double loom, me an' another'n. I never had wove any. I had t'take one side an' keep up with n'other girl. I wus weavin' an' I missed them pedals an' skinned my ankles. That's where I started my weavin'. I done pretty well, though.

"I worked for Mrs. Hambidge only a little while. I liked workin' there but I didn't like workin' th'wool threads an' no cotton.

"Soon I went over t'Mrs. Norton's, over in North Carolina, an' I learned how t'make th'dogwood flowers an' weave them. Then I got my loom an' did my own.

"I never had no trouble weavin' an' fixin' out patterns. I can weave 'bout anything that's down on paper. I like th'pattern weavin' better'n any. I *love* th'pattern weavin'. I just like t'see 'em come out. When that pattern comes out right y'feel good."

The cat paw is Mrs. Darnell's favorite pattern to weave and she enjoys making bedspreads the most. "Before our house burnt, I had seven bedspreads t'get burnt up! I hain't done too many since. I sold three I reckon."

There was one particular piece of material she wove and became very attached to. With a proud look on her face, Mrs. Darnell said, "I weaved it fer somebody else." In her bedroom, though, sits a framed picture of that bedspread she cherishes and loves so much.

You would think that after weaving all these years, Mrs. Darnell would have done some work for herself. This is untrue in her case. She said, "Everything I've done someone else wanted it and I'd just sell it, but I'm gonna weave me somethin'. I'm makin' me a little house, a place where I can keep all my stuff to itself. My house is crowded so."

Mrs. Darnell expressed the importance of having patience to weave when she said, "I've always been patient in workin' weavin'. I've always had lots o' patience with m'work. Even th'loom threadin'—I've never had anyone t'show me how t'thread a loom. I just did it by th'pattern myself. Threadin' th'loom an' puttin' th'warp on is th'hardest. It takes lots o' time t'put in a warp. When y'get that through, yer done. I don't mind t'do it, though. It just takes a little longer. I learned t'put m'warps on myself. I can roll one plumb across —about fifty yards—all by myself, comb it an' all, and hold it an' roll it."

The time-consuming and hard work put in to weaving seems to be nothing compared to all of the joy Mrs. Darnell gets out of it. "I'd still weave even if I didn't sell anything. I'd rather weave as eat. When

PLATE 317 Gertrude Keener.   PLATE 318 A woven bedspread.

no one's aroun', you can be a weavin' your pattern an' a hummin' an' a singin' while you're sittin' there.

"When you're troubled y'go t'weavin'. Y'can just set an' be happy when yer weavin'—'r I can. I don't know whether ever'body can. Anything like weavin'r quiltin', I'm just as well concerned as I can be."

Gertrude Keener is a very remarkable person. She is rather quiet, but she always has a smile on her face. After visiting her, we were truly amazed at all the beautiful work she has turned out. She has been weaving since the age of ten. We were amused by her story of how she learned to weave: "I learned myself off my momma's spinning wheel. She didn't want us messing up her spinning, and I remember very well one day she wus cookin' dinner and I went to th'spinning wheel an' started spinning. And I didn't draw my thread out quite long enough an' quite thin enough an' I had a great big lump on my thread. An' I rolled it up an' Mommy came back an' undone it an' redid it. But that's how I got interested in it. Then Mommy taught me weaving."

Mrs. Keener seems to think bedspreads are the nicest things to weave. "I like th'whig rose pattern an' th'pine pattern—they're both very pretty patterns. For rugs, th'dog track pattern an' for placemats I think th'log cabin is th'prettiest an' th'goose-eye pattern is a nice pattern t'weave materials with like coats. These are all real old patterns."

In her early days, Mrs. Keener had to weave to enable her to get an education. "After my first year in high school I went t'Camp Dixie as an assistant to a craft's teacher. An' that's where I helped th'children weave. But then during th'rest of my time at home I wove coverlets for money an' made my own money fer high school an' I made my money fer college—weaving during th'summer months an' weaving during my spare time. Y'see, I would take orders at Camp Dixie. People would give me orders an' that would be all I could do t'fill those orders. I'd always fill my orders an' have money enough fer school."

Weaving was an inspiration to Mrs. Keener, as well as to those she taught. "Weaving may have helped me t'be more patient. It gives me a feeling of accomplishment. An' when I taught the children at Camp Dixie, I found that wus one o' th'best things to help them to enjoy it. A lot of 'em would be homesick. But if I could ever get one of 'em started workin' on somethin' like that, their homesickness would fade away. An' that taught them t'be more patient. Weaving is really good for you. You have t'have patience t'weave and I've been quoted as havin' a lot of patience. I don't think anybody would be successful with weaving if they didn't have any patience."

Weaving seemed to be something very special and relative to Mrs. Keener's personality. Quoting her feelings seems to be the only appropriate way to end our talk with her. "I've always been real interested in weaving an' I think it's one of the greatest crafts ever an' I just *love* makin' a pattern an' weaving different things. I think it's an art that we need t'keep. That's th'reason I want t'get started back. And my daughter wants me t'teach her t'weave all these different designs. She said she wanted me t'do all that while I wus able—before I got too old t'do that kind of work. I love t'weave. I think it's th'most relaxin' thing you can do. When you watch your pattern grow, t'me it's like life, more like living. It's more like building character than anything else I can describe it with. It's like teachin' a child from th'beginnin' to grow—as your pattern grows'r as your cloth grows, it's just like a child growin' up. You weave your life into somethin' beautiful. That's the way I see it."

HOW TO WASH CLOTHES
IN AN IRON POT

"Th'place of th'washin' is by a branch. That's where most ever'body washes. Now, my great uncle lived up away from a branch, and they built what they call a wood pump. In other words, they took little logs and they took an auger and bored a hole all th'way through that, and then they joined'em together. And they made a line for th'water t'come down to th'house from th'branch."

Even as he said this, Mr. Dickerson led us over to the pile of wood he planned to use.

"And some of'em that maybe couldn't do that, they'd dig'em a trench around th'side of th'hill and run th'water around out there. There's one feller up here in Wolfork, he built his house out where he could see over th'valley. Well, he didn't have any water there, and it was rock and he couldn't dig a well, so he went up about a thousand feet to a branch and he made him a wooden trough from that branch around th'mountain down there to his house.

"These spouts we'uz talkin' about—they's two'r'three ways t'make-'em. But when th'first settlers moved in here, they didn't have any lumber—couldn't get any—so they'd take a pole like this and they'd cut'em a 'v' trough down th'pole, and they'd build a dam out in th'branch and let th'water come down this 'v' pole and pour out.

"And then another way they would do it: when th'sap was high, and we had plenty of chestnut trees, you'd get a chestnut tree, take your axe and split th'bark, and then you'd start spreadin' that bark off. Peel it off th'whole pole and lay it out and let it dry and they'd use

PLATE 319   R. M. Dickerson and his wife watch intently as Mr. Dickerson's sister, Mimi, re-creates a scene they haven't watched in years.

that bark there for a trough. Takes a pretty big tree. When it comes off
th'tree, it's pliable. You can bend it. So they'd just bend it and take a
piece a'bark or maybe a bit of hickory withe and tie it up and lay it
out in th'sunshine. It'ud fold up and dry and stay that way.

"Y'see, water is runnin' in it all th'time, and that keeps it from air
crackin'. We had a spout at home, and ever' night when we'd been
goin' barefoot we'd go out there and wash our feet.

"That wooden trough, they dig it out of chestnut because it's easy
t'work and th'grain's straight. I've seen some old troughs made that
way that'd last maybe twenty-five years.

PLATES 320–322 Mr. Dickerson notches the ends of the three legs to fit the battling bench, and then nails them into place. The bench has three legs so that it will set steady, even on rough ground.

"You can take timber and keep it in water. I bought a place over here in th'Depression and I had to recover some ditches. And they'd put some sycamore poles down 'fore I got it. I pulled out one sycamore pole that was just as green as that apple tree. It'd been down there in that water 'bout twenty-five years. But you cut one down and lay it out. In a year, it's just all to pieces."

By then he had a large oak log that he had split in half lengthwise to make the top of the battling bench. The flat surface formed a counter approximately twelve inches wide and four and a half feet long. It was left rough.

"Y'want it kind'a rough, y'see? When you're battlin', it'll knock th'dirt out in th'cracks. If it's perfectly smooth on top, you'll beat th'dirt back in your clothes."

He then took three pine poles about five inches in diameter and thirty-two inches long. Notching one end of each, he nailed them into place as legs for the bench as shown in the photographs.

"Y'make three legs to th'bench because three legs'll set steady on any kind'a ground. Sometimes th'wind's blowin' smoke over in your face and y'want'a move your things around. Y'move it and y'don't have t'level up your bench. It just sets there.

"And your bench goes out from your tub so y'can work from either side. The single leg won't be in th'way. It's not a'stickin' out."

Both the paddle and the battling stick are made of pine. Though their lengths are different (one is about four feet long and the other one foot), their shapes are basically the same. The end of the longer paddle, however, is tapered and rounded "t'fit with th'bottom of your pot so y'can scoop ever'thing up."

Also, "Y'want th'handles flat so they won't turn in your hand. That paddle might turn over in your hand and spill your clothes.

"With your battling stick [the short one], y'don't want square corners. Y'round them off because when y'hit with a square corner, y'might injure your clothes."

Mr. Dickerson then made the paddles that we would use that afternoon. Both were of pine, as it is light, soft, and easy to work.

First he shaped the handles using his hatchet, and then he smoothed up the handles and paddle blades with a drawing knife. "When you're cuttin' a straight line like this [the handle], you use your drawin' knife like this [with the beveled edge of the blade up]. When you're comin' into a curve, you turn your drawin' knife over. See, this edge is beveled. If it was straight, you'd dig in."

PLATES 323–324 Here he works on the two paddles that are needed. In *Plate 323,* with a drawknife, he shapes in the handle for the stirring paddle. In *Plate 324,* he hews out the handle for the battling stick. The handle will be smoothed as in *Plate 323.* The blade of stirring paddle will be tapered and shaped to fit the bottom of the pot.

While he worked with the drawing knife, the paddle was clamped in a vise. A shaving horse could also have been used, though.

Additional smoothing was accomplished with the edge of a small piece of glass.

Then, using a large black iron pot and two pairs of bluejeans, we began the actual washing.

"Well, let's get our water started then. Get our bucket and we'll put some water in there and we'll build a fire. That water'ud run all th'time at th'old-fashioned wash places. People usually kept a bucket settin' under there so if y'happened to want some water right quick, you'd always have a bucket full when y'went t'th'spout.

"Now, y'have t'put a little water in [the iron pot] before y'start th'fire so th'heat won't crack it. Here th'wind's kindly wrong, but I guess we can make it, maybe. Y'need t'stack your wood under your tub kindly, and y'have t'keep it a'goin' all th'time. If you'll put some a'those chips up in under there, she'll come."

PLATE 325 Now Mr. Dickerson pours a bucket of water into the pot before lighting the fire so that as the pot gets heated, it won't crack. Then he lights the fire.

PLATES 326–327   As the water heats, Mimi Dickerson alternates rinsing and battling until most of the heavy dirt is dissolved out of the clothes.

Mimi Dickerson, carrying out the process from there, began to fill the pot with water as the fire caught. While she was waiting for the water to boil, she took the clothes and rinsed them out in cold water at the end of the battling bench. Then she took each piece separately, lifted it sopping wet onto the bench, and battled it with the short paddle, turning it over and over continuously as she worked. Then each piece was rinsed, battled again, and then rinsed again. Had there been any heavy stains, they would have been scrubbed out.

When the water was boiling, soap was added and the battled clothes were put in to boil.

"It helps to keep'em stirred so th'soap can go through'em and get th'dirt out of'em. Workin'em down with th'paddle helps it come out better. Now we just rench'em and hang'em out."

The clothes were then lifted, steaming, out of the pot and carried over to the tub at the end of the battling bench, which had been re-filled with fresh, cold water. After being rinsed there, they were carried over to the second tub, under the spout, and rinsed well a second time. Then they were shaken out well and hung up to dry while still completely wet.

PLATE 328 Having battled much of the dirt out of the clothes, and having removed any stains that might "set" in the hot water, Mimi boils the clothes for about twenty minutes in soapy water. She keeps them stirred as they boil so that the soap can work its way into every crease.

PLATES 329–330 Now the boiled clothes are run through three rinses to make sure they are clean. The rinsing is done in two separate tubs: one at the end of the battling bench, and one under the water trough. In the old days, these tubs would be made by cutting a wooden barrel in half through the middle.

PLATE 331 The clean clothes are then hung out to dry.

PLATE 332 When the job is done, Mr. Dickerson inserts the ends of two sticks through the eyes of the pot in order to turn it over without burning himself.

PLATE 333 Water is then poured over the bottom of the pot to rinse off any ashes and soot that might have accumulated there during the washing operation.

"We used t'rench our clothes three times, and then hang'em out wet.

"Y'usually turn'em after y'rench'em so th'inside of'em can dry better. It's better t'hang'em out a'fore they start dryin' 'cause they won't be so wrinkled and they're softer."

On each side of the pot is an eye. Two poles are run through these to empty the water out of the pot without getting burned.

"Th'pot has little eyes on th'side. Th'reason for those eyes: y'can set th'pot off and on your fire. When y'go t'set it down, you're out here where y'can see when you're hittin' your rocks. When y'get through your washin', turn your water out. Then turn your pot upside down on these pillars here t'keep your pot clean. It won't rust then, and y'don't have t'scrub it out ever'time y'wash.

"It's a job washin' for a whole family. All your bed clothes, all your towels, and if y'live on th'farm y'have extra overhauls, shirts. If th'weather's fit, you wash once a week. Y'try t'pick a day when it's not rainin'r'somethin', but if there's snow on th'ground, y'just have t'go on and do it anyway. I'll tell y'what I did: bought me a boiler and put it on my kitchen stove and boiled mine in there.

"I *have* washed about all day. Used to wash till dinner time and go fix dinner and then come back and finish washin'. It didn't take too long t'wash a load. We'd boil th'clothes say maybe thirty minutes'r'so, and sometimes not quite that long dependin' on how much dirt they was in'em. But y'see, you rubbed'em some before you put'em in th'pot, and got th'worst out. Now if you'uz gonna boil a pair of real dirty overhauls, you'd have t'boil'em a little longer than you'd boil a sheet.

"We had flat irons then. We'd set'em down in front a'th'fireplace, or on th'stove, and heat'em and then iron. They'd weigh about five pounds—six pounds—and some seven. You could iron five'r'six pillow cases—maybe a little more'n that—and then you'd have t'heat your iron again. Y'kept *one* heatin' all th'time though.

"Now that's th'whole bit!"

ANNA HOWARD

Anna Howard is ninety-three years old. She was born in Franklin, North Carolina, and still lives less than ten miles from there.

When I first saw her, sitting by her little wood heater, I knew I wouldn't forget her. Anna is the type of person that is the same every time you see her. She had been sick and in the hospital for over a year. I guess one reason why I love Anna so is that despite her illness, she has a tremendous ambition to go on and work. For over a year she was unable to walk, and yet she went on and cooked and kept house and even made her garden, getting around in a homemade wheelchair (a little straight-backed chair without arms that had four small wheels from a child's wagon mounted on the legs). A person who, among other things, would go on and work when she couldn't even walk is special to me.

Like our other contacts, Anna grew up in a self-sufficient age. Her father raised both wheat and flour which he had ground into meal. She tended their chickens and stock, often spending long periods of time in the woods rounding up their cattle. Even as a young girl, she churned butter, helped can food in large, homemade churn jars, and entertained herself by making rag dolls, tiny flower pots, and play houses with little rock chimneys. And she used to ride the dirt road to town on a black mare, once getting so bogged down in the muck that some neighbors had to get rails and planks and help her haul the mare out.

PLATE 334

PLATE 335

Her parents were strict, but she minded them carefully—all except
in one area: snuff. "They whopped me for dippin' snuff. I craved
snuff. We'd make it out of Pa's homemade tobacco. I bet you I
couldn't even tell you th'times [my mother] whipped me for that."

With her own age as perspective, she has a special feeling for older
people who are left alone. She remembers with a chill recent visits to
the home of an old friend, taking her a little glass of jelly, or of pickled
beans or kraut each time. "But she ought t'see more people than my
old ugly face. Her neighbors aren't a'doin' their duty." Another
friend, also living alone, shakes so bady she can't fill her pipe un-
aided. "She'd crumble tobacco up in her lap and put it in her pipe,
and ashes and all'ud pour out. I asked her if she wanted me t'fill it up
fer'er. 'Well,' she said, 'honey, I'd just be glad, for I'll never get

t'smoke.' I filled it up fer'er, and every time we went over, I had t'clean her pipe up. And she was so proud of it, th'poor old thing. I just felt sorry fer'er."

Anna is luckier than most. An old childhood friend named Will lives with her now, and they help each other. Even so, she is sometimes depressed. Recently she told us, "I made do with what I had . . . Now I just set here waitin' t'leave this country." But more often she is happy, open, warm, busily engaged in little needlework gifts for friends. And she remembers: "Life was sweet. You enjoyed every minute of it."

RHONDA BLACK

[We asked Anna to begin by telling us the kinds of things from her childhood that she remembered most vividly.] We never had a dose a'medicine in our house to give young'uns. There was herbs they'd get and make tea for us. And my daddy'd go out and get new nails out of th'store, put'em in a bucket, pour water over'em. And when they got that water rusty, that's what we took for blood medicine.

And [a woman that was pregnant] never went to a doctor. Their mother learnt them t'have children. They never went to a doctor. And a woman that was pregnant wouldn't of got out for a man to seen her. If she was by herself when a man walked up, she'd bow up and stick her head out th'door thataway t'talk to'em.

If we all went anywhere, we were charged to behave ourselves. "Now I better not hear a thing. Now you'uns behave." And now it was "uncle" and "aunt" everywhere we went. Yes, sir. And if there were people sittin' around to hear, and my daddy was a'talkin', and us young'uns over there, well [pointing a finger], that's all he had t'do if we spoke to one another or moved. There was no talkin' done.

But Daddy was funny too. He had us t'play, and he'd play with us —blindfold in th'house when we were young. And on Christmas when th'children would come in—th'neighbors always visited one another then—he would play a finger game. He'd make us put our four fingers down thataway [hanging]. I forget just this minute what he called it. And he'd count'em, y'know, and whichever it came out on, he had somethin' we had t'do. We'd have t'go foot [go and do it. Apparently there was some sort of rhyme or verse that went along with the counting, and the person's finger that the verse ended on would have to go and do some little thing. Then the counting would start again until all the players had had to do something].

Then he'd play club fist. Stack up, and he had a great ceremony
he'd say. He'd knock it off, or take it off. [The person who starts
makes a fist with the thumb of that fist sticking up. The next person
makes a fist around that thumb sticking his own thumb up for the next
person to lock onto, and so on until there is a vertical stack of fists, all
interlocked. Then the person whose fist is on the bottom removes it,
says, "You want me to knock it off, take it off, or let the crows pick it
off?" The person whose fist is on top grips the thumb beneath it
tightly, tells how he wants the other to try to remove his fist, and then
tries to keep him from doing it. The game continues like this until all
the fists have been removed.] If we said, "Knock it off," you bet he
knocked it off!

And there was another game [called "slap, hug, and kiss." One
player would sit in a chair blindfolded. Another player would stand
behind him, and the rest of the players would be in a line in front of
the blindfolded person. The one standing behind would make a silent
signal that meant either a slap, a hug, or a kiss. Then he would ask the
blindfolded person to call out the name of one of the players in the
line. The blindfold would be removed, and that person would have to
go to the player whose name he had called out and do to him whatever the silent signal had dictated.]

And he just played with us, and enjoyed playin' with us like that.

Sometimes my grandmother came to visit. She always went horseback, and she'd come to our house. Lord, we thought she was
th'queen of th'world. Oh, we were so proud she couldn't hardly get off
her horse. We just nearly pulled her off, y'know. And just loved her.
And she'd bring us a biscuit, and now you talk about somebody bein'
proud—and stick candy. Oh, we'd be so proud to see Grandma. And
sometimes she'd bring us apples when they'd come in.

And whenever we come in from school, we had t'take our clothes off
right then and do whatever chores they left for us t'do. Then we had
chores th'next mornin', and then we'd put our school clothes back on
and our mother combed our heads and see'd that we was perfectly
clean. We got panties, and they was made out a'bleachin', and they
had t'be ruffled around th'legs down here at th'knees. They had t'come
under th'knees. And in th'winter we went barefooted, and when we
did get shoes, they were homemade shoes. And you got your stockin'
t'come up over this knee here, and your bloomers went down in
th'stockin'.

The first hat I ever had on my head was bought for me. They made
bonnets for th'women and bonnets for th'children—little stitch bon-

nets with ruffles around it. And th'first hat I ever got—I guess I was about ten. It was just a straw hat, and it had just a cotton band. And there was a sort'a spotted ribbon that crossed there and hung down a little bit off th'brim, y'know. They weren't too wide. Boy, I'm a'tellin' you, I was th'proudest thing in that hat that ever was a'comin' t'Sunday School. Where there was a window, I'd turn my head and check that ribbon. I was richer over that hat than anybody would be today of a fine car.

[Here Anna remembered something that happened to her when she was about five years old.] One time, me and my mother was started across Middle Creek. We went t'go up there t'get peaches. They had orchards, y'know. Plenty of'em. And we got there before it started t'rain—awfullest storm they'd been.

We got over there about milkin' time, and th'creek was up just a'rollin muddy—just as muddy as could be. Well, there was a woman tendin' a corn mill, and she wanted t'go across. Her cow was on th'other side of th'creek. And they had a two-plank footlog across th'dam where it poured over. And I wanted t'tote her bucket that she was a'gonna' milk in. I thought that would be a help to her. I was just a little feller, but I was big enough t'tote th'bucket.

And we started across there, and I had t'go in front, and Ma was comin' behind on th'footlog. And th'water a'pourin' down here. When I got about th'middle, th'footlog, me and th'bucket went off down th'river! We went just over where it poured off.

My mammy waded out, and that woman bent alders over from th'bank of th'creek fer her t'hold to, y'know. She got t'th'middle of th'ford, and I had sunk, and I was a'holdin' to a rock clenched in th'bottom of that creek. And th'water come t'her chin right there. But she waded to me, and my bonnet—I had on a homemade woolen dress made on a old wooden loom, and a bonnet and big sack apron buttoned up my back—and I can remember that dress just as good! And she pulled me out, and her a'screamin', and th'other woman—she had t'get down in it and get wet all over, y'know, pullin' me out and up over that big rock. She pulled me out under one arm, and th'woman then bent th'bush back to her and she got a'hold of that and waded out. And I was dead, y'know—water runnin' out of my ear and out of my mouth. And I was limber as a dishrag, and she just had me a'hangin' across one arm. And we went up to another family and they stripped me and shook me—and I never knowed anything till three o'clock in th'evenin'. And I've never heard out of my left ear good since. If I've got that ear to you, I can't hear you as good as I can out of this'un. And since then, my head swims every time [I have to cross water]. If there's anything I can get t'chew on—a stick or anything—I can cross a broad log [but unless she has something to chew on to keep her from getting dizzy, she can't cross water].

[Thinking about her own childhood got her thinking about young people today.] They want different things, y'know, that we never seen and never heard tell of. And a young'un ain't as proud of a big bicycle'r'tricycle'r gun or things like that as we were of a stick of that old "Long Tom" chewin' gum, or a stick of red candy.

They've got money now. It's not so important. It's good t'have, but if you're gonna lay it away and worship it, you just as well go down there and pick up as many rocks as you have dollars and lay *them* away, and they'd do you just as much good. If you worship your money, you're not worshipin' God.

It's like livin' in a new world. Oh, Lord, it ain't nothin' like—well, look at church. Why, they're turnin' in their seats lookin' back t'see who comes in. They ain't listenin' t'th'preacher. Or lookin' t'see what kind of dress you wore today or how good it's made.

We used t'have t'get th'Bible and take and read a verse and get it by heart and say it in Sunday School. And we had t'get th'preacher's text in church. We had t'look at him and get his text and tell my grandma when we went home where that text was at, and she'd read it t'us by heart. We had her t'tell it to. If we didn't, she'd say, "Now ain't you ashamed of yourself t'go t'church and not know where th'preacher's text was from?"

And she'd say, "Children, nobody knows your heart, only you'uns, and you better keep it good. You have t'stand on it; we don't."

[She also believed that no person was perfect—not even the preachers.] They put on their britches just th'same as your daddy puts his on. That's exactly what Grandma always said.

[Her advice to young people today]: Live close to the Lord and let him put it on your heart. And don't tattle. I don't say you do, but you asked me for my opinion. Live and be truthful and honest whatever comes. Tell th'truth. Sometimes it hurts, but let'er pop. I'd tell th'truth on my daddy just as quick as I would on a rank stranger that I've never seen. Some people would do some other way [besides telling the truth] to save'em if it was just their own kin, and if it was somebody else, they'd tear'em all to pieces. Now, that's just exactly th'nature. And my advice is t'any young person to take th'Lord first and be honest and truthful. And never you lose confidence in nobody [cause them to lose confidence in you]. You'll never get it back.

I try my best to learn just what th'Bible said. You can't [be perfect] all th'time. You'll maybe do a little somethin' that don't please God, but you don't get forgiveness for that, all th'same. And be friendly and good to ever'body, and especially to old people, folks you love.

God can put it on your heart or mine anything he wants you t'do, and I know he can. He has mine. Pray about things you don't know what t'do about. It'll come to you just as plain.

And I try t'be all th'same alike. I don't talk about people. I don't say no harm about nobody and all they do. It says in th'Bible t'do unto others as we wish t'be done by, and I feel that way about that. And I feel like if you're in earnest and you got faith in th'Lord and ask him for anything, he'll put it right on your mind.

[But if you're bad] and slip and hide and steal somethin' from somebody and don't want them t'see you, well, now, that's against God. You'll be caught up with sooner'r'later. You can talk with people and from their talk tell that lots of'em's tattlers. We have lots a'long-tongued people; lots of'em. And you can just sit and listen, and you can catch'em. I just wait and never say a word about it. I just wait, and sometimes it ain't no time till they're caught.

Kindness and love is th'main thing. Now that's my advice. It's good t'know you've got a friend. It's love. Just like I made [a friend] out of you. I see people that their looks and their ways just a'gives t'you, and you love'em. And th'next time you see'em, you love'em better.

I've not had too much of a happy life since my old man died. And after my children left, I just felt like I was alone in th'world. And when all my people died—everyone that passes on out, I just feel like I'm further and further away. Yes, sir.

So now I knit socks a lot. I just love t'do that. If I ain't got anybody t'talk to me, now I'm bound t'have somethin' in my fingers. If I'm able t'hold my head up, I'm bound t'have somethin' in my fingers t'employ my mind.

[But despite the fact that Anna has weakened somewhat with illness and age, and despite the fact she is often alone, she is a long way from surrendering.] I've been made fun of for bein' old-fashioned, but it don't matter t'me a bit in th'world. If anyone tries t'run over me, they'll find they've run up against a stake that won't budge 'cause it's made out a'locust! I've always done th'work of a man. God's been good t'me. He's given me strength.

MIDWIVES AND GRANNY WOMEN

This chapter on midwives and granny women was most revealing and even startling to me. Too often I assume that the modern hospital, adequate transportation, and medical doctors were available to my ancestors just as they are to me. This was not the case, as these interviews so vividly illustrate.

Back in the days when doctors were scarce, it was essential that a midwife be near. I realized the dependability and usefulness of a midwife as she delivered a healthy baby. With kindness, consolation, and determination, she carried on her work—always willing to help a family in need.

This article was a challenge and an inspiration to me, and I admire these women for giving up their own personal lives, with little pay, to bring new lives into this world. It showed me a rare human quality possessed by so few people today in their work. The midwife of bygone days had what it took to be successful in her work: true devotion.

KAREN COX

Perhaps the best way to start—a way that will put much into perspective—is with an interview from an extraordinary Registered

Nurse, nurse-midwife, and teacher, Mrs. Josephine K. Brewer. "Jo" Brewer was directly involved in the formation of a maternity clinic in this county that, among other things, worked to train midwives, many of whom had been practicing without professional training.

E. L. Bishop—M.D. and Director of Health, TVA—talked about the clinic in depth in a pamphlet published on August 15, 1943, as part of the "New Dominion Series" from Charlottesville, Virginia. Commenting on the fact that the Atlanta daily papers had been editorializing on the need for maternity centers in rural Georgia, Dr. Bishop expressed the irritation of the Clayton community "that the proposal was treated as a brand-new idea brought up by city folk for their friends in the country." He quoted the Clayton *Tribune:*

> *We have had here in Rabun a full-fledged county maternity home for the last eight months. That's where the movement originally began. The big city papers don't seem to realize that Rabun County is in Georgia.*
>
> *. . . Rabun County is in Georgia. It is in the extreme northeastern corner. It is entirely rural and largely mountainous. Except for the small town of Clayton, the population is scattered. Many families live in isolated hollows or on mountain farms separated from their neighbors by high ridges and poor roads . . . Rabun is the kind of county in which people could easily sit back and say, "But we can't do anything about it." They have not done this, and the reason seems to be that a few forward-looking citizens have helped others to see that it can happen here in Rabun.*
>
> *. . . The Maternity Center is a bit of real pioneering. It is one of the very first of its kind in the rural south . . . No one had any idea of setting up a charity institution [but] no one was to be turned away because of lack of funds. The Center was for all mothers. An arrangement for payment in fruit, vegetables, chickens, or day labor by a male member of the family made it possible for even those without cash to meet their expenses.*
>
> *Use of the Center has exceeded the most optimistic hopes . . . Rabun County not only is recognizing the right of every baby to be well born but also is finding many ways to assure its continued well-being.*
>
> *The three local doctors are also among the beneficiaries . . . They are relieved of long drives over mountain roads; of tedious hours spent in isolated cabins; and of the need to struggle with facilities inadequate to their needs in the best of homes and a menace to life in the worst.*

MRS. JOSEPHINE K. BREWER: Mrs. Effie Dickerson and Mrs. Etta Owens were about the best local midwives I've ever known, and I've known them in different parts of the state. Midwives [also known as granny women, or neighbor ladies] used to serve each section of the county. We did have granny women in nearly every valley of the county, like Persimmon, Liberty, Bridge Creek, Germany, Chechero.

Sometimes the neighbor lady was not a trained neighbor lady. She hadn't had the first elements of what to do in a situation like that. And then, on the other hand, we had some good midwives. And out of those, I'll talk about a few I remember best. Mrs. Effie Dickerson and Mrs. Etta Owens—I think they were very well loved. And I'll say this: they were the ones that came to the regular monthly meetings—classes held at the Health Department—beginning in 1939. They came in, had instructions in anatomy and what to do at the time of delivery, and they were taught noninterference. That means not to do internal examinations, because mothers could and did die from what we called "childbed fever"—puerperal sepsis. Some midwives would examine the mother with unscrubbed hands—no sterile gloves. They'd give examinations, and many times the mother died later from childbed fever. What I'm getting around to saying is that our ladies [the ones trained at the clinic] had a very good record. I think they did do as they were instructed, and they didn't do these examinations that were really illegal as far as granny midwives go.

Mrs. Etta Owens lived in Mountain City, and Mrs. Dickerson lived out from Tiger on the Liberty Road, and when she was getting ready to go to a place, the husband would come for her. But she preferred, and so did Mrs. Owens, that they contact her ahead of time so she could say to them, "You know, you must be examined by a doctor to see if you are a normal case, because granny women are only supposed to take normal cases." They shouldn't take anyone with high blood pressure or with infected kidneys or swelling, and other abnormal symptoms, because these are three symptoms of toxemia, which means the mother might go into convulsions at the time of delivery. The blood pressure could get very high, and that's why these women liked to be contacted before the actual delivery date.

Now these women that they attended could go to the private doctor, if they wanted to, or they could come regularly, without cost, to the Health Department clinic and get their checkups. Then the granny midwife would feel that she was safe in taking these cases because they'd been very well taken care of during their pregnancy.

The midwives had little midwife bags. Mrs. Dickerson and Mrs.

Owens had very clean bags—we had bag inspection. Certain materials were supposed to be in them. They weren't supposed to have any unauthorized drugs—any kind of thing that would make the patient sleepy during confinement—and they were supposed to keep the bag very clean. And after each delivery they had to clean their bags—wash them with soap and water and launder the towels and things that they carried—and put them out in the sun. They were also taught to put their dressings in the oven of the stove and bake them. That would kill the germs.

To train them, we had a very large wooden box. At the bottom and on the top, there was a simulated abdomen and perineum—just like the mother—so we could actually teach them the mechanism of labor, and so we could teach them what was going on inside. There was a little baby doll with the model too, which we could pass on down through the birth canal. We also had a lot of books and pictures for them to study, and we had a blackboard that we used in the lectures. Those women knew pretty well the anatomy when they got through with the classes. They also knew some signs and symptoms of abnormal conditions so they wouldn't get too far along in a delivery before they'd see if they needed to call in a doctor.

We used to go out on home deliveries with them when they would be called. We had a special project here—we would go out at night or day, anytime we got calls—and we would have actual teaching at the bedside, too. But I didn't teach them in such a way that the patient would lose confidence in the midwife. That would have been a bad relationship. So we just worked together on the delivery, and just when we could, we'd discuss about certain things relating to that delivery. I'm talking about learning scientifically rather than something they've just grown into from young girls.

I would also like to tell you about when the midwives kind of went out of practice here in Rabun County. Some of them had gotten sick, some had died; and the ones that were still working weren't able to carry on many deliveries, so it looked like we had to make some kind of plan for the people of Rabun County. So we worked with various clubs and governmental officials. Miss Lula Smith, who was also a Public Health nurse, worked with me on it. And the Welfare Director, Mrs. Vassie Lyon; and the Ordinary of the county, Mr. Frank Smith; and Dr. Green was interested. And we decided that we needed a little hospital or center where people could be looked after. They could be given more care than they could get in the home. Then we decided to make it a maternity center.

So I went to Atlanta to see Dr. Abercrombie, who was then Director of the State Health Department, and he said, "If you'll go back up there, and you all will start something on your own with no outside help, I'll guarantee you that in six months' time, I'll put you in touch with a foundation that will help you financially. But you've got to show that you can do something on your own."

So we did start. And just a few days before we opened, we ran over to Greenville, South Carolina, to see their "Maternity Shelter," as they called it. And they wanted us to say that we got the idea from them, but we had to say no. We'd been thinking about a place like this for a long time. They offered us a hundred dollars a month if we would say that we were an outgrowth of them, but we didn't accept the money because we were not. We were ready to open, almost, and we knew we could do as well.

We started out with laundry baskets for little babies to be put in. Each time a little baby was expected, we had to run out, or ask Mrs. Lyon or Miss Smith to scour the countryside for another laun-

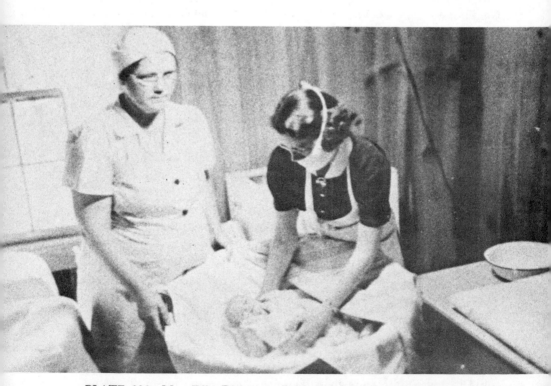

PLATE 336 Mrs. Effie Dickerson (left) and Mrs. Josephine Brewer caring for a newborn in the county's maternity hospital.

dry basket so we could have some place to put the baby. One of the doctors thought that we could never fill this place up and that it would never be used. He didn't believe the women would come to it. But we learned right away that that was not true. They *did* like it! Dr. Green and Dr. Neville were real helpful and anxious for us to open this place.

Mrs. Dickerson at this time had to quit doing a lot of deliveries, and I needed some one person to help me start the maternity home because we knew we would be working night and day to get it started. I asked her if she would help. She and I were the only ones that were working full time, and we worked there for days and nights, and we had to be on call all the time. One of us was there all the time, and we nearly worked ourselves to death.

So next we had Mrs. Vickers, who was employed as a cook, because before that, "Miss Effie" would sleep during the day, but she'd get up and fix the meals and then go back to bed because she had to be at work at night. She'd get some sleep between times, and I was the nurse on duty. That couldn't work that way, although outside people gave us a lot of help with sheets and pillowcases and blankets, and helped us get laundry baskets for the babies. But they weren't there to do the actual work. It was just the two—then the three—of us.

And as time went on, we got so busy that we had to have another person there, so we hired a young woman who had never had any nursing training at all, Miss Leila Belle Wall. She had worked in a dentist's office. And she became an excellent nurse's aid. And as time went on, we got more people.

Mrs. Dickerson worked a while, and she saw that she couldn't hold out because she had to go up and down stairs, and they were so narrow that when a baby was born and the upstairs rooms were filled, we had to wrap the patient in blankets, and the doctor and Miss Effie and myself would take her on a stretcher, outside the house, downstairs to a lower room. We had to do that regardless of the weather because all three of us plus the patient couldn't make the narrow staircase.

We needed that maternity home. One day [before it was opened] I went out to make a home visit, and this lady was practically out of her head, and her blood pressure was very high. And Mr. Clyde Ramey had loaned us a bed that we had in the back of the Health Department. I knew this lady would probably die if something wasn't done, and soon. So I came back to town and called the doctor and Mr.

PLATE 337   Dr. Tom Dover standing in front of the first Health Department building in the county. The building is now the office for the Highway Department. The first baby known to be born outside the family's home in this county was born here in September 1940.

R. E. Cannon. They had a stretcher, and they went so far in their van, and then they had to take the stretcher out and take it to the house— quite a distance—and they stretchered her back to the vehicle and brought her to the Health Department and we started working on her. Dr. Tom Dover was the doctor we could reach first. We began to get her blood pressure down, and she delivered, and the lady still doesn't remember about it. She was so far gone into her toxemia of pregnancy that all she knows is what we tell her. That was our first real maternity home patient, even though it was in the Health Department. As far as I know, that was the first woman in Rabun County whose baby was born outside of her own home. That was September 1940.

The first woman who had her baby born *in* the Home was Mrs. Robert Singleton. Mr. Singleton was the postmaster who just retired here in Clayton. Their son, Bobby, was the first child born in the maternity hospital. That was on November 22, 1942. We opened the home on November 20, 1942. In fact, we were hardly ready with anything.

It's kind of sad, in a way—the passing of an era, you might say. The fast life we live now, and all the transportation, all the roads that we have. I'd like to add this postscript: people used to be proud to be born in Rabun County. In fact, they came here from North Carolina, South Carolina, Hiawassee—every surrounding town and county—to born in the maternity hospital. They liked to come to our place, and they'd beat a path to the door. There were magazine articles all over the U.S. about the teaching program and the good care the people got there. The doctors would look after the mothers themselves, and if they couldn't get there, they told me to go ahead and do the deliveries rather than calling another doctor in. So I had many deliveries myself in the maternity hospital. People wanted to come to this hospital.

Now there seems to be a kind of fad to go away from Rabun County to have their babies. I wonder why, because we still have a good place and local doctors. And the funny part is that even those who do go away to outside hospitals will come in and ask Mrs. Martha Thomas, the Health Department clerk, to have the baby's birth certificate recorded in Rabun County! Well, that's impossible. We think that if they would like their children to be said natives of Rabun County, then those babies are going to have to be born here to say so. In cases where the mother's condition is bad and the doctor thinks she will need surgery, I think it's fine to go to an outside source. But we have good ways of taking care of them here—good hospital, doctors for deliveries—much better facilities than we used to have; that's for sure. But, still, the education of the patient about family nutrition, home hygiene and sanitation, baby and child care and other health topics can't be taught in the busy, overcrowded hospitals of today like they were back in the good old days.

Midwives in the area had a rather checkered career. There were some women, for example, who never bothered with them. As Ethel Corn said, "Now some women'ud have their babies by theirself and take care of'em and get up and go on back to th'fields t'work. I've heard Mommy tell of one woman she knowed a'doin' that. She said she'd had some of her babies out in a field and brought'em up and layed'em in the shade and went on about her work."

And, of course, there were times when the poorly trained midwives were completely at a loss as to what to do to save either the mother or the child. At such times, a doctor was essential. Anna Howard's terrifying experience with just such a situation occurred when, "I got hung and fell over th'fence. Th'baby was lodged in my side and had t'be turned before he could be born. They had an old midwife with me, but I'd suffered so long they said I wouldn't live and they went and got th'doctor—an *old* man who couldn't even go horseback. But they was a man that just married and moved close t'us, and he had a buggy, and so Paw got that buggy and went off after th'doctor and wrapped him up in a blanket and brought him. And that old [midwife] sat in th'corner.

"And I said, 'Doctor, I want you t'tell me. That old midwife didn't know what was th'matter did she?'

"And he said, 'No. There ain't a woman in th'world except a doctor that could remove that. It sort of growed to your side.' He had to take th'baby."

For many people, however, midwives were the ideal solution; and for some, they were the only solution. Women were having babies faster than doctors could get to them, and they simply had to have help. The midwives were there, and in the course of their heyday, they touched an amazing number of lives:

Mrs. Robert Avery: "It used t'be all they had nearly back in my early days. About all my family was delivered that way."

Mrs. Andy Webb: "I'd rather have a midwife anytime as a doctor. They know their business, and a doctor don't care. You *got that,* did ya'? I ain't no hand fer a doctor. I want ya' to know and understand it. I ain't. He might do somethin' t'help your back, and then he'll reach out and get your pocketbook and that's all he wants. When I get in pain and get t'hurtin' or get sick, th'midwife's th'one I go to. That's th'only one will help anybody if they ain't got a big pocketbook."

Mrs. Jan MacDowell: "My mother was a granny woman for about all of th'community. They come after her 'cause she was their doctor. People'd come after her, and she'd just always go. They just depended on her same as th'doctor."

And Beulah Perry remembered one of the most vivid scenes of all: "Most of th'old womens in those days smoked cobbed pipes. You'd see those old ladies comin' down th'highway smokin' a cobbed pipe and with that little black bag in her hand. Our favorite old lady was called Aunt Haddy Corner, and we would see that old lady comin' way off—I guess as far as from here t'th'highway. Well, if we saw that old lady comin' down th'road with that smoke from her cobbed pipe, we'd know that it was Aunt Had Corner, and we would watch and wait till she got near, and we could see that little black bag in her hand, and we'd say, 'Yonder comes Aunt Had. She's carryin' somebody a little baby'"

Some families regarded their midwives so highly that they gave baby girls the first name of the midwife as their child's middle name. And there were thousands of midwives in the mountains. As Jo Brewer told us, "Over Georgia alone, we had thousands of granny midwives. They are dying out now, though. In the state today there are about eighty-five granny midwives who are over sixty-five years of age, and there are only 196 total. They used to be up in the thousands. Even when I started in public health in 1939, they had thousands doing their part in the delivery of children. Rabun County dwindled down to absolutely nothing several years ago as far as granny midwife deliveries go."

We asked a few women what the old midwives carried around with them, and the replies ranged from more elaborate midwife bags to nothing at all. Mrs. Jan MacDowell said, "She didn't carry a thing but herself. They was always prepared for ever what they had t'have, and she never did take a thing." In agreement with this was Mrs. Andy Webb, a midwife herself, who claimed she didn't carry around anything at all. Anna Howard almost became a midwife who carried a well-equipped bag, but she decided against it finally: "Well, you carried packs of literature of different kinds. Th'nurse came here t'see me and she fixed me up a bag. I give mine all back, though. They just ran me crazy." Mrs. Lawton Brooks, on the other hand, knew one granny woman who carried "scissors, thread, cloverine salve. That's about all they ever carried."

Mrs. Elizabeth Patterson, whose mother was a midwife, carried a number of things with her whenever she made a call. A story that Mrs. Patterson told us about her mother not only detailed the materials she carried, but also gave some insight into why her mother was so careful and conscientious: "She said one reason what started her to being a midwife—she'd had children, and once she had a midwife that really let her suffer a lot. After that, she had a good midwife— 'Aunt Lizzie' Keason* they called her. And she was such a good

* "Aunt Lizzie" Keason was one of the most well-known of the Rabun County midwives. She is gone now, but when she was still alive, at eighty-seven, Billy Dilworth wrote of her in an article for the *Anderson Independent*: "A little old mountain lady who used to know every family within miles of this peaceful but busy mountain town [Tiger] is taking on a new pastime these days . . . spending these Spring mornings in her garden. Or watching after several of her cows . . . 'Many's the time I left home before daylight and returned after dark,' she related. 'I remember bringing nine children into the world for one couple. I walked through snow and ice—more than two miles . . . I didn't lose a single mother or baby in those more than 525 times. I thank God for that.'

"She knows what poor financial conditions mean, too. 'When Harve and I got married, he was making fifty dollars a year. That was big money,' she recalled. 'Back then, twenty-four pounds of flour and a half gallon of kerosine did us a whole year.'

". . . The little mountain lady, whose hands showed work, had built a city of more than 525 persons—an average American small town."

midwife, Momma copied her, and said, 'Well, when she's not here, I'll help th'ladies. I won't let'em suffer.' She said right then she made up her mind she was going to help th'poor women if she could.

"Aunt Lizzie delivered me. That's who I'm named after. They called her 'Lizzie,' but my name's Elizabeth, and that's who I was named after. But Momma had a lot of experience and caught babies before she kept a record of it; but then she went to a school . . . and then she got her license out here in Rabun County at th'Clinic up there. Momma got her a bag and always had her certificate in it so, you know, if anybody questioned her or anything. A lot of times she was scared. Sometimes with all you can do, even a doctor can't save a lady. If they take childbed fever or milksick or somethin' like that —Momma was always scared somethin' like that'd happen. Or blood poison 'ud happen pretty much back then, and she'd carry her license.

"And like I said, some of'em was careless and wouldn't wash their clothes clean—wouldn't wash'em at all, hardly—and she'd carry enough sterile clothes, you know, while th'woman had th'baby, to put next to her. And she'd pack'em up beside that woman's bed and tell her not to use nothin' else but that.

"And sometimes she has went to places they didn't even have a diaper to put on th'baby, and she'd take old sheets—most of it was linen, you know, they're good'n'soft—and she'd go and they didn't have diapers, so she'd sit down and notch'em instead of hemmin'em. Take her scissors and notch that baby a bunch of little diapers out of what she'd carry."

Though some midwives were trained extensively, others had little training at all for their job. Ethel Corn said, "It'uz a thing they just got in by themselves. They didn't have no medical trainin' ner nothin'. It was just their custom."

Mrs. Avery agreed: "No, she just began her work. She'd be caught somewhere and have t'do th'work, and from then on she'd do it." And Mrs. Andy Webb, who delivered over a hundred babies, said, "I had no teachin' at all, and I know it'uz better then because they ain't near as many women were dyin' then as they is now. They was took better care of. I can't read, nor I can't write. What I've got, God gave it t'me. And I'm proud of it, and I've saved many a life. What God gives y'is right. I never lost a patient because I had th'Lord with me, and I was willin' and ready t'do all I could t'save th'lives."

Our other contacts agreed that there was little, if any, formal training before the opening of the Rabun County Clinic. Most remem-

PLATE 338   Mrs. Andy Webb

bered, however, that after good training began, the picture changed considerably. Mrs. Don Burnett said, "They didn't have t'have a license when they first began, as far back as I can remember. I didn't know of'em havin' t'have'em until up later years. Then they got t'where if they delivered babies, they had t'have a license. And then they were finally just completely cut out of th'job at all. Weren't allowed t'do th'job at all."

The appearance of midwives varied as much as their training. Mrs. Lawton Brooks remembered that "they always had on a big white apron and a white bonnet." Margaret Norton remembered them as "looking like regular people, unless sometime they put somethin' on th'top of their head, y'know—or put somethin' 'round their hair, and sometimes partly around their face. But they didn't have no special costumes that they wore. Just had on a clean apron—a white apron."

Mrs. Harriet Echols said that the midwives dressed ordinarily, "But they had t'be clean. We didn't know anything about sterilization, but they did know enough t'have ever'thing clean."

Curious about what kind of transportation the midwives had, we asked Mrs. Marinda Brown, who told us that she always kept up with what was going on, and she always knew just about when she would be called on. Then, all they had to do was provide her some sort of transportation (usually a buggy or a horse), and she'd be ready immediately.

The others agreed, but said that sometimes they didn't even have the buggy and horse. Mrs. Howard said she always walked, whether it was at dinnertime or after midnight. Beulah Perry said, "Then the granny women either walked, or they went on a wagon'r'somethin'. Most all I can remember walked, or either there would be somebody go get them in a buggy. There wasn't any cars in that day. And sometimes it would take at least a half a day to get there."

Mrs. Webb showed her deep faithfulness for her job when she said, "I went if I had t'crawl. I had no way t'go only walk. And now th'doctors has got a way t'go but they won't go. And they lose a whole lot more patients just by that. I know I'm right."

In advance of the birth of the child, little was done in the way of prenatal care before the advent of public health. A few precautions, however, were taken by some mothers. Ethel Corn remembered, "Well, now, old midwives, when somebody was pregnant and after they was so far gone, they would give'em sulfur and wine of cordia. And they'd give that so they'd be nothin' wrong. You bought it at

PLATE 339 Ethel Corn

th'drug store. It'uz nineteen percent alcohol. And it works in th'female organs altogether. And it'll clear'em up . . . and th'baby can be born without any trouble . . . And they'd always want y't'eat a balanced diet. They'd try not t'eat nicknacks and sweetenin', but they'd eat a balanced diet of vegetables and pure farm-grown stuff."

After the midwife clinic was formed, Mrs. Lex Sanders attended and remembers, "They [expectant mothers] had t'go and take a checkup within three months of their pregnancy. Well, this mother, if there was any germs, y'know—certain diseases about her body—she would take a blood test within three months of her pregnancy, and when the baby was borned, it would be clear of th'diseases and she would too.

"You know, they'd treat her—give her shots and things. If we run into a case like that, we had t'take an oath and not tell it t'nobody, for th'doctor said that it would skip—I believe he said to th'tenth generation. And he said probably a germ of this would pop up in some honest mother, and he said they weren't allowed to say anything about that in order to take care of our patients. To take care of honest mothers, we weren't allowed t'get out and talk about that to nobody. We had t'take an oath that we wouldn't say a word about that."

The time for the delivery was always a big affair. Almost everyone we talked with agreed with Margaret Norton who said, "They'd have women in t'hold their hand, or heat water'r'somethin'. There was always somethin' t'do. They always had four, five women plus a doctor [midwife]."

Ethel Corn said that the old midwives didn't put towels on the mother's head, but they held her hand. She also noted, "They had t'have somethin' t'pull fer. They didn't have nothin', in one sense of th'word, like they do in hospitals that they put up for'em to pull to that'd give'em strength to bear down t'th'pains. They never did give'em nothin' fer pain, and if th'pain stopped, they always had t'have a doctor to start that labor back up. If th'labor stopped and didn't come back on, they'd both be subject t'die.

"And midwives would help when they'd have pains and bear down just like th'old-timey doctors did. They'd work down there to spread them bones, y'know, till th'baby could be born."

Mrs. Anna Howard told us that she put towels on the patient's head and examined her, making her sit up or lie down flat on her back. She also said, "We held her hands and knees. They had t'be three—one t'each knee, and one give out sometimes. And we'd hold'em just as tight. She wasn't t'kick her feet out. We have t'sct'em up and get her feet up in bed." She also stressed washing one's hands well before the delivery.

Mrs. Webb noted the importance of cleanliness too. She said that she always washed her hands well with "disinfect." In addition to this, however, she had a certain prayer that she would say both before and after the baby was born. She would not, however, tell us the prayer itself.

At the time the baby was born, a number of activities began. "Back then, when a midwife went and delivered a baby," said Ethel Corn, "they'd cut a long cord, and it'uz tied, y'know, with a string so it'd fit. And they'd scorch a piece of cloth—put it on a shovel and put it over a fire, and they'd scorch it right brown. And then they'd put that next t'th'navel. They'd cut a hole in it and pull th'navel cord through. They'd leave that on till that navel cord'ud come off. It generally took from three, to five or six days for that. 'Course it had t'rot off.

"And then they would grease a cloth with mutton taller, and they'd scorch th'cloth and put on it, and they'd always pin bands on it. This day you never see a baby with a band on it.

PLATE 340   Florence Brooks

"Baby's'ud rupture themselves, y'see, because that's a very thin place [where the navel is], and so they'd put that on till it healed and growed up firm. [Otherwise] if they cry hard or anything, it would rupture'em and maybe ruin th'baby fer life. It'ud always be ruptured."

Florence Brooks told us that after the baby was born, the midwife would cut the cord and tie it and then dress the baby. Then she'd wait for the afterbirth [placenta, umbilical cord, etc.], carry it off, and bury it. We asked her if there were any certain instructions as to the care of the baby. Her reply was, "No. Nothin' only just t'keep its navel cord greased with castor oil till it come off. And I don't reckon they was such a thing as alcohol. We'd always put a little powder on its navel after its cord come off t'dry it up." She also said there was no tea given to the mother—only to the baby.

Anna Howard told us about a disease a baby could be born with called "croupy." We asked her what it was, and she replied, "Choke t'death. And, buddy, I've seen'em born black as tar. Sometimes you'd have t'pick it up and shake it. You shake'em, pull their mouth open, and blow in their mouth . . . But we'd take them that come a'chokin' —we'd throw'em up and blow in their mouth—I would. And then take homemade syrup—jest a half a spoon full—and put a little water in it and put it in its mouth with a teaspoon, and when we could get it

290   FOXFIRE 2

to swallow it, that would cut that phlegm loose and it would get its breath."

She also told us about cutting the baby's umbilical cord: "I learned to cut th'baby loose. You had t'cut it loose and tie its belly. You'd take th'scissors and cut it. If you cut it right, it was all right. And that was what scared me so bad. I was afraid I wouldn't cut it right. But I did. I never missed it a time."

She also indicated the importance of breast feeding when she said, "You never put a bottle on. Y'never heard tell of a bottle."

Apparently, at the time of birth, a common thing among most babies was the hives. Mrs. MacDowell told us about her mother's cure for the hives: "She made lots of tea. She believed in tea. She made red alder tea for that."

Florence Brooks said, "Catnip tea, ground ivy, or red alder. It was supposed t'break'em out and make'em have th'hives—which th'doctors don't believe in now, and I don't either."

Mrs. Andy Webb told us that she used castor oil, black snake root, and rattle weed to make teas to break the hives out. She said of hives, "It looks sort'a like th'measles, but it ain't measles. Them's bold hives. I've got mouse ear to make tea out of and save lives. It grows on a rock sort'a in th'edge of water. And that'll cure th'bold hives. Right smart a'difference. Th'bold hives works around th'heart, and th'other hives just makes'em cramp and jump."

When we asked Mrs. Webb what she did after the baby was born, she said, "I had t'take th'afterbirth with m'hands. I just washed m'hands with disinfect and cre'lin (some kind'a medicine y'put in water). I'd rather have it as t'have th'disinfect."

Ethel Corn told us the midwife would give the child catnip tea to break the hives out and clear up the liver. She said, "They'll have'em after they're born, and if them hives don't break out on'em—if it's th'bone hives—it'll kill'em. You've got t'do somethin' to clear th'liver up. And if you don't, they'll get yeller lookin'."

She also told us that when the baby was just born, the midwives would often "feed him butter to cut the phlegm out."

Beulah Perry also agreed with the use of catnip tea. "If th'mother didn't have enough milk, why they'd make catnip tea—go out and get that catnip and make a little weak tea and feed those little babies maybe two tablespoonsful till it got satisfied."

When asked what the mother was given after she had her baby, Ethel Corn's reply was, "Always after they delivered a baby, it was a big dose'a castor oil."

Mrs. Brooks told us the mother was given a dose of castor oil before she had her baby, and sometimes paregoric after she had it.

Nearly all the women we talked to affirmed that a good long rest was the best thing for the mother. Ethel, for example, said, "Well, now, before I was grown, I heard Mommy tell of'em havin' their baby and gettin' up and goin' on to work. But now back when mine was born, the doctor didn't allow me out of bed for nine days. And he wouldn't allow me t'eat'r'set up in bed for three days. And you know, women had a lot better health when it'uz done thataway than th'way they do'em now. That's one thing I think makes th'women so weakly now when they have a baby. In one sense, it works like a cow havin' a calf. You'll turn her out of her stall and she goes on a'pickin'. Well, that's th'way th'doctors does now. They take'em to a hospital— they won't go t'a home—they have t'be at a hospital. And th'baby's delivered there. Well, in a hour's time after that baby's born, they'll have'em up again and goin' and doin' and th'next day send'em home. And I *have* knowed of'em sendin'em home th'day th'baby's born. And they'd go back home and go t'doin' their washin' and ironin' and all kind'a work like that. Well, that's against'em, and it's really dangerous."

Mrs. Andy Webb agreed. "I never let my patients get out a'bed in nine days. And now they turn'em loose th'next day. I *know* it's bad. It ruins their health. I'd tell'em not t'eat no apples ner nothin' like that that would hurt'em. I'd tell'em t'eat cooked fruit. And now they just let'em eat what they want!"

Mrs. Brooks said, "Eat anything y'want except kraut and pickled beans, and stay in th'bed for ten days. No gettin' up for ten days. It sounds like a nice rest, but y'get wore out. I stayed in bed ten days and I never had no back trouble—that was t'take care of your back."

Anna Howard agreed also: "That's th'reason women ain't stout. They make'em get right up."

Mrs. Brewer's clinic also kept the mothers in confinement for a long period of time. They used this period to advantage, however, as a training period. The mother was kept seven days, and she paid two dollars a day. The purpose of the program was to help the mother so she didn't feel like she'd gotten into something she didn't understand. "We had seven days to teach her to bathe the baby, handle the baby, and let her learn health facts about the baby: why she should put the baby down on the abdomen instead of on its back, for example. Many babies can be found dead from choking on their own milk."

Anna Howard added some additional customs: "Now if it'uz a miscarriage, you could go and take apple tree bark and make a tea out of it, and give'em a cup'a'tea. But no other time." She also told us about washing the mother with a yellowish salve after she had had her baby. "There weren't nary one a'mine that ever went through but two good washin's until she got up." The mother was put on a very light diet, but with good food to eat.

The amount of time the midwife stayed on at the home after the child was born varied. Mrs. MacDowell, for example, claimed that she usually stayed a week after the birth. Mrs. Echols remembered that if the mother wasn't feeling well, "she'd be there for two weeks to watch and see. They usually had someone else in t'do th'housework, and th'older children could do th'other work."

Anna Howard said, "If it'uz born in th'mornin', you'd stay all day . . . I've stayed with several—stayed a week, and then sometimes I've stayed nine days. It was just accordin' t'how they got along."

In other cases, however, things would go along so well that the midwife would only stay from a few hours to a day after the baby arrived, and then go on to other jobs. Margaret Norton said, "Sometimes they'd have t'stay more than a day, or maybe they'd have another case t'go to and have t'go and come back. I knowed that t'happen lots'a times."

Almost none of the midwives were paid a great deal for their services. Mrs. Marinda Brown told us the midwives were sometimes paid in food or things they could use. Mrs. Algie Norton said that they usually didn't charge anything. Mrs. Lex Sanders said that she wasn't allowed to charge anything, and that it was the person's own decision whether they wanted to pay her or not.

Mrs. MacDowell told us that people didn't pay the midwives, but Ethel Corn said, "Yeah, they'uz paid, but it'uz just two or three dollars. It wadn't no big prices like it is now."

Mrs. Howard claimed, "I never charged. I always was too sorry for th'wife t'charge. They meant for me t'charge five dollars, but I never did. But they'd give it t'me sometimes."

Mrs. Webb said, "If they wanted t'give me anything, I accepted it. And if they didn't, why, it'uz all right. I was workin' for th'Lord— not for th'people."

If they were paid at all, it seemed that it was seldom with money. Few could afford that then. Mrs. Parker stated that sometimes they would be paid with a twist of tobacco, but "they didn't have th'money back then, and they didn't expect it."

Mrs. E. H. Brown said, "The family gave them money if they had a little money. If they didn't, they gave them something else. Maybe somethin' t'eat. Half a gallon a'syrup, or a pumpkin'r'two, or some corn, or somethin' like that."

Mrs. Echols agreed: "They usually charged about five dollars, but a lot a'times if you had meat and molasses and anything that was raised on th'farm that they didn't have, they'd take it in produce."

Deaths? They happened occasionally, but they seemed to be fairly infrequent according to most of our sources. Mrs. Sanders, for example, claims that she never lost a patient or a baby during her career, and many of the others claim the same. In fact, many of them believe that the patients did better then at home than they do now at the hospitals. Mrs. Corn, for example, said, "You hardly ever heared of one a'dyin', and you very seldom heared of one a'bein' deformed in any way. My mother had nine children. They'uz nine of us. Most all of'em had big families then. And they done better at home than they do these that went and had they'rn at th'hospital. Now I had seven, and ever' one a'mine'uz born at home!"

But superstitions regarding death were common, and certain signs were much feared. Aunt Nora Garland, whose mother was a midwife, talked at length about the "news bees" that are so common around here: "Well, now, there's yeller ones—that's *good* news—and they's black ones, and that's bad news. And you know, I hate to see them things, too. I was in th'bed nine days before that baby was born, and there's a little window right at th'head of my bed. And I watched that news bee go out ever' day—that black news bee. He'd come in and stand over my head (they go like they're a'talkin' noise, y'know), and it'd go out th'window and go right across toward th'cemetery. Of course, we thought we could keep that baby, and it was a eight months baby, and there wasn't any hospitals then.

"So we lost our baby. It was buried right out here at this little cemetery—right th'way the news bees went. So I believe in news bees."

Other superstitions were also common. Jo Brewer talked of some of them at length. "When a person was hemorrhaging, the old thinking was that if you turned an axe with the blade side up under the bed, it would cut the hemorrhage. Now how that started, I'll never know. I mean, it's just so ridiculous on the face of it that you wonder how intelligent beings could believe it.

"Another thing that they believed was that if a mother was nursing a baby and had to quit, and her breasts needed to be dried up, if she would milk some milk on a hot rock, this would help dry up the breast. Now I can see how that might have started. Expelling a little milk gradually *will* help. But milking them on a hot rock! They could have milked it in a towel or on the ground and it would have been as good."

Mrs. Harriet Echols said, "If you put a knife under the pillow and an axe under the bed, it will cut the pains. And they put a pan of water under the bed when you had a temperature. That water was t'cool th'atmosphere and make the fever go down."

But Mrs. Echols was quick to claim that she didn't believe them herself—they had only been common in the neighborhood where she had been raised. "That's just all in th'makin' because there's nothin' to it. Because birth *is* a trial. It's a travail. With anything that's born, th'mothers have t'suffer. And nothin' will prevent it until th'birth is completed.

"Back then, those people made a livin' on th'farm. I'd stop in where th'new babies would be born, and they'd talk about how much pain they had until they put th'axe under th'bed . . . but that was just an old wives' tale because it wasn't true. Nothin' that's born is born without sufferin'. Some give you less pain than others."

Still other superstitions were those that were the result of stories parents had told their children concerning birth. Beulah Perry, for example, can remember vividly when parents didn't talk about such things and would tell their children that "you went in th'woods. That's where you'd find little babies—in th'woods."

We've come a long way since then; but still, there is something immensely attractive and appealing about a midwife that will come and stay and hold one's hand for as long as is necessary to make everything all right. But perhaps more effective than anything we could tell you about them are the stories they tell themselves.

RICHARD NORTON: I went after Doc Neville one time, ridin' a horse. He had a Model T Ford. Well, th'roads was s'bad up here that I come back t'his father's and got his saddle horse and took it back [for him to ride].

They hauled lumber with wagons then, and they just kept that road cut up till a car couldn't get up here. And then too 'cause a'that awful cold and freezin' weather, it was just cut all to pieces. It was so bad that th'horses would break through th'ice and th'mudholes and just nearly pitch on their heads, y'know.

So I brought him up here on that horse. It was s'bad that we just couldn't make no time on it then. We got here. We came right on th'two horses; but they was really freezin' t'death cold, and they was just wet with sweat. It'uz s'hard on them t'travel, y'know, through that ice, and breakin' through it and fallin' and strainin' and goin' on.

People don't know what hard times they was!

HARRIET ECHOLS: Well, y'know, honey, since th'olden days, there's s'much about midwives—you ought t'get in on all this. The old-time people thought that young people shouldn't know all th'facts of life and ever'thing till they were grown. Well, if you're not gonna' learn it while you're little and your parents teachin' it to y', how are y'gonna get all this? Ever'thing about th'birds and th'bees?

My great-grandfather was a doctor—th'old-time doctor that rode horseback through th'mountains. And my grandmother married when

PLATE 341   Harriet Echols

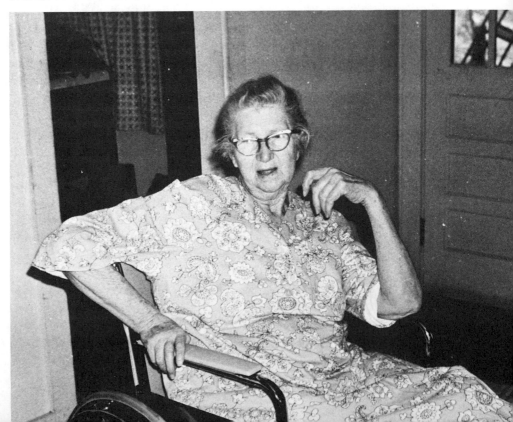

she was young and took up th'practice of nursin'. And bein' a midwife was her specialty. 'Course she took care of any kind of sick patient that come along, 'cause as a small girl, from th'time she was eight'r'nine years old and began t'do things, she went with her father. Said she'd set up on th'horse and ride with him t'see patients.

And so she learned quite a bit. And she raised a family of nine, and that midwifing was her main work t'make money. Her husband died, and they had a farm, and th'boys worked th'farm.

Well, I learned how. I have delivered one baby, and I've helped at a lot of home deliveries. When I delivered that baby, th'doctor came about thirty or forty minutes after and examined ever'thing. That is th'essential thing. You have t'have your water, wash your hands, and you have t'examine th'mother t'know that ever'thing is normal. You have t'see if th'baby's in th'right position to be born normally. And if not, then you've got t'know what t'do t'straighten it out. And if you can't turn th'baby t'get it straightened out and it comes feet first, then it usually dies because it strangles t'death—unless there's a doctor there t'take care.

It's a pretty scary affair. I wouldn't have wanted that t'be my lifework whatever. Midwives used t'didn't have instruments. They just had t'work with th'know-how. If anything was wrong, they tried t'get a doctor. If they didn't, Nature just had t'do th'best it could.

But when I delivered that baby, th'doctor come; and when he got there, he said I did a wonderful job. And a'course I was scared t'death. But somebody had t'do somethin', and th'other ladies . . . they just expected th'neighbors t'come in and help.

But there's not too much t'do because it's usually over in an hour'r'two. When Nature starts, it's a pretty tryin' time. But yet, and still, it makes y'mighty happy when things are all right.

ANNA HOWARD [The following story unfolded when Anna Howard and her mother were summoned to deliver the baby of Mr. and Mrs.—we'll call them Jones for the purpose of the story]:

I went to a family up here on this creek—they call hit the old Curtis place. The man was a Jones, and he was married and they had two children.

Well, when they sent for me an' Mother t'go there, he [Mr. Jones] had got th'milksick [a disease thought to have been caused by drinking milk from a cow that had eaten a certain plant that grows in dark coves]; and *his* mother was there too.

Well, it was a night—do you'n's remember way back the comet was gonna pass? And that was th'greatest excitement that had ever been. And they come the awfullest storm that I have ever see'd in my lifetime. And it was awful steep up there—part of th'way t'that little log house—but me and Mother went.

[By the time we got there] the little girl'd got sick [Jones's eldest daughter], and the old man [Mr. Jones] didn't know anything at all. They had him on th'floor on a pallet, and th'little girl, just alive, on th'other side of th'room. [There was a younger daughter there too, but she had not gotten sick yet.]

So she [Mrs. Jones] was gonna have a baby. Hit was a six months baby. His [Jones's] mother went and she got apple bark and made tea for Mrs. Jones. That was to keep her from havin' th'baby. And it wasn't an hour till she [the wife] took that milksick too.

[Mrs. Jones had the baby soon after she took sick.] Well, I'uz a'settin' over in th'corner, and they gave me th'baby t'hold. His [Jones's] mother done th'work a'takin' th'afterbirth—she just had it t'do. My mother had t'oldest girl t'watch, and she was crazy as she could be. His [Jones's] mother, then, had t'tend to her [Mrs. Jones], and she'd put her head against th'headboard and she'd climb. She'd climb that headboard and get up in spite of creation. Well, that eldest girl died of that milksick, and my mother took her and laid her out.

And th'man [Jones] got *gone,* and was nobody knowed where he was. I'uz there and I had t'hold that baby, you know. It was a'breathin'. It was a fully developed lookin' baby, and I'll bet you a dollar hit would'a weighed six or seven pound. The biggest, fattest, prettiest baby I ever saw. Well, it wadn't long till *hit* died in my lap. Then I had hit t'dress, and my mother helped lay it out.

And then we got t'huntin' for th'old man, and he'd crawled off from behind th'stove and crawled clean around there, and he was a'lyin' under th'bed that girl had died on. And we had t'get down on our knees and get him by th'feet and sneak him out. He didn't know what he'uz doin'. He'uz crazy with th'milksick.

[All of a sudden they discover that Mrs. Jones and her youngest daughter have disappeared too.] Well, when daylight come, we got t'huntin' for them, and we couldn't find them nowhere. It thundered and lightened and I don't see how she lived. We was just a'sweatin' —me and m'mammy. And th'water goin' up th'hill and hit a'comin' down. Hit wet us way above our knees.

And about time for sunup I said, "They've been a'loggin' in there, and they've built a shed way down below th'house." And by gran-nies, she'd took that young'un and went down there and stayed. Ever'body was scared t'death.

Well, they'd sent after th'doctor, but he never come that night. Not till th'next mornin' when th'sun'uz shinin' and hit had cleared off. Th'doctor come and hollered "milksick" before he got in th'door. You can smell it. Well, there was two funerals, both of'em children. And he [Jones] lived, but he's been dead a year now.

That milksick, they'd get it from cows, y'know, back up in th'mountains. And back here towards Mulberry there's a place, but nobody's never found it. And they've tried all these here experiments, and they've never found out yet how it come. It's bound t'come from some mineral and settle on th'vegetables of a mornin' with th'dew. But hit'll kill'em. They ain't no doubt about it.

MRS. ELIZABETH PATTERSON: [My mother, Mrs. Effie Dick-erson] went to one place up here, and they had a boy who was men-tally retarded, and he was grown. And they had a lot more children besides that, and they had some other back in th'bedroom.

And they [the family] said that if they wronged him [the mentally retarded boy] in any way, he'd get serious mad, y'know. And they just couldn't do anything with him.

So he would come and sit and try t'watch Momma borned that baby, and Momma just wouldn't have children'r'men around—ex-cept she'd have their husbands—she thought that was all right t'help if they wanted to.

But this boy just kept on, and th'mother kept on sayin', "You go on out, son," beggin'im, y'know, and tryin' t'have her baby. And th'baby just couldn't be borned.

So Momma, she just got kinda aggravated, and I'm tellin' you, she got onto'im. She said she was scared to, but she knowed that woman was sufferin' and needed to have th'baby. And she got onto'im. And it kind'a didn't do no good, so she *really* got onto'im and fussed'im out.

And she said they had old rails that they used to build fences with just piled up out there by th'house. Anyhow, he went out there and got an axe and went t'cuttin' them rails. She said he just cut and never stopped.

Th'mother thought he would turn on Momma, and Momma said, "Nah, I don't think he will. I think y'all haven't been quite hard enough on'im. We all know you'll be sorry fer'im, but you've got t'make them mind, y'know—even if they are a little bit off."

It wadn't long, while he was a'cuttin' them rails, th'baby was borned. After that, she got th'baby cleaned up and th'mother, she runned out there and called'im. She said she was afraid he would get too exhausted—he was sickly anyway. And she called'im and told'im to come and see his brother. . . . So he come in and was Momma's friend thereafter. He would just see her in town and he just loved her.

Lots of times when she went th'baby wouldn't be ready to be borned, and she'd be hungry. She was always wantin' t'go eat. And she'd get in that kitchen and go t'cookin' for all of th'family, and feed th'rest of th'little children; and if it was nighttime, get'em fed and ready for bed and out of th'way so th'baby could be borned.

And then, if they didn't go t'bed, she'd get'em fed and let th'husband take'em someplace t'get'em out of th'way. Oh, she's seen some hard times durin' that period of time, but she enjoyed it so we couldn't do anything with her. After her health got t'fadin', we begged her not to, but she went off lots of times when she wadn't able. But finally she saw th'light, and she had t'give it up.

She told me some things they don't tell y'now—I mean, th'doctors, y'know. I think they give you shots tryin' t'hurry you up, but Momma said, with th'first one [baby], they always need t'take all th'time they need. For God made'em to have that baby, and if they took a lot of time, it wouldn't injure'em nowhere, y'know. And Momma would make'em hold back to keep'em from tearin' when th'baby was born.

I was with her when Allen was born, and it couldn't be borned on th'bed at all. And she'd heard tell of way back, th'midwives put'em on the husband's lap. But Momma wouldn't do that—'fraid it'ud tear th'woman. So she made us fix quilts down in th'floor so it would be hard. Th'bed was just too soft—mattress a'givin'—and we needed some place hard. So we fixed it down in th'floor. And th'mother that'uz havin' th'baby, it wadn't but five minutes after we put her down there, th'baby was borned.

When she passed away [her mother], you never have seen th'flowers from places she'd gone! And some of th'children would come up to me and say, "If it hadn't been for her, I wouldn't a'been here, y'know."

PLATE 342   Marinda Brown

MARINDA BROWN: I was delivered by a midwife, and my younger sister was delivered by a midwife. When my sister was born, I was right about three years old.

We had been out. They sent us out somewhere. I seem t'remember we used t'rake th'leaves a lot, you know, to bed our stock. And I don't know why we'd be doin' it in June [when the sister was born], but I've always gone through th'years with th'impression that we were out in th'woods on th'side of th'road rakin' leaves.

And when we went back t'th'house, my sister was born: and this midwife picked me up and helt me t'look at th'baby.

Now that is an impression that stayed with me all these years. And I've talked t'my older sisters about it, and they say, "Oh, no! That isn't right. That isn't right because they sent us off to th'neighbors t'spend th'night."

But I've still got that impression.

MRS. ANDY WEBB: Well, one winter, I come up here t'my daughter's. And th'snow was that [knee] deep; and I had t'walk. I had no way else t'go but t'walk. And I was might'near froze t'death when I got there. And th'wind a'blowin'—they, my goodness!

I stood on my knees at th'poor side a'that bed and took care a'her when I was s'numb I couldn't hardly stand up!

LEX SANDERS: I done midwife work just 'cause I had it t'do, y'know. Russ Anders' wife, when she was borned [gave birth], it was a awful stormy night. They couldn't get no doctor. That was my first experience. I took care of Pearl.

Then they was a orphan girl, and none of her people would keep her. She just stayed in town. Well, she just went up and down th'streets ever' daytime; and ever' night, John Mills let her sleep in th'jail.

PLATE 343   Lex Sanders

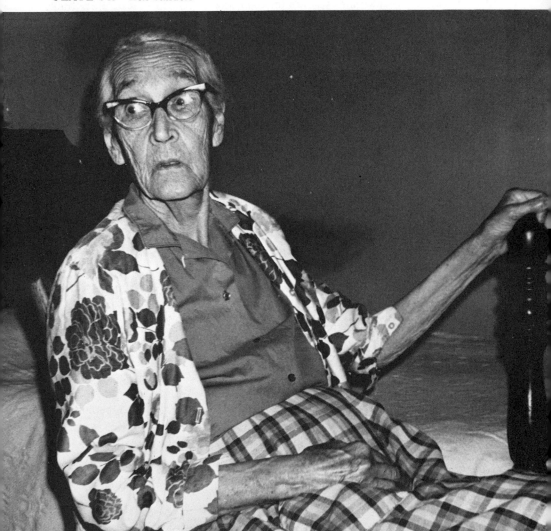

Somebody come t'me one day and said, "Why don't you keep her till after her baby's borned?"

And I said, "Well, I don't know."

Well, we had t'see th'Red Cross, y'know. So we went, and she had a office there in th'courthouse. We went in there and seen her. All my children was grown, y'know, and I didn't have any at home, so I told them I'd take th'girl and take her t'th'doctor and see that she was clear of diseases. And they said to take her to any doctor I wanted to . . .

And I brought her home with me and kept her for six months.

Well, when her baby was due, she took sick. I called th'doctor and he come and he said it was only in her head. Said he didn't think there was a thing in th'world wrong with her—she just had it in her mind that she was gonna have her baby [but he didn't think she was].

Well, he left her three pills, and he told me how often t'give'em. I give her th'pills, and just before I give her th'last'un, she was awfully sick. I told her, "Now, th'doctor said if you took this pill and there wasn't nothin' wrong with y', it would kill ya'."

She said, "Honey, give it t'me. I'd rather be dead than th'shape I'm in."

Well, I gave it t'her and I waited two hours. I see'd that th'pill wasn't goin' t'do no good, so I just [went ahead] and I delivered her.

And the next morning, well, my hands was kinda tired. I wasn't licensed at that time. And I had this orphan girl there, y'know; and I had t'be kinda particular about it. So I called th'doctor again, and he come back up there. I was settin' there in front of th'fire with th'baby in my arms, and when he come in 'at door, I said, "Well, her mind is done delivered her!"

She had one a'th'finest baby boys that you ever looked at. And I went t'th'Red Cross woman and said, "If they's any money in th'treasure for that, give it t'some poor widow woman or orphan child. That doctor's not entitled to it."

She said, "Miss Sanders, you get your license. We can't pay you. We've *got* t'pay th'doctor." She said, "You get your license and you can charge just th'same as th'doctor."

She told me I could meet her in th'courthouse, and I met her and she granted me my license.

Well, then I'uz licensed for twenty years, but they depended on me too much, and I got nervous sometimes . . . so I got th'doctor t'sign for me t'have a rest. [On one occasion she found herself in a cabin high on the side of a mountain alone with an expectant mother, four young boys, and the mother-in-law, and no other help in sight. She felt too much could have gone wrong.]

We was taught th'only wound there was about th'baby's body was th'navel. And when we fixed up that navel, we wasn't allowed to touch it. We had t'pick it up by th'cord that it was tied with, for he said if it got infected, that'd probably cause th'death of that baby after it was growed up.

And that, in essence, is the way Lex and others worked. Some of their practices and beliefs have now long since been outdated, but that hardly makes them irrelevant. By all counts midwifery was a fascinating art that few people today realize even existed. Having read this chapter, perhaps you were able to more fully understand the hardships and responsibilities a midwife shouldered back when there were no doctors. She successfully performed in an area that would seem impossible for many of us to undertake today. For this and more, the midwife of former days, who had the strength and courage to do that which was needed to be done, should long be remembered.

OLD-TIME BURIALS

"When I was a child on up till I was grown," said Ethel Corn, "seemed like I was drawn to go to any funeral whether I knowed the people or not. I just had th'urge to go. What finally stopped me from wantin' to go to funerals was when [a friend's] wife died. And she had a baby. It wadn't but more'n a year old. And that was th'pitifullest thing and got me the worst of anything I ever went to. They took that baby up to see her, and when it did, it went t'reachin' and cryin' t'save mama. And you know that backed me off from wantin' to go to funerals."

Many superstitions and ghost stories have had their beginnings at old-time burials and wakes and graveyards. Maybe it was the way some of the supposedly dead people suddenly woke up, or the way the bodies were hauled to the church for the dramatic ceremonies held there. Nevertheless, the fascination was fact. Aunt Arie told us in hushed tones of a neighbor who was shot during a fight and died with his eyes open—"blared," she called it. "And you could see th'devil in 'em—them fightin', y'know."

And Ethel Corn told us of a neighbor's wife who had to be dug up and moved from the old family plot to a graveyard nearby: "And she'd been dead for about twenty-odd years. They said when they took her up and opened that lid, there was glass over it so no air couldn't get in. And said she looked just exactly like she did when [they buried her]. And then they raised that glass, and when they did, said it all just went down flat to nothin'."

Dr. Rufus Morgan, a retired Episcopal minister whose interview concludes this chapter, told us that it was easy for him to see how superstitions and ghost stories might arise in this connection. "I might tell you one little story," he said. "Up here at St. John's Church [is where it happened]. I was born in a log cabin the other side of the church. One evening, my mother had been down to visit her parents and was on her way back and was passing the cemetery at late dusk. As she passed, she saw a white figure in the cemetery. She was rather surprised. She stopped, and the figure just stood there. Then she started on and the figure started after her. She stopped again, and the figure stopped. She started on again, and it repeated the movement. Finally she stopped for a longer time. Most people would have beat a hasty retreat, but she waited and the figure came up to her. And it was an Indian mother who had been at the grave of a child that had been buried there.

"That's the way superstitions in regard to ghosts arise. They can develop very easily if you are afraid.

"Another thing—my longest hike, which was something over two hundred miles in five days, went from up above Albany, New York, into Boston—the length of Massachusetts. I had a blanket and a frying pan—just bare necessities—and I'd camp out overnight.

"Well, I got along toward the eastern part of Massachusetts, and I couldn't find open space which was suitable for camping. It was getting dark. By the time I left one town, I'd be in another.

"Finally I came to a cemetery by a church, so I said to myself, 'That'll be safe. Nobody'll bother me there.' So I went in and found a nice place between two graves, and, wrapped in a blanket, I went to sleep.

"Along ten o'clock or so at night, I felt something, and I couldn't tell at first just what had waked me up. I listened and felt, and finally I discovered it was just beginning to rain on me. So the disturbance wasn't the ghost at all. Just the rain."

While working on this chapter, we learned to value the qualities of unselfishness and concern that people had for others in the time of death and to appreciate the unlimited time they gave of themselves. Showing their genuine sympathy, respect, and love for the family of the deceased, people traveled great distances in wagons and on horseback to attend wakes, help dig and fill the grave, make the coffin, wash and dress the body, and to help the family in any possible way. And they did it, usually, free of charge. As Margaret Norton said,

"Th'family didn't have t'pay nothin'. They dug th'grave free of charge. Men went in together and dug th'grave. And you made th'buryin' clothes, and you made th'box t'be buried in, and there wadn't no payin' goin' on. Th'preacher never charged for a funeral— for preachin' a funeral. They'll charge for funerals now, preachers will. They're not supposed to. See, most preachers is paid by salary, and that's one of his jobs. He ain't supposed t'charge y'. But many of'em'll take anything."

We gained a new insight into people from seeing how they acted during time of death and in comparing these old-time funerals with today's, we were amazed at the differences. You'll see many of them yourself.

BETSE WHILDEN and KAREN COX

1

As soon as a person died, a number of things were traditionally done almost simultaneously: a bell was tolled announcing the death; a neighbor was contracted to produce a casket (unless it had been made in advance under the supervision of the person who had died); relatives who lived away from the community were notified as quickly as possible—sometimes by means of a letter edged with a black border; and the body was washed and laid out in preparation for the wake that would take place that night in the home of the deceased. The "settin' up" was held in the home since, as Maude Shope said, "they didn't have no funeral homes t'take'em to, y'know. If one was t'die here last night, we laid'im out. What neighbors was already here 'cause somebody'uz sick would strip th'bed off and put'im on a plain plank till y'got yer casket."

Most of our contacts told us that the number of times the bell tolled depended on the age of the person who had died. Ethel Corn, for example, said, "Quick as the news went that they was dead, why somebody would go and ring th'bells. And then they'd toll th'bells for however many years old they were. You could count th'bells a'tollin' and you'd know just exact how old that person was."

Maude Shope went into even greater detail. "They'd go and ring th'bell soon as they could—toll it. Like if I was t'die today, however many years old I was, they'd toll it. You'd go t'countin' if you heard th'bell toll, and if you knowed they'uz somebody sick in th'neighborhood, you could count th'bells and tell pretty well who it could be."

th new mon feaver i Stood over him tell the verry last i done all i could for him to know ...

March the 23, 1885
Hayesvill Clay Co.
NC

Mr. J.F. Palmer   Dear Sir

You rote me that you wanted to know what had becom of Josef Palmer i hav neglectd to rite you i can know tell you wher he is he lies bared at the babtis church in hayesvill and Clay Co. he was bared at 12 o clock to day the 23 Jacob he live on brastown [Brasstown] he lay sick 6 days before they sent me word he was all most ded when i got their so far gon that Dr. Killion could knot doo him know good he had some fool Dr. tending on him so he is gone he died with the new mon feaver [pneumonia fever] i stood over him tell the verry last i done all i could for him Dr. Killiam saꝺd with me tell he died but we got ther too late to doo any good Jacob what will be done with them 6 litle childern oh do tell me Sos was sick so. she could not come to the berill to day the three bigest came with me oh what a sad thing hit is to think a bout it Jacob i had to come to town to get the coff [coffin] made i had him a fine won mad hit was made out of the finest of walnut and trim- med as land [?] as triming would do any good I bout him a fine soot to be bered in so I put him away nise as any man could be put away Jacob the berl cost 19.55 Jacob i want us all to make up the maney and pay the bill will you help us if so let me know Jacob les not let her take what litl she has lef from them litle childern if so they will suffer shore that will never doo don' you say so Jacob he died Saturday the 21 jest at 5 o clock eavning he was franzy at times but he could tolk tell the very lost he turned over on his side was ded in a minnet never srugle but wanst Jacob i did want you their so bad but their was none of us their but me and Rbe when he died Thomas got their in tim to see him bered that was all that was their i had no time to sand after any of them i had to wait on him Jacob we laid the 2 half dollars on his eys thot lay on our pore old mothers eys he had kep them all the tim him self come over or rite me soon i cant hardly rite thes lines i feel soo bad i could give hiss wife beter was not for them lite wans oh which won of us neset [next] oh i am trublte so Jacob i will move her out of that plase soon get her close to me Sam wus her baby is about 6 week old dont you know se had a bad time jest out of the bed and waiting on him tell she is down sick rite me soon for i dont know what to do
                                        J.H. Palmer

but wanst Jocod i did want you their so bad but their was nan of us their but me and Rbe when he died thomas got their in tim to See him Bered that was all that was their i had no him to Sand ofter any if them i had to wait an him Jocob we laid the 2 half dollars an his eys thot lay an our pore old mothers eys he had kep them all the tim him self come over or rite me Soan i cant hardly rite thes lines ifeel Soo bad i cauld give him up beter was not fỷ them lite wons oh which won of us neset oh i am trubte so

PLATE 344

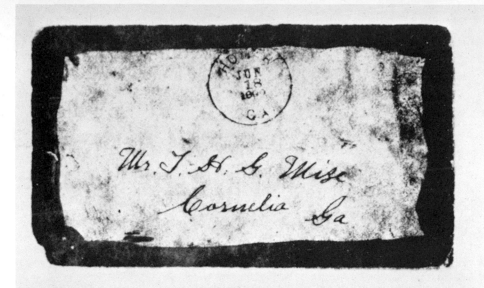

Homer Ga, June the 17 1890.

Dear Brother and family

I write you this morning
to inform you of Mothers death she passed away last Friday the 13

Homer Ga. June the 17 1890
Dear Brothers and family

I write you this morning
to inform you of Mothers death she passed away
last Friday the 13 about 10 minutes before 5 o-
clock in the evening. She gradualy grew weaker
and weaker untill the last and died without a
strugle. Just seemed to fall asleep. She ask to
be raised up in bed we raised her up her breath
got slower and weaker till it ceased. didn't
seem to suffer any pain in several hours previous
to death. She was buried at Homer Sunday evening
and the funeral was preached by Rev. T.O. Rorie.
We are sorry that you all could not come to see
her. Albert didnt come either we wrote for him
but he could not come Juliar was sick: The rest
of us are tolerably well and hope this will find
you improving in health. . Hamby when you get able
you all must come down and stay awhile with us
its very lonely here now seems like half of the
family are gone and all of home I don't feel like
I could ever make it home again. We are spending
the day today with Rev. Rories family. I'll close
write soon and come when you can. I remain as ever
Laura Mize

ing she gradualy grew
d without a strugle
ised up in bed we
eaker till it ceased.
hours previous to death
y and the funeral was
that you all could not
we wrote for him but
rest of us are tolerably
promis in health.
ist come down and
stay awhile with us its very lonely here now seems like
half of the the family are gone and all of home I dont
feel like I could ever make it home again. we are spending
the day today with Rev. Rories family. I'll close write soon
and come when you can I remain as ever

Laura Mize

PLATE 345

Annie Perry described the tolling in this manner: "Slow, th'toll of th'bell would be. Slow. 'Dong, dong, dong, dong'—however old th'person was."

And Anna Howard said, "They tolled th'bell as many times as they were years old. If a child were two years old, it was two; 'r if they were eight'r'twelve'r'twenty—'r just whatever. And fer th'old'uns, it'd toll fer half an hour. If you could count th'strikes, you'd know how old they were, and you'd know that somebody had passed away. Then ever'body'd begin t'try t'learn who it was."

Few of our contacts agreed on the length of time the family waited before the burying. Florence Brooks said the person was buried two days after he died. Happy Dowdle said the family would leave the body out until all the family that was going to be able to come got there.

Almost all agreed, however, that since there was no way of preserving the body for any length of time, the service usually took place with as little delay as possible—often, in fact, the next day. And washing and dressing the body took place at once. As Mrs. E. H. Brown said, "Usually we waited till th'next day t'bury'em. Or we'd wait till th'casket was ready. 'Course we'd go right ahead and get that dressin' done as early as we could before th'rigor mortis, I reckon they called it, set in. Y'see, after th'body'd get stiff, it was awfully hard t'do anything."

We soon became curious about just what it was the family or friends would do when they laid a body out. Aunt Arie said that it was essential to work fast or the body would stiffen up and swell. She talked about hearing arms break "in there" after the body had stiffened. They would massage the person's cheeks to get the eyes closed, and then put a silver coin over each eye to keep them shut since, "lots a'times with homemade fixin' and th'jostlin', they'd come open." Silver was preferred because copper might turn the skin green. In one of the most touching moments that took place in our interviews, she revealed that when she washed her husband, Ulysses, before his "buryin'," she found a birthmark that she had never known was there.

Anna Howard gave us information along the same lines as Aunt Arie: "When they died, they laid'em out and closed their eyes and straightened'em. And if their eyes wouldn't stay shut, they'd lay a nickel on each eye. Then they'd wash'em and dress'em at home. They didn't have no funeral home t'take'em to."

Mrs. Lex Sanders talked about a man who had had a heart attack and died: "He was blue—his whole body. They said th'men who dressed him said he was layin' on his side, and his right side was perfectly bloodshot. Well now, I'll tell you what they done. Th'old system was they'd keep a rag layin' over their face wet in soda water. Then they finally got t'droppin' aspirins in it. It kept their color. It kept their face from turnin' darker."

Dressing the body, an essential part of a burial many years ago, was also done by the family and friends. Ada Kelly revealed, "When my parents were raising their family, they'd usually take the body back home. They'd dress the body at home and keep it overnight. They always dressed them in the best they had. Sometimes somebody died and didn't have decent clothes to be buried in. Then somebody in the community furnished them—helped out."

Aunt Arie said that shirts were split down the back to get them on, and she echoed Ada Kelly when she said that her father had to be buried in one of her husband's shirts because he didn't have any good ones of his own.

In Anna Howard's community, the preacher would dress the men ("Sunday clothes—their best'uns. A white shirt, tie with a few flowers down th'middle of it, nice pants."), and the preacher's wife would dress the women ("in long dresses down to your ankle").

Others of our contacts, as they talked, revealed more and more variety:

MRS. LESTER NORTON: "My mother's dress was homemade, and I mean homemade. She already had th'cloth, but they made th'dress after she died. She told me that th'dress would be all right t'bury her in if she never did wear it, but we could make it and bury her in it. So I had that done. And we carried her t'th'graveyard in a wagon—a two-horse wagon."

MRS. E. H. BROWN: "Women was usually buried in black or white material—and it was cheap material. It was made accordin' t'th'condition of th'body. Children was usually dressed in white. Th'men was buried in a suit."

ETHEL CORN: "They'd generally make their clothes. Sometimes people'ud be buried in th'clothes they had. They'uz generally all black then. When I'uz just a young'un, they'uz buried in what they called shrouds. They'd just make a shroud, y'know, and bury'em in it. They'd choose different colors and make'em. A shroud is similar t'what y'see these Catholic people wear, y'know—kind of robe-lookin' with belts is what a shroud is. And they buried th'men just in suits. They wadn't things t'choose from much, and when anybody died, they'uz generally always buried in black. That was th'main color."

MARGARET NORTON: "They had t'ask for it t'be—if they wanted t'be buried in blue'r'pink'r'white'r'whatever—and that was fixed for 'em."

MRS. TOM MCDOWELL: "Sometimes special clothes were made from cloth donated by friends and neighbors."

And sometimes, in a stroke of individuality, a person would make the clothes for their own funeral. As Lex Sanders said, "Lord, I've dressed so many. That was back when they used t'be no undertakers. They was some people that had their buryin' clothes made for twenty-five'r'thirty year. They made'em and just put'em back, and of course I don't guess they was ever ironed'r'put on. But I know that. I know Granny Bingham had her buryin' clothes made, and she made'em with her fingers. And they buried her in what she had made. And they buried Arie Sanders—she wanted her buryin' clothes made. And she made'em and they buried pore old Arie in what she had made."

Just as there were no funeral parlors, there were also no professional casket makers. That work, like the preparation of the body, was done by friends, relatives, or men in the community who did it either for free, or to earn a portion of their living. Harley Thomas, for example, a genuine craftsman, was paid about thirty-five dollars. "I've made hundreds of caskets myself. Oh, Lord, yes. Back in th'depression, I made caskets for the county. They had t'bury a lot of people, and they give me a job makin' caskets for'em. I had my shop right out there on th'branch where we had a water mill t'grind corn and stuff. They paid me t'make'em."

Others charged about five dollars to cover the cost of the handles and a copper plate on the lid. And many others simply did it as their contribution to the mourning family. Mr. Mize, the director of a local funeral parlor, said, "Back in those days, they'd make their own caskets. Neighbors would gather around some carpenters, farmers, and they'd make the caskets." Mrs. Lester Norton's father made the caskets for her community: "Parker made as many as six caskets for people, and he had his lumber all ready to make his when he died. He already had John Wilburn to make the casket—he had asked him to make it before he died."

Caskets were made out of poplar, pine, oak, or chestnut. Their shapes varied widely, but usually they were body-shaped—wide at the shoulders and narrow at the feet. Ethel Corn remembers seeing some that had a glass built in through which you could view the body. In Lex Sanders' younger days, however, they were not as elaborate as any of the above, being "just simple, square boxes."

Maude Shope remembers that "the lids then, they put so many screws in it. It sat down flat on top—not bulged up like the caskets they have now. I don't think they had any divide t'take it off. Th'whole lid came off as I remember. And they wasn't no glass in it like nowadays."

Fidel Crisp talked about his father who made caskets: "My daddy used t'make coffins when I was a little boy. And he'd make coffins for anybody that died. And th'size—for a little bitty kid, he'd make it smaller. And if it was a bigger, grown feller, we'd get his length and ever'thing and make th'coffin t'fit him. We'd make it out a'lumber."

Ada Kelly's father did the same: "Seemed that he always kept some lumber put up dry somewhere. And he'd make th'coffin; usually varnish it. Make it look right pretty."

Mrs. Lex Sanders told us some interesting facts about coffins for babies. "Well, now, I've furnished cloth a many a time fer little infants . . . some of'em premature. But they'd make little square boxes, and then they'd line'em and pad'em with cotton. And then they'd paint'em black with jet oil—shoe shine'r'shoe polish. Then they lined th'inside with broadcloth. People used t'be so much poorer than they are now."

Mrs. Sanders got us thinking about linings, and so we pushed the point with the rest of our contacts. Ada Kelly remembered the coffins she had seen as being lined with white cloth. Since it was the most commonly used cloth in her day, she said that someone always had some.

Florence Brooks said, "They'd take cotton and white cloth and bleach it for th'babies and little folks, and for th'older folks, they'd line it with black material."

Mrs. Don Burnette, on the other hand, said they used satin or white or blue linen—whatever they could afford, and whatever they preferred most.

Mrs. E. H. Brown went into still more detail: "They padded the coffin with cotton, and lined it with what we called plain white silk. And then they took carpet tacks and tacked that down. It was right pretty. It was fixed very nice. It wasn't painted; it was covered with some kind a'black material. My father was buried in a casket like that. And my grandfather was buried in one too. But it was his request that his coffin be made out of undressed lumber. He didn't want it dressed, and so it was made that way. That old man out yonder [pointing to a picture] made'em. He made nearly ever'body's casket around."

Harley Thomas discussed some other ways to line one: "We lined'em with white cloth—what y'might call linen. Padded'em with shavin's. Excelsior, y'know. Sometimes they'd cover th'coffins in black. They did lots of'em that way when I was makin'em. They'd just cover'em with black cloth. They wouldn't even dress th'lumber. They didn't have nothin' t'dress it with only by hand. I had a plane along then, and I planed my lumber." He also remembered painting some of them black, which was a lot easier because then the lumber didn't have to be varnished.

Anna Howard remembered the lumber being dressed with an adze and then covered with a white bleaching. And then sometimes "they was little things they put on th'coffin—handles, brass. It was brass, and they were shiny—new, y'know. They had them t'sell in th'stores."

And Ethel Corn added this: "They was all homemade caskets, and they'd cover and line'em and pack'em. They'd line'em with cloth they called canebreak, and they'd put cotton sometimes in that. They'd always line th'inside with white canebreak. That was th'name of th'cloth. It'uz kind'a satiny lookin'. And they covered th'outside with black cloth. It'uz th'same for both boys and girls and men and women."

By the time the casket was delivered at the home of the deceased, many of the neighbors in the community would have gathered around those who were mourning. "They'd go spend th'night, y'know," said Mrs. Tom McDowell. "They'd go set up of a night and sing, and people'd come in. And when they died, somebody'd go and toll th'bell at th'church. And that let th'community know. If we'uz workin' in th'fields and somebody died, we quit and we went. Tom's grandmother had a big old sheep horn. And when she died, they got up and blowed that horn. Now we heard that all around. They blew th'horn that noon, and when th'horses heard it, they all come in. People didn't work no more till she was buried."

"The neighbors usually did everything," said Mrs. E. H. Brown. "Usually they'd be someone go spend the night with them the first night. They thought they'd be lonesome or something."

The night following the death, it was customary to have a wake, or a "settin'up with th'dead." In fact, this is often still done today. When we asked Fidel Crisp why, he remarked, "Show your respect to th'dead man is all I know. It's th'respect they have fer you after you die. And they set up with'im on that account. But now if y'die, they don't give a damn whether you live or walk."

Mrs. Lex Sanders told us a short story concerning wakes. "There come an old man t'my house one night t'spend th'night, and died. And we set up with him about three nights tryin' t'get his people, and they never *did* come."

In Mrs. Lester Norton's experience, "Usually a great big bunch come in and stay till along towards midnight. They usually wouldn't be but one'r'two left when daylight come. But somebody stayed all night with'em. And set up with'em."

The following excerpts from various interviews go into even greater detail:

AUNT ARIE: "Friends would come in, stay all night, bring food. Twenty-four or thirty stayed at Poppy's [her father]. It was a comfort to th'family in case they should need anything. Along about midnight, they'd sing some hymns soft. And they'd stay until th'body was taken to th'church. Now they sit up all night in th'funeral parlor, but they still stay with th'body."

ANNA HOWARD: "And then you'd have company and sit up all night. Say th'funeral would be th'next day'r'th'next. They'd just have ever'body come, y'know, comin' and goin'. Singin'. You had singin'. They'd sing till they got tired. And ever'body seemed kind and good."

FLORENCE BROOKS: "And they'd lay'em out sometimes on boards till th'casket got made. And th'people'd come and sit all night and all day until th'funeral. Sometimes th'whole house was full. They brought food—nothin' special. Ever'body brought some. They'd sit up all night and sing until th'funeral. Th'night that Howard died, they'uz so many in th'house you could stand in th'corner and sleep."

MRS. E. H. BROWN: "We called it 'sittin' up with th'corpse.' I remember I stayed at a place one time—me an' two more girls—we were young. And th'mother'd passed away. About midnight, they came in with th'coffin, and me and those girls put th'clothes on that old lady. And th'men folks picked her up and laid her in th'coffin. And she was put away th'next day. They got her in a wagon."

The next morning, the casket would be put into a wagon and hauled to the church. Ethel Corn related what happened at this point: "As they'd come up to th'church with th'corpse, they'd start ringin' th'bell, and th'organ would start playin'."

Maude Shope added, "They rung it just a slow ring when th'corpse came in sight. I don't know if it stopped when th'corpse wagon finally got stopped, or whether we'd take th'corpse in th'church first."

Anna Howard answered that confusion by saying, "They'd be tollin' that bell and a'raddlin' it on till they got in th'church."

Our contacts agreed almost unanimously that the body was carried to the church in a steer wagon—either one belonging to the family or some neighbors. If steers weren't available, mules were used.

They usually wore black to the service, and though the profusion of flowers common now was rarely seen, sometimes women were buried with flowers in their hands. The services were sometimes held in the homes first, but more often they were held at the church, and some of the men in the community would have already gotten together in advance to help dig the grave. All would be ready.

The services were usually simple, lasting between a half hour and an hour, after which the body was viewed one last time, and then carried to the grave.

As Anna Howard said, "The preacher was all there, and there was two men who seated ever'body. They'd take it up there and set th'casket right there before th'pulpit, and th'preacher was a'settin' up there. Sometimes, if th'person was old, the service was long. And if they wasn't, it'ud be short. Th'preacher'ud read a chapter in th'Bible, and then he'd pray. Ever'body went up and looked at th'coffin. And they had a nice white silk rail—it would be a great big thing—cover from here down t'here. They'd cover th'face. And th'one who made th'casket took it off and opened th'casket. The people would look at th'casket and then go on out. They'd bring th'family last. And then they'd take and close it up and they'd take it out, and ever'body'd follow it to th'cemetery."

Maude Shope said, "They opened th'coffin at th'church, and th'neighbors, they went around and looked first at th'corpse. And th'family come around last. Th'closest relation was th'last one t'come around t'see'em. If you was a brother and I'uz his mother, well you'd go first and I'd come around th'last one t'see'im. Then they'd close'em up and take'em th'way they do now.

"And all children went. Children that'uz not big enough t'look into th'coffin, they'd pick'em up and say, 'That's Grandma,' or, 'That's Grandpa.' If one o'your neighbor's children died, somebody'd take care a'her children and take'em around and show'em."

Digging and filling in the grave was a sacred act that was often reserved for friends and neighbors who were close to the family. Ada Kelly verified this by saying, "Friends dug the grave and filled it up afterwards. And some do here now. [On several recent occasions when students who attended our school have died, our principal has helped

PLATE 346

with the grave.] They used t'be a bunch a'men had tools, shovels, and ever'thing that they needed t'dig graves. And some one person usually had charge of those tools. Different ones in th'community would dig th'grave. It was always very sacred. It'uz just a custom."

Mrs. Lester Norton also agreed, saying, "They'd always be plenty there t'dig th'grave and look after that. They didn't have anybody special back in them times. Just neighbors."

Florence Brooks added, "They'd just carry th'casket up t'th'cemetery, and they'd have th'grave already dug. All th'neighbors helped dig it. They'uz a lot a'difference back then. Seemed like people had better feelin's for other people than they do now. Now they don't care if y'set up by yourself all night or not."

One fascinating account of a funeral came from Ethel Corn. "I was at one Mason funeral. Uncle Tommy Vinson, he'uz a preacher. He belonged to th'Masons, and they buried him over here on this hill above Earl Vinson's. And I went to it, and th'Masons buried him. And it'uz'a beautiful funeral to be at. And they had th'flags and things. And as they brought him out, they arched th'flags out over th'door 'fore they come out at th'edge of th'porch.

PLATE 347
Carlton's
picture

"And then when they laid'im down, they'd put all of his things in there. And I don't remember what they said. Then they made a link around th'grave—a chain like, y'know. And of course it'uz'a password of some kind that they passed from one to th'other till it went plumb around. Then they read over'im, and then they started out th'first one —th'highest rank one. And each one'ud say, 'Ashes to ashes, dust to dust, sleep all night here, brother.' And they'd throw just one shovel a'dirt. And that went around all th'way thataway till they completely covered him up.

"They say if you belonged to th'Masons—a man that belonged to th'Masons—if he died, the Masons would look after his family, and they would get them money to live off of. They'd take care of'em. And they'd help th'people of th'community that was in need a'help that they knowed of. And they's nobody ever tell what their secrets is.

"Like th'Woodmans, now. Th'Woodmans was a lodge, y'know, that they could belong to. And you never could get kicked out, but it costed so much to belong to it. But then when they died, or sickness come up, they'uz money put in t'keep th'family goin'. But I stole Uncle Bill's book. I knew where he kep' it. I'uz just a chunk of a girl, but I wanted t'know that password s'bad, y'know. And I got it and I tried t'read it, and I couldn't read it ner understand a thing about it. It'uz all mumble-jumble t'me. I never did let'im know I did it."

When the service was over, people from the community often went with members of the family to stay a day or two. As Ada Kelly said, "Not ever'body, but close relatives—close friends—somebody like that. Oh, it affected everyone. We'uz close t'ever'body that died. And every family, nearly, had deaths. 'Course, ever'body dies sometime."

Soon after the funeral, a tombstone would be set up. Often it was a simple, rather crude, but honest affair. Ada continued, "They usually carved out a rock—nearly always somebody in th'community that did those kind a'things. They'd smooth up a rock and make tombstones out of a rock—just out of the rock here in the country. They didn't charge anything. Ever'body did things for the other fellow then."

And sometimes the markers were of wood [some of which still survive in this county today]. Anna Howard confirmed it: "The children would bring his horse up, and him and his wife would ride off together. Then you heaped the grave up and padded it hard. And then they'd put up—sometimes it would be a gray rock—sort of soft. Then they'd write on that their name and the date they died.

"And some just put up a plank and marked on it in big letters" (*Plate 349*).

2

In an effort to find out if the burial customs were any different in the black community in this area, we interviewed one of our favorite sources, Beulah Perry. We found that in many ways, their way was identical to that of the white community. Again, there were no funeral parlors, and so the burying usually took place the next day. In addition, the burying clothes were often made for the occasion, they were of whatever colors the people chose, there would be a wake to which people would come and stay all night and sing and pray, the coffins were often homemade, the lumber was left rough and often covered with cloth at the church, the coffins were often padded with cotton, neighbors dug the grave and filled it in, and so on.

But there were differences, as the following excerpts from our interview with Beulah show.

On care of the body: "We just kep' th'body in a cool place like on a porch or in a back room where there's no heat. You see, you couldn't keep th'body after they were dead where there's heat, so they'd keep th'body in a cool place."

PLATE 348

PLATE 349

On tolling the bells: "Not in th'country 'cause you wadn't that close to a church in th'country. But now in towns they would. Somebody would toll th'bell, and it didn't make any difference what time they died that night; why, somebody'd go an' toll th'bells maybe about two'r'three times, and you'd know. You'd say, 'Oh, they must be somebody dead. I hear th'church bells.' But I don't guess th'church bell was ever tolled [where we lived] 'cause people was always so far out in th'country. Lot a'times it was as far as from here t'Mountain City [about seven miles] to a church. Very seldom you was real close to a church."

The funeral procession: "Most people walked, and a lot of'em would go on [early] to be there because such few peoples in those days had ways t'ride. Some people'd ride with th'wagon, but th'ones that'd walk'd go on early and be there."

On viewing the body as part of the funeral service: "After I got t'be a big girl, they passed a law that you couldn't open a [look at] body any more if th'body hadn't been embalmed. They passed a law that you couldn't open a body—but then, seemed t'me like real early too. Because I do remember, and I was very small then, when we'd go to a funeral, and we'd wonder why we couldn't look at th'bodies. I remember they said that th'law wouldn't let you open th'body if it hadn't been embalmed."

On what took place after the funeral: "Th'next day they'd go and clean up and wash yer things and put out th'beds—sun an' air an' disinfect. Y'know, back in those days, peoples was very particular about cleanin' up after someone died'r'had a long sick spell. They would go an' clean up with all kind a'disinfect. And back in those days, they had lots a'lye soap, and they'd just wash and scrub up ever'thing. And scald th'bed th'person lied on. They were more particular back then about things like that, I believe, then they are now. Y'see, all th'sickness was at home, and then after that person died, they was very particular t'get ever'thing just as quick as they could washed and boiled. Had them great big pots out in th'yard, and ever'thing that could be boiled was boiled. And they'd even scald th'walls of th'room where th'sick lie. Most ever'body had large families, and they had two'r'three big pots, and if they didn't have pots, they had big tin cans—you buy'em at th'store, I reckon. And they'd just put'em on th'rocks and pile wood around'em and get those pots boilin'. Just th'time one would be empty, you'd fill up another one until that room was scalded. Walls'n ever'thing. Even th'bed."

On clothing: "The womens would wear black, and th'mens would wear th'black bands 'round their arms on their coat sleeves. It'uz somethin' like a chiffon'r'a voile band they wore 'round their arms just on top of th'coat—pin it on. It was a piece a'crepe a couple a'inches wide. If they was a teenage daughter, she would wear mournin'—a black suit to th'funeral and maybe a few weeks'r'a month'r two after. Youngsters wear white. I think when my mother passed, we all wore white—all of us girls wore white. And if it was th'mother of th'one that died, she'd wear a long veil way down t'here [across her chest]. And she'd always wear a little veil for maybe four'r'five months."

On flowers: "It depended on what time of year they died whether they'd have any flowers. Peoples used t'go to th'woods and get some holly'r'cedar and make wreaths. And, y'know, back in those days, peoples had a lot a'ribbon they wore. People's children and mens, they wore a lot a'ribbon things like neckties an' belts an' sashes. Why, they'd take a lot a'ribbon things and make a nice one. Sometimes they'd make a cross out a'it."

On superstitions: "I was raised in one a'them old-time Christian homes, and we didn't hear a'too many fairy tales like y'do now. Peoples was too religious. They'd think it was silly. My parents taught me th'real things. We didn't know too many fairy tales. Y'know, back when I was a child, peoples didn't do them type a'things. But now after I got on up in th'teenage, people began t'get stories, and they had several sayin's: a black cat crossed th'street, you'uz gonna have bad luck, or you better turn around and all. But nothin' like that back in my early child days. My peoples didn't believe in those kind a'things, and they didn't teach it. Now my grandfather would tell us that if you go out at night and see a light, t'not watch that light because if y'did, that light would draw y', and you'd just walk and wander and follow that light and you never would get to it. Now I remember that 'cause we all used t'go out in th'yard after night for somethin', and we wouldn't look at a light for anything."

On death affecting the whole community: "Yes it did. Because peoples was so close back in those days. Even th'white people. Now my parents and th'older white people back in those days, they were close t'gether. They was just th'same as one big family. If they was anything t'be done, they would just help out like we all was one. Very close. So much more than we are now."

3

Dr. Rufus Morgan is a retired, native Episcopal minister who lives near Franklin, North Carolina, and is a noted botanist and Appalachian hiker. He has climbed Mount LeConte over a hundred times, and he

still does, despite age—he is over eighty—and near blindness. His elo-
quent and moving statements about burial customs seemed to provide a
perfect conclusion to our article.

I really wish that the same burial customs prevailed now as then.
As you indicate, the neighbors would come in during a sickness, and
then in death, and they would lay out the corpse and dress him—get
him ready for burial. And a neighbor carpenter would make the coffin,
and neighbors would dig the grave, and the coffin would be taken to
the churchyard or cemetery in a farm wagon drawn by horses or
mules. Then the remains would be buried by the minister; sort of a
very simple—and to my way of thinking, more reverent than the
present—practice.

There wasn't any idea of a metal casket or a means of preserving
the remains because, as the scripture says, "Dust thou art, and unto
dust shalt thou return." And I'd much rather think of my body as
just going back to the earth where it came from and fertilizing some
tree or the grass or flowers, than just having a metal box with me
inside preserved like a mummy. We've gotten away from the farm
wagon. We have a hearse now, and a funeral home to look after
things. Instead of the neighbors coming into the home and comforting
the mourners, they go to the funeral home the night before the funeral.

And there are other things connected with our funerals that are of
interest more and more. Many people are turning to cremation. Mostly
it was people from the outside who got it started here. People ask
me, "Do you think cremation is Christian?" I tell them I don't know
of anything against it, except that I don't want to be cremated.

They say, "Well, what about the ashes?"

I say, "Well, when the ashes are ready, I advise somebody to bury
them just as they would the body of somebody departed." The little
church up here is becoming more and more popular, and in several
instances, the people who are left behind have asked that their ashes
be scattered up here at the cemetery. They love the place—it's a nice
place. So I just scatter the ashes instead of burying them.

I had a service for one lady up near Highlands who lived up on
Bear Pen Mountain in the sight of a lovely waterfall called Highland
Fall. She wanted her ashes scattered there in sight of that waterfall
near her home, and so I did just that; and I held a service right
there on the mountain top.

Another change I've noticed is a distortion of emphasis. That is,
you go into the funeral parlor and into the church, and there's a

casket, and it's open for people to see if they want to—I don't—
and then banks of flowers all around. Well, the center of attention
ought to be the departed person instead of that. You have it all
dolled up to pretend that he isn't there—just the flowers, the beautiful flowers. When I die, I want the money to be spent for something
to carry on the work that I've been interested in instead of spending
it for flowers. If the flowers are in bloom—and I love wildflowers
—I'd like for the children, or somebody that I've known, to pick
some along the way as they come. Bring them along in their hands.
If the wildflowers are not in bloom, then sprays from the hemlock
trees, or the balsam, or pine. Or, if they're in season, dogwood berries.
Or any other for that matter.

Being an old man, it just strikes me that we have changed the
emphasis for the worst. And in the way of music, I don't want any
mournful songs. Saint Paul says, "Be not sorry for those who are departed." A Christian has hope and looks forward to being with
Christ. The faithful servant of Christ lives on. He doesn't just depart
and wait until the Judgment Day. I like a prayer that is in one of our
services which says, "Oh, Lord, we bless thy holy name for all thy
servants departed this life in thy faith and fear, beseeching thee to
grant them continual growth in thy love and service." That, I think,
is perfectly consistent with the New Testament idea that we're starting
our eternal life here. And if we live that eternal life, which is com-
panionship with Christ, then we don't dread the future.

I like one translation that I ran across a few years ago in a
passage from Saint John's gospel. The commentator gives us this
translation: "If any man observe my saying, he shall not notice this
until eternity." Then he goes on to explain. It's like a man sitting under
a tree reading a book. As he reads, a leaf falls on the page of the book.
And what does he do? Become disturbed? No, he brushes the leaf
off and then goes on reading. And he said that death is like that. It
had no more significance for a Christian than that leaf which falls
on the page.

When I die, I would like Easter hymns sung at my funeral because
they are so joyful. They're hopeful. They reflect our belief in the resur-
rection of the dead. They're not morbid and weeping and depressing.

I have one hymn that I very often repeat. I could sing it, but my
voice isn't what it might be:

> "Now the laborer's task is o'er;
> Now the battle days are past;
> Now upon the Father's shore
> Lands the voyager at last . . ."

BOOGERS, WITCHES, AND HAINTS

P robably my earliest memories are of the times when
the power would go out
and we would have to get down the kerosine lamps. My grandmother
always used these times to the best advantage by telling ghost stories—
or "booger" tales. I don't remember the tales as such, but I can remember the lamp that lighted only her face as she recalled the choicest
horrors of her childhood.

That the people of these mountains should have a rich supply of
"haint" tales is not at all surprising. They had conquered the land
—but only in a small area around their doors. No matter how friendly
the woods seemed in daylight, there were noises and mysterious lights
there at night that were hard to ignore if you were out there all
alone.

We tape-recorded the following stories in an attempt to let you
share a singular mountain experience—a night of ghost tales by a
slowly dying fire.

DAVID WILSON

1

To be absolutely truthful, most of the people we talked with did not
believe in ghosts or witches or anything of the sort. They had either seen
their fears proved false (a white dog, a flapping sheet, natural gas, or
the like), or they simply had never had to have them proved false—they
just never believed. We met many of them in the course of our wander-
ings. Here are some of the best of their comments.

MRS. E. H. BROWN: Oh, I've heard a number of ghost stories. They come in here and they went out here and I didn't pay any 'tention. I never have been hainted. I didn't think I'd ever done anybody any harm that they'd bother me.

I moved t'Highlands and they'uz some people come in tryin' t'tell me how terrible th'old Methodist Church was haunted there at Scaly there where I lived. Well, I'uz raised there. I let'em tell their tales. They said that you just couldn't go in that church at night— they'uz th'awfullest thing they ever were in there.

I let'em tell their story, and I laughed at'em. I says, "Well, I've been in that church after dark by myself and I didn't hear a thing." I said, "I wasn't a bit afraid."

There'uz a boy that'd been murdered that's grew up with me was buried out there, but I never done th'boy no harm, and I didn't 'spect him t'make any noise and bother me.

And then they thought they would get me. Said, "Just as sure as you pass th'school house about midnight, you'll see a little girl and a little boy walkin' that rock walk."

"Well," I said, "I've passed there alone many nights about midnight and I never did see anything." That was just a fancy someone had told. Why, I passed that place numbers of nights. I didn't see nothin'. I believe most a'that is imagination. I say imagination, or maybe a guilty conscience. Then you might see somethin'. I wouldn't be surprised. If you'd done some dirty deed or murdered somebody or something, why I wouldn't be surprised if they wouldn't imagine they saw something.

But I never experienced no such thing. Only thing I was ever afraid of was a dog or a snake.

DANIEL MANOUS: No, I don't think there's anything like that. Do you? I don't think so. I think that's th'imagination. You think on a thing till you think it's real.

I used to hear my grandfather tell one about when he'uz a boy. They'uz a cemetery right close to where he lived, and he could hear a baby cryin' every night over at th'cemetery.

He'uz scared and didn't know what t'think about it and told one of th'neighbors. Said, "I heard a baby cry over yonder at th'cemetery every night. I didn't go about it." Said, "I'm afraid to. Are you afraid to go over there?"

He said, "No, I'm not afraid to go over there."

Grandpa says, "You come over t'my house tonight. If that baby cries, if you'll go over there and see what it is, I'll give you ten dollars."

So he came over then that night, y'know, and waited till seven o'clock. Said, "All right. If you're not 'fraid t'go, now's th'time t'go."

That man just took off and went over there, and they'uz a big basket sittin' on top a'th'tombstone, and they'uz a baby in it. Little baby boy. He just went and picked up th'basket, went on back and took it to him and said, "It's a baby."

He'd been a'hearin' th'baby for several nights he claimed. He kept that baby and raised it, and it went by th'name a' Billy Tombs—after th'tombstone. That was actually th'truth. I've heard my grandpa say that he'd seen th'boy a many a time. Billy Tombs.

The Bible preaches that th'dead don't know anything at all. After any person dies, why they don't know anything. They don't have any thoughts, don't know a thing in th'world.

Well, they *couldn't* come back here. They couldn't come back and cause trouble and bother th'livin' because they can't *get* back. They're dead. They don't know anything.

If you don't believe th'Bible, you just as well not believe nothin'. If it didn't teach that, y'might have somethin' t'base it on, y'see. But since they don't know anything, how could they come back? 'Cause they'd have t'be doin' a little thinkin'r'somethin'r'nother before they could get back and trouble anybody'r'anything.

They's mediums that say they could talk t'th'dead and all that. I don't believe that. That's just a evil spirit. Really, I don't believe in'em. They's nothin' t'base it on. They's no foundation. Cain't build a house without no foundation. Th'Bible destroys all th'foundation. If somethin' dies, it's gone—don't know a thing in th'world. You kin find th'stories, but there ain't no foundation for'em. That's what I call a myth. Just not reality.

MARY CARPENTER: There's a place over yonder at Jim Branch— they had been people said they's seen balls of fire big as these old- timey washpots roll th'road there. I forgot who it was told me that they'uz comin' there one night and said they was a big ball of fire. And they said they hit Frank Kelly's field and cut out across through th'field and wouldn't pass it.

HOYT THOMAS: I had friends treed a possum one night, and said they seen a ball a'fire that gave enough light till they seen how t'get that possum out a'that tree.

PLATE 350   Annie Perry

And then one night last winter we seen a light, but it was a weather satellite put up in fall that was burnin' up. It just looked like a extry moon. It had kind of a purple-like glow around it. Didn't last but a few minutes till it was gone. Then it trailed off in a cloud of smoke.

And one night it just looked like th'world was afire back in there. Like a big forest fire, y'know. And it come on around, and at twelve o'clock it went right square up in th'middle of th'sky and made a question mark. Just as pretty a question mark as you ever looked at.

ANNIE PERRY: I don't know nothin' about ghosts. In fact, I never was brought up t'hear ghost tales. My daddy said not t'tell children ghost tales. Said it'ud make'em afraid. Well, I'm not afraid, but I tell you I had a sister that wouldn't open a door an' go out on th'porch an' get a drink a'water at th'well. She'uz just afraid a'th'dark.

They's no such thing as a haint. It's not a thing in th'world but imagination. They just imagine they hear these things and they don't hear'em at all.

Now this is not a hainted tale—this is true. I'uz seven years old when I started school. Had t'go through these woods over here, and ever'body thought they'uz haints in th'woods.

And th'neighbors, they had lots a'big old brood sows. And if you caught a pig'r'made a pig squeal, they'd bite you. And they'd say, "Now, Annie, don't you get out there on th'side a'th'road (them pigs'uz on th'side a'th'road), an' go through there or them old sows'll eat you up."

Well, they had me afraid a'hogs.

I'd have t'go by m'self through those woods over there. I'd look way out here and way out there. There wouldn't be a thing in th'world. Directly I saw a thing that looked like a hog. I had t'go by it and I was skeered. And there wasn't a thing in th'world. Not a thing. They wasn't a hog within a mile a'there—just some old stumps a'lyin' there. But I guess it looked like a hog t'me. Imagination. That's so now. They skeered me with hogs. And I'd look way out an' I'd see somethin' and I'd make a hog out of it.

Now that's th'way ghost tales get started. Ain't no ghosts.

LAWTON BROOKS: 'Bout two mile and a half out a'Hayesville, there kind'a in a bend in th'road is where a man was killed and just shoved out onta this big old white rock by th'side a'th'road. And he died and left blood a'settin' on th'rock. That blood wouldn't wash off.

Stayed there a long time. An' ever'body passed through there got scared, y'know, seein' blood on th'rock where that man just fell out and died.

'Course people got their nerves up and got scared about it and they'd see ghosts. Some of'em said somethin' would be gettin' on behind their mules or horses an' ride with'em an' spook their animals an' make'em jump around scaired and crazy like. People was really scaired t'go by that big white rock 'cause so many people says somethin' would get on their animal an' aggravate th'dickens out'a'em.

I was a'courtin' up there, and I had t'come by there. 'Course I could'a went around, but if I went around it would'a been further out'a my way, and I decided t'go by it. It was a'rainin' that night, and I'd just take th'near cut and go down through there.

When I got pretty close t'where that rock was, m'horse got scaired and wouldn't budge nary an inch. Just bowed right up, front legs stiff like boards. I teched'im wi'm'spur and he jumped over t'other side th'road. Took a step'r'two and bowed up again, and I could feel'im a'shakin' a little even.

'Bout that time I saw somethin' white comin' off th'bank right down t'where that rock was at and stopped. I thought t'myself, "You got me!" I just knowed that'd 'bout done me in.

So m'horse, I think he found out before I did what that thing was, and he just commenced walkin' along and walked right up next t'it. I got me a match out'a m'coat pocket—they wasn't no things like flashlights in them days—and I struck me a match, and there set a big white dog—big old white shepherd dog a'settin' there in a ditch.

And if I'd a'went on and hadn't a'never discovered what that was, I'd a'always said I seen a ghost. But I found out what it was.

ETHEL CORN: They call them balls'a'fire jack-a'lanterns. It's kind of a round-lookin' thing, an'hit'll come and they'll play up—they'll go down low t'th'ground and high up. And they're see'd always over here on what they call th'Chainey Hill. And some said hit was from mineral. They's a vein a'minerals goes through there. And they'd rise and they'd go up, and they're pretty good-sized lights, and they're playin' all over th'bottoms down below there. And sometimes they'll go away-y-y up and then back down.

I'd been out a'plowin', and I'uz a'wantin' t'get th'bottom plowed out. And I plowed—hit was a dusky dark when I got in. And I went t'put up th'horse and got th'corn and went t'feed her, and right at th'back of th'stable they was jest a big light rose down right at th'back of th'stables in th'swamp.

And hit kept a'goin' higher and higher. I was young—I wadn't plumb grown—and I was awful cowardly, and I throwed th'corn through a crack in th'stable—I didn't put it in th'trough—and I run and I run and I never knowed what it was. I didn't take time t'see how high it went. I run!

And Andy Burrell'uz goin' up th'branch home one night. It'uz in th'winter time an' right cold and th'wind'uz a'blowin' right hard; and it got t'blowin' an'floppin' his tie back over his shoulder. And he never thought of it bein' his tie, and he run about a quarter mile up th'mountain till he just give completely out.

And when he did, he found out hit was his tie that'uz a'doin' th'floppin' and makin' th'rackets. He'uz scared, and he took a hard race from it!

MINYARD CONNER: This boy that lived way back in th'woods had t'go hunt his cows ever' evenin'. There was a big tree beside th'road. He'd drive his cows in there and they'd be somethin' hangin' down from th'limb up there on th'tree. Couldn't tell what it was. He said it would just be hangin' there. Just nearly dusk.

And he had some more boy friends that lived pretty close. He told these other boys about it. They didn't believe him. And he told'em a certain time of th'evenin' it'ud be hangin' there. Said it wouldn't be hangin' there when th'sun was shinin'r'anything. It would be right late of evenin'. He told'em t'come a certain time.

Well, th'night th'boys was t'come, he went up there. He kept watchin' that limb t'see if anything was a'hangin' there. He'd bet some money, and he'd lose his money if they wasn't. Well, they wasn't, so he just decided he'd get out and climb th'tree and hang down *himself.*

'Bout that time, here they come around th'curve, y'know. He'uz a'hangin' down yonder. He'd slipped down on th'limb and he'uz a'hangin' down there.

Th'boys come up and looked around. Said, "Well, he told th'truth. But he said there'uz just one. There's *two* of'em." And that boy kept turnin' his head around, y'know, and kept turnin' his head around. He turned around and seen that'un hangin' right beside him! He just turn loose and here he went! And when he hit th'ground, th'boys broke and run.

Well, he jumped up and took atter'em. He said, "Wait there, boys. I'm one of you!"

One said t'th'other'n—they was a'runnin' right t'gether said, "What did he say?"

"He said, 'Wait there, boys. I'm gonna have one of you!'"

That's th'way them ghost stories gets started.

WILL ZOELLNER: I didn't think much a'ghosts then. We told a lot a'tales—pulled off some stunts on people—done lots a'foolishness around about that.

One time we sent a couple a'girls t'get some water—needed some water. It was Christmas I think it was. They went out t'th'spring, and when they got out there, there was two fellas had a bed sheet wrapped around'em.

Well, th'girls filled their jugs—one of'em had th'jug done full and th'other had it 'bout nearly full. Th'moon was shinin' just as bright, and they'uz about four'r'five inches a'snow on th'ground—had been fer several days. And them fellas just popped out acrost th'spring on th'other side.

Those girls, they just fell down like dead. By God, I thought we'd never get'em back t'th'house. We toted'em and ruffed'em around. Even got a rubbin' doctor from Pine Mountain when they come to.

Gosh, they never played that game n'more. They'uz just scared t'death. Them girls—I heard their hearts a'beatin', and they groaned a lettle bit onct' in a while. They'uz just limber as rags!

MARGARET NORTON: They say th'best way t'keep from gettin' scared when y'hear somethin' is t'find out what it is. Go right on and find out what it is, and then you'll know. It's usually a animal'r'somethin' like that. Maybe a possum in a tree.

2

There were, however, a surprising number of contacts who had seen, or whose relatives or close friends had seen, phenomena that were inexplicable to them except in supernatural terms. Most believe unshakably that haints, boogers, and evil spirits walk the land, and after hearing their stories, one wonders.

AUNT NORA GARLAND: There was about thirteen couples of us, and we took a notion to walk out plumb to the Mountain City Blue Heights Church to a box supper.

Well, we all were coming, and there was about thirteen couples I guess, and we started back up th'mountain and in th'dead of winter. Awful cold, but y'know we were young and didn't care much, and we were all coupled up together, and me and m'husband; of course— we weren't married then.

But there was a little girl there. And there was a family that lived about a mile and a half from th'church back up th'mountain on that old road, and they was pretty well-to-do people. And I thought strange about them a'lettin' that child go—them leavin' that child at th'church.

So we started from th'church and this little child—it looked t'be about four year old and it was barefooted and it had on a white dress and a little band in it like they use t'make'em, and it had blond colored hair and curls plumb down t'its shoulders—it walked right at my heels every step up that mountain.

And I just thought ever' one of th'rest of'em seen it, and I just thought these well-to-do people had just left this child in church. Just went off and left it t'sleep there.

It kept right at my heels. It didn't walk at th'side a'my husband. It walked right at my heels all th'way up that mountain to a branch. And just before we got t'th'branch, why that child fell down and spread out its arms thataway and was just as gone as gone ever be. I said, "Lord have mercy," I said t'my boyfriend. The instant I said that, there wasn't a thing there a bit more than nothing in this world.

That's th'reason I believe in ghosts.

I wouldn't have found out such a thing as that if I hadn't see'd it with my own eyes. But of course I wasn't a bit afraid, y'know, because they'uz about thirteen couples along in front. But that little'n had walked right at my heels ever' step up that mountain till we got t'th'branch, and my mother always said that a ghost wouldn't cross water.

Her and my father used t'live right on up above there in a house, and she said every morning there was a naked baby sittin' on th'chimney. She's told us that so many times, but I didn't see that. I'm just a'tellin' y'what I see'd. It might have been th'same thing, but this child was dressed in white. But I wouldn't have thought of a ghost, and hadn't thought of one, if I hadn't see'd it with my own eyes.

JIM EDMONDS: When my gran'daddy was a little boy, he had

a aunt that died. She run a old-time loom. Worked herself t'death.

She died, and th'old man tore th'loom house down where she worked. Wanted t'get it out a'th'way. And he was goin' a'courtin' three weeks after she died—courtin' with another woman. Gran'-daddy said he heard th'boards a'rattlin' just like th'old loom a'run-nin'. Heard th'loom a'rattlin'. Said they had a big fire a'goin'—a big blaze—and she walked up t'th'door.

Th'little baby—her baby—they had t'hold him to keep him from goin' to her. Kept sayin', "There's Mommy! There's Mommy!"

And my mother would tell them witch tales. My mother said that her grandfather moved from South Carolina to Townes County. He drunk a lot and weren't scared of nothin'.

They were lookin' for a place t'camp, and they asked this feller. He said, "Go t'th'second branch. Don't stop at th'first. Can't stay there. It's hainted."

He said he was goin' t'stay there. Weren't a bit scared. They fixed their camp, got their supper, and went to bed; but he was up. He was a'feelin' good. Heard someone comin'—like a wagon. Looked down and saw it a'comin', and just like a big white sheet over th'wagon. Just a'rattlin'.

The old man just hollered at it, but it didn't go very far before he heard it comin' back, so he hollered at it again. He got t'hollerin' at it and cussin' it—even got out his knife t'cut at it—but you can't hit'em. That thing faded up and down th'road all night.

Somebody been killed. That's th'reason for it.

And old Billy Jesse claimed he was a witch. Ol'Gran'daddy couldn't shoot a thing. Somebody put a spell on his gun. He went over to Billy Jesse t'take th'spell off. He lived in what they call Bitter Mountain Cove. Told him he wanted him t'take th'spell off him. Somebody had witched his gun.

So Billy loaded that gun and went t'every corner of th'house and shot sayin', "Hurrah fer th'Devil!" Run t'every corner and shot—never did load it but once—hollerin', "Hurrah fer th'Devil!"

Billy then said, "Now, th'next thing you will see will be a great covey of quail. Now don't you shoot at nothin'. Then th'next thing you see will be a big buck. You can kill him. Just shoot nothin' else."

Gran'daddy done just like he told him, and here come a big drove a'birds. He just held still. He went on and there was this big ol'buck. Shot and killed him. Th'spell was off his gun.

There used t'be more ghosts then than now.

LAWRENCE MOFFITT: I heard of ghosts but I never did believe. But I lived one time down here, I'll tell you that, talkin' about ghosts. I don't know what that was and never did know.

I moved down t'Maysville, Georgia. The man I rented from said there'uz a house *below* there that was hainted—an old house—and nobody wouldn't go into it.

Well, th'first night I moved into this house (not th'hainted one) there'uz a racket on th'porch just like you was a'draggin' a big chain. Well, that would come right on through that house, and there was a side-box kitchen we called it, on th'far side. Well, that would come through every night. Never missed a night.

I'd get up and sit on th'hearth, and had a flashlight. Never could see anything in th'world, but you could hear it just as plain as you can hear me a'talkin' to you.

Well, I wasn't used t'nothin' like that. I talked t'th'man I rented from there. I said, "What's th'matter? Is *this* house hainted? You told me th'lower one down there yonder was, but is this one too?"

"Well," he said, "I'll tell you. There was a man killed here. You've probably seen th'stains there on the plank there on th'wall in th'kitchen."

I said that I had, but I didn't know what it was.

"That's where a man was killed, and ever since, this racket has come through th'house."

Well, I stayed there six months. There for a week or two, I couldn't sleep. I was tryin' t'find out what it was. The minute th'light would come on, that stopped. You didn't hear nothin'. You put that light out and you'd hear that. It'd come every night at nine o'clock as long as I stayed there. But I got used t'it. I got t'where it didn't bother me a bit in th'world.

But now t'*start* with, if I'd had a way, I'd a'come back home!

OSHIE HOLT DILLARD: Way over in North Carolina somewheres, they was a Indian cave when Grandpa Harkins was just a young man. And they thought this Indian went t'th'cave every day—or at least once a week. And they was a white man which slipped around after him for three days and nights until he got a chance to shoot him; and he killed him and got his waybill that was printed on a deer skin.

And he went up there, come by this old farmer's house and wanted to borrow his mattock. And th'old farmer said, "If you'll wait till I get my hogs fed, I'll go wi'ya'."

And he said, "I don't want y't'go!"

And th'farmer said, "Well, th'mattock is a'settin' out there under th'smokehouse shed. You can just go and pick it up." And he said, "Take good care of it and bring it back. It's all I got."

Said way over in th'evenin' after they got back from church, th'farmer thought about th'man. Thought he might of found some gold'r'somethin'. He'uz a'lookin' up through th'field th'way that man had left that mornin', and said he seen somebody wanderin' around up there. Said th'farmer went up there and said that man was just as gray-headed as he could be and didn't have a lick of sense—didn't even know how t'go home—couldn't even see. Said he went back and got some help t'carry him home, and th'man lived three days and three nights and died. He never spoke a word.

Th'farmer wanted t'go back and get his mattock—y'know, th'news got out all over North Carolina over in there—and he had t'have his old mattock t'farm with, so he went back up there with a whole bunch a'people. They said, "We'll dig this mountainside down [looking for gold]."

He said, "You can dig it down if you want to, but I'm gittin' my mattock and gittin' out of here."

So they went t'diggin', y'know, and laid their coats off. And it sounded like ten thousand freight trains comin' off th'bluffs. And they was a big old locust tree standin' there, and said ever' limb and th'bark fell off of it. And they run off and left their coats.

Grandpa said nobody had ever been back to it. Now he said that was th'*real truth*.

LAWTON BROOKS: Bob Meeks was his name, and he was a'workin' somewhere in Tennessee over there. He come through by Benton while they didn't have th'road then, and he had t'come across that mountain. Now I don't know whether it was Frog Mountain, whether that was th'name or not. But anyway, there was twenty-two mile there that there wadn't no houses on it—and steep and twisty, my Lord.

And it was late in th'night. His wife had a'called him. Some of his kids got sick, and he had t'come in. And he'uz a comin' along up that mountain, and he said he come around a curve and he seen this thing. Said it'uz th'biggest man he ever saw.

The man stepped out of a water ditch by th'side of th'road, and

PLATE 351 Lawton Brooks

said he just leaned over a little, and as he come by he just stepped on th'runnin' board, reached down, opened th'door, got in, set down, and looked him over. It was a old Model T, and th'way it was goin' it didn't make much more time than a man walkin'.

And he said he looked at that thing's hands and that's what he couldn't figure out. Says hit's fingers, one of'em was as long as two of his'n if they was put together, and as big again around. He said he had awful big arms, and on top of his hands was just as hairy plumb on down toward his fingers. His fingers was th'longest he'd seen on anybody. Must have been ten inches long.

He said he spoke t'him and he never did speak back. He said he didn't know whether he was gonna do anything t'him or not. He said he knowed he was big enough. They wadn't nothin' he could'a done about it. They wadn't no need a'gettin' scared because that man could'a reached plumb around him one-handed. Big tall man—all hairy.

Said he had a beard way down, an' face hairy, an' said he was a kind'a'nasty-lookin' old man. Said he looked as old as th'hills.

Said he never got a sound out'a'him. He could hear him a'gettin' his breath.

And he said he rode at least three mile with him, and he wondered if this thing was goin' plumb t'Ducktown with him. An' he was goin' around another curve, an' said that thing—man, what'ere it was— he just stepped out. And said he looked back and it'uz just a'standin' there in th'road.

Said he was th'ungodliest man he ever did see all th'days of his life. He said people might not believe him, but he said it'uz th'truth.

Now I believe it, 'cause I don't believe Bob'd tell a lie. He was a man never got excited about nothin'.

And after that man got out, Bob said he just kept drivin' on.

And me and Walter Coleman and George went a'possum huntin'. Now that's th'only thing ever I did that I never found out what it was. Now I didn't find out *what* that was now, I'll be fair with'y'.

We left, and it sounded like somebody a'takin' a fit. Jest like somebody a'cryin'—hurtin' awful bad. An' it jest commenced when we walked t'where a dog treed a possum out on th'ridge right on't'th'Hiawassee River.

An' we jest went out there t'get a possum, y'know, and when we went out there, by gosh, we just walked around t'th'end a'this old big log there—jest got a little bit past it—an' somethin' commenced.

Walter said, "Lawton?" Says, "What in th'world is that?"

An' I said, "I don't know, but," I says, "ain't that a pitiful noise? That's somebody or somethin'r'nother hurtin'."

So we took our old lantern then and walked around th'log. Plumb around it. Come back t'th'big old stump there where th'tree had been sawed off. We looked at th'stump. It wasn't holler. Looked in th'end of th'log. It wasn't holler. Well, I went up t'side of th'log with m'lantern. Shined th'light along it. Couldn't see no hole in th'log on either side of it. It still sounded like somebody a'cryin' and moanin' under th'log.

And we started a little away from th'log to where it sounded like it was comin' from now, and then it sounded like it'uz right back there at th'log. And then we'd start off out t'th'log again and it'ud be comin' from a little away from th'log. And then it commenced there right there at th'log.

And we never did find out what it was. We left there—I mean, we *left*—old George an' Walter an' me. We started off that mountain away from all that moanin' with nary a possum—into a field (Old Man Smith's field)—and we run right into a wire fence that we didn't know was there. Way we went flyin', when we hit that fence it scared th'daylights out'a us.

That was th'only thing I ever heard I never did find out what it was. Why, I wasn't skeered s'bad, but I wasn't gonna stay and them boys run off and leave me! They wouldn't stay wi'me, and I sure wasn't gonna' stay up there an' listen t'that thing by m'self.

So we didn't take time t'get any possum!

MRS. MARY CARPENTER: I've heard Mama tell about th'one my daddy saw one time. Said that there was a preacher, and there was a forks of a road somewhere near a church I believe it was.

And he said that hit was about ever' evenin' about sundown that you could go there, and there'uz a woman that—she was so high up in th'air that she looked like she was on a quilting frame—just high up. And she had on a long black dress and she'uz just a'walkin' along, and it rustled like leaves a'rattlin', y'know, as she walked.

My daddy and another man, they worked for Earl Hudson at a sawmill, and they said they'uz comin' in one night and it was a'rainin', and they was a'ridin' them mules on in home.

And that man said to my daddy, said, "I'd like t'see that preacher's ghost tonight, wouldn't you? While it's dark and rainin'?"

Said my daddy said to him, "Well, yonder she comes!"

Said they went on—just kep' a'ridin'—and Papa said to him, "You ride on one side a'th'road and I'll ride on th'other and let her come between us, and we'll see what she looks like."

And so they did. They reined th'mules over and let her come right in between'em. Said he said t'him, "Let's foller and see where she's a'goin'."

Said it was just a'pourin' th'rain down, and said they turned th'mules around and followed about a half a mile back out th'road, and said there was just a curve in th'road—a little ridge. And said she just riz and flew over that ridge and they didn't ever know where she went.

Now is that th'kind of haint tale y'want?

Well, all right. Now there's a place down next t'my brother's that they've seen things down there on that hill. My husband said they'uz a'goin' out through there one night—him and Lawrence Talley I believe it was. They'd been t'church up here t'th'Flats to a Holiness meetin', and they was a'goin' down Mud Creek goin' back home.

And he said they was goin' up along there, and he said he didn't know what it was. It didn't say a thing in th'world. But somethin' just hit them. It was as cold as ice, and he said they just begin t'shiver and shake.

And he said Lawrence said, "Are you cold?"

And he said he was just about t'freeze t'death, and it was in th'summertime.

And he said, "Well, I am too." Says, "Seems like there's ice all over me!"

And John said, "Well, seems th'same thing t'me."

He says, "Let's run."

And John says, "I can't run."

He said, "I don't guess I could either."

And said it just jumped off of'em just like that, whatever it was, and went away.

He said there's people said they'uz haints out there.

And there at my brother's right across th'creek—you've been over there on Kelly's Creek up there where Jim Taylor lives—there's a Mason woman lives over there. She said she'd seen a little baby out there that was flyin'—had wings. And she said it came up out of her garden more than once, and she'd be out there on th'back porch up in th'evenin' doin' her night work, and she said it would rise up with wings like a little angel—a baby.

And I know she seen somethin' one time, fer because her husband's [Frank's] daddy lived over on Germany and he was sick—bad sick. And so Frank—he'd went t'see his daddy. They were lookin' fer him t'die.

And she had a hog pen out in th'woods there, out toward our house, and she began t'scream. And Mama hollered t'me t'run over there fer somethin's th'matter. She may be snakebit.

Well, I went a'runnin' just as hard as I could, and Dad, he went a'runnin' over there. And you know, she'd fainted 'fore th'time we got over there.

By th'time we brought her to, she said there was a man there at her hog pen with a white shirt on and no head! Blood was all over his white shirt.

Gran'pa said they moved one time—said Mama was a little girl then. And he said they got moved all but their chickens, and he had t'go back and catch them after dark.

So he got him some sacks t'put his chickens in and went back t'th'place he'd moved from and caught his chickens up and tied'em and put'em in a sack. He was ridin' a mule.

He had some slung across his saddle—some on one side and some on th'other—and he was comin' along, and all at once there was somethin' in th'road. Said it looked like somebody in th'moonlight.

Said he said, "Whoa" t'th'mule. Said "Is anything th'matter?" And said it looked like a log. Said it started rollin' toward his mule, and his mule started runnin' back'erds with'im. Said it just rolled so far and stopped, and it rolled back up th'road.

Said he started back up th'road with his mule—back up through there—and said it'd come back toward him when he'd start.

Said he made two or three trips like that and decided it wasn't goin' t'get out of th'road and let him by, and said th'mule was afraid of'im; and so he just laid th'fence down—a rail fence—and let his mule run through th'pasture and come back out, and laid down th'fence again, and passed that place.

And Gran'pa said one time him and Uncle Dave was goin' home from a dance, and as they come around there where a pond was, why they heard something' a'sayin', "Oh Lordy! Oh Lordy!" Takin' on pitiful.

Gran'pa said he was scared—and said he was little—and he grabbed Uncle Dave by th'coat and said, "Dave, don't you run!"

He said "I ain't a'goin' to. I'm goin't'stay here. It's risin', whatever it is."

And said somethin' come up out of the water with th'moon a'shinin'. Said you could see it like a white sheet. Said it had four corners, and it just kept a'goin' on up, and it was just takin' on th'pitifulest. Said it was sayin', "Oh Lordy! Oh Lordy!"

Gran'pa said that his mother said that what caused that—there was a miller there and he'd killed his wife and put her in there, but that's been many many years ago. I don't know. It could have been. Gran'pa, I believe, told th'truth, 'cause I never did know him t'tell a wrong. I believe he heard it. I believe there's things for certain people t'see.

When we lived in that old house right down there, they shore was one down there. Harv Brown owned th'place first, and his wife was afraid t'stay there.

They'uz goin' t'sell it, so we bought it. And we could hear a horse down there. Harv was afraid of it too.

At night he'd come, and you could be just as quiet as you want to, but when you blowed th'lamp out (back then you didn't have electricity in this part of th'country) you could hear that horse —and I mean it'd come right up in th'yard just like a feller. You've heered a feller ride a horse—what a big racket they make—and it'd stand and stomp till you got up and looked, but when you got up t'look and shined th'light, there wasn't nothin' there. You didn't hear any more that night.

But it's th'truth if I ever told it—if I'm a'sittin' in this chair. I've heard it.

And Gran'pa said one time that he went t'make music one time fer somebody, and said he broke th'banjer string.

They said, "Well, we'll have t'quit. We ain't got another banjer string."

One of'em said, "John, you run over t'Ken Muse's." Said, "He's got some banjer strings—some extry ones." Said, "Get one over there." Said, "It ain't late and we'll play some more."

Said he looked out. Said he wadn't afraid, but he didn't like th'idea of goin' fer he had a big dog that'd bite—a great big ol'dog—and said he said, "It's pretty dark out there an' I'm afraid that dog'll get me."

"No!" he said. "I'll make you a board light." There wadn't such a thing as a lantern or a light or a flashlight. Said they got him a pine torch and lit it.

He said, "Now if you'll hurry along," he said—that'uz just a big ol'pine knot, y'know, and they just keep a'burnin' and a'goin'—said, "If you won't stay too long and hurry along, it'll last you till you get there and back."

And so he did. He started out with his pine knot, and said he got nearly there and somethin' just rared up on him and put his hands up on his shoulders and pushed him back'erds and blowed his breath in his face!

Said he reached like that t'push it off and couldn't feel nothin', and said that he plodded on pretty fast till he got over there, and he said to him, he said, "Is your dog loose tonight?"

He said, "No. I've got him tied up."

He said, "I *thought* you kept him tied at night." He said, "Now you tell me what that was that rared up and like't'pushed me down out here." And said. "He'uz 'bout as big as yore dog." He said it was a big thing, "And it put his front feet right up on my shoulders and like't'shoved me back'erds!"

"No," he said. "It wadn't my dog, John," he said. "Come here and I'll show you. I chained him tonight."

Said he went around t'th'back of his house to his cellar door, and that ol'big dog was tied up there. Said he never did know what that was, but said somethin' shore pushed him back'erds. And said he had th'light and could have seen if it'd been somethin', but he didn't see no dog.

And I know another'n. I know one more I'll tell'y.

Gran'pa said that one time they moved t'a place, and Mama

was their baby. Th'old man that owned th'place lived off in an older house—and his *good* house, he had it for rent.

Said, "Why do you reckon th'landowner lives in that old house and rents this good one?"

And [Gran'ma] said, "I don't know."

"Well," he said, "I don't know either, but there's somethin' sorta fishy to it. Maybe he gets more pay fer th'better house though."

Well, Gran'ma done th'milkin'. She went t'milk that evenin', and when she started milkin' in th'bucket—you know milk in a tin bucket'll make a racket—right out from a big rock pile a baby begin t'cry.

Said that Gran'ma just milked on a little while, and said she just took her bucket and went t'th'house and told Gran'pa. She said, "I want you t'come out here and listen." She said, "When I go t'milkin', there's a baby goes t'cryin' in that rock pile."

"Why, now," he said. "There ain't."

She said, "Come on out here and hear it!"

She poured her milk out t'where it'd make a racket in th'bucket, and she went back and she started milkin' and th'baby commenced t'cryin' again.

They talked t'th'man about it, and he said, "Nah. There wadn't nothin' to it." Said, "People just imagined hearin' things."

And Gran'pa, he was a little bit afraid of it. He stayed on a while —just milked and let th'baby cry.

Said that some of th'neighbors around there, they got t'talkin' to'im. Said they didn't nobody ever know what become of that man's wife and baby. Said he had a baby and a wife and they just disappeared and nobody ever knowed where they went to.

And Gran'pa said that he didn't know, but he sorta thought they might be in a rock pile up there. He said, "When y'go t'milkin', th'baby goes t'cryin' out there."

A bunch gathered up t'gether out there, and they went t'milkin', and th'baby cried. They moved a big pile'a rocks and dug down there, and he had—he killed his wife and baby and buried'em there and piled rocks on'em.

Gran'pa and Gran'ma, they moved away from there. But that's why that man couldn't live in th'house. I reckon they'd come back t'him in th'good house there.

ALEX JUSTICE: One night we just wanted t'camp out, and we saw haints all night. All night. 'Long about ten o'clock I guess it was

—th'wheat mill was down there and they'uz a old sawmill down there —somebody come ridin' a mule up, and somebody come right up t'th'bridge, y'know.

We run out there, and it was gone as quick as we got there.

Then along about four o'clock, there was a yoke of cattle— yoke of steers come down th'road hitched to a sled. They'd get 'bout as close from here t'th'porch there. We saw it all. We'uz just boys. It did scare us. There'uz big old white dogs just a'trottin' along, and a man—he had on a white shirt and didn't have no head. Chains a'rattlin'. Then it'ud go away, and then it'ud rise up again. Just a bit down below us—and here it'd come. We'd grab corn stalks and run out there, and there wadn't nothin' there.

Then I saw a sled with a load a'wood on it comin' down th'road, and they wadn't nothin' pullin' it. I could see th'standards on th'sled, I could.

And once my wife was sick—we'd had a dead baby and been t'bury it that day. There'uz snow on th'ground, and somebody come up on th'porch and knocked on th'door.

And old Aunt Katherine Adams was there, and I told some of th'boys that worked with me, I said, "Open th'door."

And Miss Adams said, "They ain't nobody there."

It just walked up and knocked on th'door just as plain as anybody was there, but they wadn't nobody there.

She told me, she said, "That ain't th'first time!"

CALVIN TALLEY: Back when I was a young boy—I guess I was about ten year old—I was headed t'church one evenin', and I rode down th'highway with my brother.

And we got out and I started walkin' up toward th'church, and all of a sudden a somethin'—there was somethin' that come around from th'side a'this old building. And it was kindly dressed in white, and I couldn't hardly make it out. I had always heered that this old building had ghosts, and I couldn't really understand what it was, but it made me pick up speed!

MYRTLE LAMB: Well, it was up near Sunburst, North Carolina. It was a house nobody wouldn't live in. Ever'body would get scared, and you would hear all kinds a'rackets.

They said a girl had a baby, and said she didn't want it so she took it and fed it to th'dogs—or hogs—and when it rained, on a cloudy night, you could hear that baby cry just as plain.

Then in th'house you'd hear all kinds of things—like stockings rubbin' against th'wall. My mother said ever' night somethin' would come
and kick th'cover off her. And she would git up and sit up scared
t'death, and this other woman got afraid and come and stayed with
her and'ud sit and dip her snuff and talk and go on.

MRS. R. L. ELIOTT: Well my mother, y'see, she was raised in a
house 'at was haunted. She said ever' rainy night that there was always noise to be heard.

And her daddy would send'em out, y'know, 'cause a lot of nights
would be like hogs under th'floor; and he'd send'em out with lanterns,
and they couldn't see nothin'—but they could hear it. It was just like
hogs. And when you'd get around there, why you wouldn't see nothin'.
They'd just hear this noise.

And then maybe a night'r'two later it'd go like horses, y'know—jest
different noises all th'time.

And her daddy was just kept a'runnin' all th'time. They'd go just
like a big bunch a'hogs under th'house—rootin', y'know how they'll
do. I don't believe you can see a spirit. I think you can just hear'em.

And where anybody is killed, there's always a noise t'be heard.
That's really true. Now I've experienced a lot of that myself, and I
know that is true. I've been around a lot of these places, y'know, where
people has been killed.

I've lived up here at th'hotel where Mr. Ramey was killed. One
night I was up there. I was out alone—jest me an'm'son—and we
heard a bunch a'people comin' down th'highway a'cryin'. Moon was
shinin' jest as bright as day. And I stood out and listened—kept listenin'—and they kept comin' closer and closer, an' come on up
t'th'house. Seemed like th'sound jest went around th'house, but I never
did see nobody. But it went like a whole bunch a'people.

So I jest went in th'house. I got scared an' went in th'house,
y'know, and locked th'door.

Then one night across th'road from my house it looked like a little
calf out on th'side of th'road jest playin' around, y'know. And they
shot at it an'ever'thing, and it jest kept dancin' right on—playin'
around—and they never could hit it'r'nothin'. Jest a spirit, y'know.
Mr. —— and his wife, they saw it too. We all saw it. Th'moon was
shinin', and hit was jest across th'road there. It was jest playin' over
there jest like a newborn calf. It'uz jest a spirit of some kind.

And my uncle, he said he lived in a house over yonder, an' after his

mother died, one night him and his brother was in th'bed and somethin' woke him up a'chokin' him. And he said he tried ever' way t'get
his brother awake and couldn't get him awake, and he lit th'lamp.
And he said when he lit th'lamp, it looked like a big animal that had
black hair. And it was a *big* ol'animal. And he said it made another
dive at his throat, y'know, t'choke him again.

He never did get his brother awake, but he follered this thang in
th'front room, and he said then that thang went up jest like a
ball'a'fire through th'top a'th'house.

You see, that was a spirit. That wasn't nobody. It went up through
th'top a'th'house right there in th'room where his mother'd died.

They's been a lot a'things seen, and I believe in ghosts.

Now up here right above Rob Williams' they's a house there where
a old man poisoned his wife. They's always thangs t'be see'd there. My
mother saw a man with no head on there.

We used t'go up there an' play. They had a downstairs and a upstairs in it. And we—a bunch of us children—was upstairs playin', and
they'uz a baby cried downstairs—cried just like a real baby. So we
tore th'top out an' come out th'top a'that house!

And one night my aunt was comin' up t'our house and this big
ol'thang caught her in th'road and choked her like a bear. Well, hit'ud
sleep on that porch at night. They could hear it lay down on that
porch. But they never did know what it was. And her husband's
brother hit it with a axe handle one night, and hit jumped back across
th'fence, but they never did see what it was. It was a big thang like a
bear.

So I've always believed in'em m'self.

And at Miss Maggie's house they's always a noise to be heard there
at some time. She lived there for years and years, an' she'd tell us lots
a'times about bumblebees in th'winter time. You never hear bumblebees in th'winter time, but she'd hear'em swarmin' in th'house,
y'know.

And my uncle lived in a place where some nights it would go like
ever' dish in th'cupboard would fall out. Said he'd get up and look,
and ever'thang was just like it was. Said maybe th'next night it'd go
like somebody poured out a bushel a'corn right on th'floor, and it
wouldn't be a thang.

Now up on th'mountain, my grandfather killed a man. They was
both drunk, and he killed him up on th'mountain. They got t'fightin'
some way over a still that was cut down on his place, and he cut his

head off and laid it up on a stump—cut it plumb off an' laid it up on a stump—and then he served twenty years in prison.

Well he got rich in prison. He waited on a train robber, an' he brought back—I don't know at th'money.

But on that mountain you can pass that stump an' you can hear things of a night. Anybody on a rainy night, if they want t'hear'em, ought just t'walk down that road an' they can hear'em.

I took my baby up on th'mountain one time an' was comin' back—bringin' him in a little ol'carriage. Just as I got even with that place I heard a singin'. You never did hear such a racket. An' boy I drove him off that mountain in a hurry. I brought that carriage *down th'road*—I got away from that place. I was scared teetotally to death!

MRS. ARDILLA GRANT: I seen'em with m'own eyes. 'Course th'woman that was with me is dead. I couldn't bring y't'her, but if she was alive I could. But they's a house at Hewitts—I guess you've heared tell of there in North Carolina—there's a big house they call th'white house up there, and ever'body that stayed there would hear somethin', 'r hear somethin' say somethin'.

Well, one night we went out there on th'end of th'porch, and th'lights was shinin' out th'windas, y'know; and they'uz a barn out yonder. Great big ol'barn they had.

We'uz out there on th'porch, an' this ol'lady, she come out from under that barn now. I'm tellin' y'th'truth exactly th'way we seen it.

Well, I didn't say a word, nor she didn't either. We watched her till she just came up close t'us, an' she had her hands out like that [Mrs. Grant puts her arms out like a sleepwalker in front of her], and she'uz just as quiet an'th'purtiest thing. She was old, y'know, and she had her hands out like that, an' she came up close. And this woman that was with me, she said, "Lord, child, do you see that?"

And we run back in th'house an' we told th'men—it was a boardin' house then—an' we told th'men what we saw, an' they got up and went out on th'porch. They thought maybe someone had stopped out at that barn t'camp out'r'somethin'. But they didn't find nobody. Not a sign of anybody. No tracks nor nothin'. Now that did scare us!

And then down below there—what they call th'Mud Cut—there's a curve in th'road, and a railroad went aroun' down there. An' down below there you could see a man—his legs and a lantern. Y'could see th'lantern an' his legs; an' he'd come up on that railroad an' he'd walk down that railroad t'th'top of th'grade they called it; an' he'd just get out'a'sight till he'd pop up right in th'same place.

That starts about nine o'clock, and I'll bet you go right up there to-night at nine o'clock an' see th'*very* sight. He'd go along and disappear an' start right back where he started from. He'd just keep a'goin', y'know. You could see th'lantern swingin', and his legs, and right back down th'railroad he'd go.

Now lots'a'people seen that. Now it must a'been in time—some time'r'nother—they'd been somebody murdered there.

[At this point Mr. Grant said that he had heard that a Bill McCathey had killed his brother there by mistake, thinking he was a groundhog.]

Then on up th'road they was a second house that th'railroad men boarded at, y'know. Now I didn't hear that. This is what they told me; but now they told it, an' I think it was true: somebody—just went like somebody'd come in an' thrown down a load a'lumber an' got t'hammerin'. Just like he was makin' a coffin.

Well, it just worried somebody that lived there. It was that way continually. An' it sounded like it was in th'wall, y'know, at times.

An' he went an' tore th'ceiling off and he found a little baby skeleton in there!

JUD CARPENTER: One night I was passin' along, th'moon a'shinin' pretty bright. It'uz along about ten o'clock at night.

Directly I heard somethin' come scra-a-a-a-pin' along behind me. I turned around and looked around. 'Bout that time that thing hit me right in th'bend of th'legs. Felt just like a old dry cow hide.

I danced away, but couldn't see a thing. I stood around there a while, kept lookin' around, but never did see nothin'.

Finally I just walked off'n'left it. Never did find out what it was.

And we used t'live in old John Sanders' house there. They'uz a winder there at th'chimbly end—right next t'th'chimbly. And they'uz somethin' ever'night'r'two would come there at th'winder and moan an' groan an' make funny rackets.

One night it climbed up in th'winder—th'winder was made out a'planks, y'know. He just come up there on that winder an' scratched and went on an' kept jumpin'n'scratchin'.

After while, my daddy decided he'd get up and see what it was. When he got out there, it vanished away—couldn't see nothin'.

They said they'uz a man killed in there—claimed it was hainted. They was right.

And I passed along by th'Methodist church one time. It was 'bout eleven'r'twelve o'clock in th'night, but th'moon'uz shinin', and th'church doors happened t'be open.

So I heard somethin' runnin'n'jumpin' across th'benches in there an' makin' th'awfullest racket I ever heered.

I didn't have no light a'no kind'r'nothin', but I went on in'ere—went plumb back in th'back a'th'church. That racket disappeared then and I couldn't see nothin'—couldn't see a thing in th'world, and th'moon'uz a'shinin' in at th'doors an'through th'winders too, so I could see pretty well.

So I walked on down th'road a piece, an' directly I heard a li'l racket behind me. I just turned around and looked. It'uz just like somethin' a'draggin' a little old sheep skin'r'somethin'. But I never could see a thing.

HILLARD GREEN: Ghosts are just th'Devil after somebody, and they're seein' these things for some lowdown meanness that they've done. It's in their eyes and in their mind is what it is. People will see things where they ain't nothin'. A ghost is a spirit or something that comes t'somebody that they've done evil to—harmed them some way'r'other. Maybe killed somebody.

They're things that way that can be seen and heard, y'know. Th'Bible speaks about these ghosts and witches and so on. You may not believe in a witch, but they are, for th'Bible tells us.

I've heard of'em. I've *seen*'em. I've seen people that could witch. They can do just anything they want to.

Now I've seen an old woman down on Cowee where I lived, and I know she was a witch. Alan, down there, he wanted t'go and plow somebody's garden, and his mother said, "No, you're not a'gonna plow that garden." Says, "You're gonna plow mine first or you won't plow nobody's."

And he said, "I'm a'gonna plow over there and then I'll plow for you."

She says, "You'll not do it."

And he went out there t'get his old steer t'go plowin'. You know, that steer just fell over like he'uz dead nearly. And he lay there three days and he never eat a bite ner nothin'.

Well, Alan took on about his steer, and he tried t'doctor it and ever'thing and finally at last he says, "I'm gonna have t'kill that steer t'get him out a'my way."

His mammy says, "Oh, you don't have t'do that. I can go out there and lay my hand on him and that steer'll get up *if* you'll go out there and plow my garden."

He says, "Well, Ma, I'll plow it then."

She just walked out there t'that steer and laid her hand on it, and that steer jumped up just th'same as there wasn't a thing in God's world th'matter with it.

I've seen a lot of things that she done, and I know she could do anything in th'world she wanted to that way t'destroy you. That was forty-seven years ago when that happened. I'uz livin' right close t'them.

I seen her get mad one time and witch a baby, by gosh, till it died 'cause she got mad at th'parents. There's somethin' to it. You don't know when it comes t'their power.

Be like old Mrs. —— over here was. Lived right over here across th'ridge over here. She got her a book and was goin't'learn how t'witch.

And somebody come t'her, y'know. Told her where t'go to out there on th'ridge and set down on that log and then they'd come and learn her.

Well, when they come to her, they said, "Now you put one hand under your foot and one on top of your head and say, 'All th'rest belongs t'th'Devil.' "

She said that she couldn't do that at all. They'uz somebody standin' there but she didn't know who it was. And she said, "All that belongs t'God-a'-mighty." And that person was gone and she didn't see nobody and didn't know nothin'. She just got up and went t'th'house and throwed her book away.

A spirit can appear to you any time that way if you'll serve th'Devil.

3

In addition to the retellings of personal or interfamily experiences, we were also told a number of pure ghost tales—tales that have been told and retold throughout the Appalachians for years. They are a part of a rich oral mountain tradition. And they're also among the wildest stories we've ever heard.

ETHEL CORN: There's an old tale told; I don't know who it was, but said there was this hitchhiker. He wanted a place to stay all night, and they told him that he could stay in that house, but it was hainted. He said he didn't believe in'em. There weren't no such thing an' he'd stay in there.

Later on he heard cats around, an' this cat with no head jumps up on th'bed. That feller, he jumped out of th'bed an' he started t'run-nin' t'get away from it.

Said he run down th'road till he give out—till he thought he was fer enough away that there wouldn't be nothin' around. He'd sit down t'rest, and said that directly somethin' said, "We've had a hell of a race, ain't we?"

He turned around an' there set th'no-headed cat by him!

GRADY WALDROOP: Man said, "I got a house over there on th'edge a'town. You can stay in there all night—all winter if y'want to. Won't cost a dime. There's plenty a'wood, books an'ever'thing in there." Says, "I'll tell y'th'reason it's thataway." Says, "Ever'body that's ever stayed there says it's hainted." Says, "There's a ghost comes in there an' they all afraid a'it."

"Aw," he says. "I don't care nothin' about that. I won't be afraid-'r'nothin'. I'll just go over there. May stay a day'r'two."

He went over an' fixed him some coffee an' lunch an' ate it. Got a book and'uz settin' readin' when a big ol'cat come down an' went up an' wallered in th'fire an' says, "Don't know what t'do about attackin' y'now." Said, "I reckon I'll wait till Martin come."

Said he didn't like that much. Said he got him another book.

Directly here come another'n down th'steps. Big ol'angoran cat. Said he got under th'forestick an' rambled around an' knocked fire all over th'place, an' he kicked th'fire back'n said, "Y'wanna com-mence on'im now or wait till Martin gets here?"

"Well," [the man] says, "I don't know when Martin'll get here, but when he comes, you tell him I've been here and gone!"

JIM EDMONDS: There was a man one time—had a lot of money, all silver. Had no greenbacks then. Had about half a bushel of silver—sold his place out, y'know, an' was goin' t'go out west—out of th'country. So he was gettin' ever'thing ready. Had his money he got from th'place, y'know.

So he got this feller t'come and give him a shave as he was gettin' all fixed up and ready t'go. Well, th'feller got him half shaved, an' then he took th'razor and cut his throat an' killed'im. But th'feller couldn't find th'money 'cause th'guy had it buried.

Well, they find this guy dead. They didn't know what happened ner nothin'. Somebody killed'im, but they didn't know who did.

When people way back then would start t'go from one country t'another an' they didn't have a place t'stay, they would just go on an' find a empty house. Some folks came drivin' by one day lookin' fer a place and asked a feller about it. He said, "I got a place down there. Can't nobody live down there. Tell what I'll do. If you live in that house fer twelve months, I'll give it t'you. Can't nobody live down there. Don't know whether you can stand it'r'not. You can move in th'house if y'want and live there."

They just had one child, y'know. Th'little feller, they just laid'im on th'bed. Th'old man, he was out workin' around gettin' wood and fixin' up—goin' t'stay all night. Th'woman, she was a'fixin' supper, and here come a man runnin' in with his head half cut off and a razor in his hand startin' like he was a'goin' t'th'bedroom.

That woman was scared t'death and said, "Lord have mercy; don't kill my baby!"

He just stopped right quick and said, "Fine thing you spoke t'me. Tell you what I've come fer. I want you t'do somethin'. You do what I tell you."

He told her th'man's name that cut his head off. Said, "I was fixin' t'leave here and he cut my head off t'get th'money. Tell what I want you t'do. You go and swear out a warrant for that man and get him to come to court for a trial. You don't need no witnesses. Don't need no witnesses. You just have him come to court. You'll have a witness. And I'll tell you what I'm goin' t'do. You'll have some money. You come and foller me."

He just went down a little ways t'where a big rock was a'layin' there. Said to move that rock, but th'woman said she couldn't. But he said, "Yes you can."

So she reached down and that rock just turned over real easy and there was all that money down there where he had dug th'hole. He said, "Now you get all that. That's yours. You do what I tell you—you have a trial and have him come t'court, and when you get ready t'have a witness, you'll have a witness."

She went ahead and had that man arrested—got that man and told him what he was guilty of. People didn't understand at all. Th'judge asked him what he was charged with. "Murder," he replied.

Th'judge then asked him if he was guilty or not guilty. About that time, here come that feller walkin' in th'courtroom with th'razor in his hand and his face half shaved and his head half cut off.

When that man saw him, he just tumbled over dead!

MRS. MARY CARPENTER: There'uz a man one time—him and his wife was a'travelin' along, and he said they went t'a house and they went in. Said that it was a'rainin' and they was a'goin' t'stay all night.

And he told her t'stay in th'house—light a lamp and stay—and he'd go t'th'field and see this man and see if he cares if they stay all night in his house.

Said she went in and scrambled around and found some matches and lit th'lamp. Th'house had furniture in it. Said there was a Bible layin' there on th'table and she just opened it up and set there by th'lamp and was a'readin'. She just kept a'settin' there waitin' fer him t'come back. Said it was rainin' harder, y'know. She thought that when it slacks he'll come back.

Her husband went over in th'field and they told him th'house was hainted and that you couldn't stay there.

She just kept a'settin' there, and directly a great big drop a'blood just hit th'Bible there and just splattered out on it.

She looked up and didn't see anything. She just read on. Pushed her book up a little and read down below it.

Another drop dropped on it.

Said she just set there and read on till th'third drop dropped. When th'third drop dropped down, said she heard somethin' a'comin' down th'stairs and she just looked around. This haint, he just set there and said, "Well, you've been th'only person that's ever stayed here when I come back."

"Well," she asked him—however it was to ask him—"Well, what do you want? Why did you come back?"

Said he was killed fer his money there but they didn't get it. He said that they'uz a fireplace in th'kitchen, and they killed him and buried him under th'hearth rock. He said his bones was under there and asked if she'd take them up and get a coffin and put them in it and bury'em in th'graveyard. Told her where t'bury'em.

Then he said, "You come back and look out there at th'gate under th'tree and dig down so fer"—I forget just how fer. Said his money'uz buried there and he wanted her to have it.

Th'next morning th'old man come back at daylight and asked her if she was ready t'go. He wouldn't come in.

She said no, she wasn't ready t'go, and wanted to know why he didn't come back. He told her th'house was hainted.

She said, "You just go along if you want to. I've got a job to do." And she just dug that ol'hearth rock up and got him up and took him and buried him and dug th'money up, and it was shore'nough money. Said he had a *lot* a'money buried out there.

But I don't know if I could have read with that blood a'droppin' or not. I'd be afraid somethin' was upstairs hurt and would've come a'tumblin' down!

I don't know who told me this'n. Somebody said they was a preacher and he had a boy that was awful mean, and all he done was hunt—fox hunt, y'know. Ever' evenin' said he'd gather up his ol'pots-'n'pans and his dogs and his gun and go out campin'.

And said his daddy thought if he could just scare him, maybe he wouldn't go. So he went up to th'church and left his Bible up there. He'd hired a man t'scare him, y'know, up there at th'church.

Th'boy was a'gettin' his food and stuff up ready t'go, and he said t'him, said, "Son, you goin' a'huntin' tonight?"

And he said, "Yeah, I thought I would."

And he said, "I wonder if you could run up to th'church and get me my Bible before you go."

"Oh, yeah," he said. "I got plenty a'time."

So th'boy, he went runnin' up there to git th'Bible, opened up th'church door and walked in. Said he got good'n'started, and said there'uz somebody in behind th'pianer said t'him, "What are y'after?"

And he said, "I come after my pa's Bible."

Said he said, "You're not a'gonna git it."

And he said, "I'll git it too."

And he said, "You ain't a'gonna git it."

Said th'boy just kept a'walkin' and went on up through there. Said he was just a'cussin' as he went, th'boy was.

And he come on back, and th'preacher was sort'a surprised that he got th'Bible. He said, "Well, did you git it?"

And th'boy said, "Yes. I got it." And cussed again and said, "I had a time a'gettin' it. They'uz somethin' up there said I wadn't gonna git it, but I showed'em anyhow. I got it."

So he laid th'Bible down and got his dog and went on and went to a old house. He was a'makin' his coffee and fryin' his meat, and said his coffee boiled and he set it over in th'corner. Said th'stairway come down in th'corner there, and said they'uz a box like a big size tool box come a'slidin' down'n slid right up on th'hearth rock right by where he was.

He looked around and said, "That's a mighty nice thing t'set my coffee pot on." Said he just picked it up and set it down on it.

Was fryin' his meat and th'lid began t'come up. He said, "Wait a minute! Hold on! You're gonna spill my coffee!"

He set his coffee pot down and said somethin' come out. It was somebody with a white shirt and no head on, and said he told th'boy about his money. Asked if he had a sister and he said he did.

Th'haint said, "I want you t'divide it with her. If you'll give her half of it, you'll never hear from me again; but if you don't divide it with her equal, I'll be back every time when you don't want me t'be."

So he went and dug th'money up and went on back and sent half of it to his sister, wherever she was.

Now I believe I'd run when somethin' began t'spill my coffee!

MINYARD CONNER: There was a boy that went possum huntin' one night. Took his dog and his lantern, and he'uz a'goin' along up a holler, and they'uz a old tiny log house up there. It was about fell down, y'know.

He seen a little dim light in it, and he just put his light out, y'know. And he just kept easin' up and easin' up, and atter while he peeped through a crack, y'know.

He looked in there and he seen five'r'six oh awful pretty women in there just a'dancin' around, y'know. Around'n'around. Just watchin'em.

Atter while one come up t'th'chimney, reached down and got a'hold a'th'hearth rock and turned it up sideways. She rubbed her hand down on th'back side, y'know, and rubbed it on her chest and said, "Up and out and over all; up and out and over all." He said she was gone like a flash then.

Said th'last one done that. Said when she done that, she kicked th'rock back.

Well, he got a'hold a'that rock and he begin t'hive and hive, and directly he pulled it up—yanked it up sideways. Put his hand over there where they had been a'feelin'—where they had been rubbin' their hand. It felt sort'a greasy to him.

He just rubbed th'rock, y'know, and he said, "Up and out and *through* all. Up and out and out through all." They had said, "*Over* all," y'know.

And he give th'rock a kick and he just out th'window he went just like a flash, y'know. Out through th'hills and briers and bushes, y'know, just a'knockin' and bangin' and slammin' and cussin'. And he kept goin' and goin' and he went across a big wide river and ended up where they was havin' a dance. Big fine place, y'know. Said they was big white horses all around there.

And said he went in and he danced with'em. Said one of'em come t'him and said t'him, "*Now don't say th'Lord's name at all!*" He give hisself t'th'Devil. Said they went up ready t'leave then.

Said they went back out and they all got on their horses and here they went. Said they pointed to a bull calf and he began t'stamp. Said, "There is your horse."

So he jumps on that little devil. Said here they went just a'keepin' up with them big white horses, just a-lip-a-tee-lip tee-lip tee-lip— goin' right on.

Said directly they come to a great big creek. Said they all jumped it and that bull calf just laid right in there and went across with'im.

Said directly they jumped a big wide river. Said he said, *"God Almighty* what a jump!" and he was in th'*dark!*

4

Logically enough, the kinds of phenomena described here have given rise to a number of superstitions, many of which are still firmly held as fact by individuals here. Ed Watkins, for example, claims that if you rebuild or repair a part of your house with new lumber, any ghosts that are there will leave. Others follow.

JIM EDMONDS: A witch will come t'borry somethin'. If they don't get nothin', then they can't do nothin' to you.

I heard about a man—a witch said he'd make a witch out a'him if he followed him. They come t'this door and th'witch said, "Hi-ho, hi-ho! In th'keyhole I go." He went on in and got all he wanted.

Th'other feller said th'same thing and in he went and got all he wanted—ate all he wanted.

Th'old witch came and said, "Hi-ho, hi-ho! Out th'keyhole I go," and went on out.

Th'old man came and thought he'd do what th'other did and said, "Hi-ho, hi-ho! Up th'high hole I go," and fell t'th'floor!

You just had t'pay no 'tention t'witches. They can put a spell on you, but they can't turn you into a witch if you pay them no mind.

ETHEL CORN: I was livin' in Charlotte—we lived off in th'backwoods. There one night about eleven o'clock we looked up an'thought th'house was on fire.

I got up and looked out, and back in th'east it looked like th'sun a'drawin' water—but it looked like streams a'blood a'comin' down. And it went straight a'towards th'north and it lit up till you could'a'-picked up a pin in th'house. I guess it'uz ten'r'fifteen minutes goin' on.

And it looked like that was blood comin' plumb down t'th'ground. They was a lot a'people see'd it, but nobody knowed what it was. It lit up th'whole house, and it like t'scared th'young'uns all to death.

I wasn't scared because I believed it was representin' a fulfillin' of

PLATE 352   Ethel Corn

places in th'Bible. An' I got th'Bible and got t'readin' in Revelations where it speaks of all these things and wonders that we'll see—it was somethin' that God had sent. It wadn't intended fer us t'know just what it was all about.

And before Uncle Jake Collins died, he see'd a light, and it looked like a torch. It was just two'r'three days before he died—er nights rather. They was a trail come from th'house down through our swamp, and he watched hit, an' hit come on down right at th'end of th'swamp and went up by his bee gums and come down nearly t'th'kitchen door, an' hit went out.

It was just two'r'three days after that that he fell dead, and we always thought it was a "talkin'" of his death, because "talkin's" will be of things t'happen like that.

Looked like somebody just a'carryin' a pine torch lit in their hand, an' it come down t'right at th'kitchen door and it just vanished.

And another "talkin'"—we had been workin' in th'fields up behind th'old Union Chapel Church, and hit went like benches and everythin' else turnin' over in that church. And I thought there was somebody in there who'd broke in, and I went and th'doors was still locked; and I looked in th'winders and we never could see nothin'. There was no benches ner nothin' disturbed.

And I went on home. That evenin' late they come and told me Gertrude Norton was dead. They'uz goin' up there t'ring th'bell.

PLATE 353

PLATE 354

PLATE 355

AUNT NORA GARLAND: My mother and Aunt Jane—they was young girls then—they were a'goin' some'ere t'spend th'night with somebody, and they were goin' together, y'know. They was t'meet in a certain place.

Well, she waited and waited and waited there in that place, and she never did come. And she started up th'road and she looked back and seen her a'comin just as plain as she'd ever see'd anybody in her life.

But it wasn't her. She was dead. That was th'reason she wasn't comin'. She was dead.

She said she'd see'd her plainer than anybody in this world, and stopped and waited and thought that she was comin' on, but she never did come—some kind of a vision.

And they say t'never look back, y'know. They say t'never look back 'cause if y'do, you'll be th'next t'die.

MYRTLE LAMB: I always possum hunted. We would always go on a rainy night in these old fields. That is th'place t'go. They would always go up in a old tree that is growed where nobody lives. Go on a dark, drizzly night. I always had th'best luck with'em.

I was comin' back, and m'shoes was hurtin' m'feet. I set down t'pull m'shoes off. I just felt like somebody was right behind me. I looked back, and he was just a little ways from me. He said he wanted t'pray fer me.

I said if he wanted t'pray fer me t'stay right there. I wadn't a'goin' with'im.

Then a night'r'two after that, he claimed he'd been to Franklin. I believe he was tryin' t'come up Middle Creek and said he got lost. Then he come—said he wanted a lantern.

I didn't feel like he was gone, and I went upstairs and looked out th'window and he'uz standin'—his light was shinin' out from under th'porch.

My mother and my brother went out and he run through th'corn fields.

Later it was like somethin' up in th'upstairs jumpin' up and down. I heard it twice. People said that was a warnin', and th'next day, my mother got bad off with pneumonia.

MRS. MARY CARPENTER: I reckon I must be superstitious'r'-somethin', whatever y'call it. If a rooster crows of a night, th'older people said somebody'd be sick. Or if somebody went t'bed a'laughin' and a'cuttin' up and a'havin' fun, somebody'd be sick in th'family, or your neighbor'd be sick'r'some one of'em dead.

One night —— and —— went t'bed a'laughin' and a'cuttin' up, and their mama said, "Cut that out in there." Said, "Somebody'll be sick in th'mornin'."

And said next mornin' 'fore they got up that somebody was knockin' on their door. Their closest door neighbor, one of'em was dead.

And you heard about my boy fallin' on his shotgun and gettin' shot? Well, about two'r'three nights before—now I don't know if that had anything to do with it or not—but that rooster crowed at midnight and I thought it was time t'get up. They wake me up when they crow, so I jumped up—thought it was time fer'im t'get up and go t'school.

And I got up and it was just midnight. And John, he told me that chickens crowed anyhow at midnight, and I said, "Well, maybe they do."

I didn't think too much about it, but it wadn't too long till I was back asleep and they waked me up a'crowin' again. Well, I bounced out t'see if it was time t'get up and go again, and it was between two and three o'clock. And I *knowed* then. I thinks, "Well, somethin' must be goin' t'happen t'us."

And two'r'three days after that, LeRoy, he started t'huntin'. And there was snow on th'ground, and ice, and he stepped on a log with ice on th'log and his foot slid and he fell off backards off th'log and shot his foot in two.

I don't know. I guess there's nothin' to it, but I couldn't help think it was because that rooster crowed. I killed th'rooster. Yeah, I killed that rooster before he ever got out of Greenville Hospital. Took him off out yonder and dug a hole and buried him.

PLATE 356

CORN SHUCKIN'S, HOUSE RAISIN'S, QUILTIN'S, PEA THRASHIN'S, SINGIN'S, LOG ROLLIN'S, CANDY PULLIN'S, AND . . .

"They'd come in and shuck m'corn, sing, and have th'best time. You've never seen such a good time as they had! I wish you could go to a corn shuckin' sometime."

Thoughts like this one expressed by Aunt Arie were what really kindled our interest in researching this chapter. When we got into it, we became truly fascinated by the various community activities that people were involved in back in the "old days." Simple things like candy pullings and ice cream parties and singings delighted people no end—particularly young people.

What really amazed us, though, was the way people took a dull, arduous task and turned it into a time for fun and warm fellowship. Corn shuckings and house raisings and log rollings became a time for neighbors to pitch in and have the best times of their lives while working with and helping each other.

We decided that the best way to get the real feeling across would be through the words of the people themselves. Here is what they had to say.

LAURIE BRUNSON

CORN SHUCKIN'S

FLORENCE AND LAWTON BROOKS: We used t'have them old shuckin's. They'd just pile up their corn in their barnyard, y'know, instead a'puttin' it in their crib. And then they'd ask all their neighbors around t'come in. And they'd always bury a drink right in th'middle a'that pile and pile their corn on top a'it. Then we'd have t'shuck all th'corn t'find it. We'd shuck all night t'get t'that half-gallon a'liquor. Then we'd all have a drink and probably have a dancin' th'rest a'th'night, if we got done in time.

God, you never seen such shuckin' corn.

Then sometimes they'd have it where th'man that found th'first red ear got t'kiss th'prettiest girl, and sometimes he'd shuck like th'devil tryin' t'find a red ear a'corn. Somebody'd find one generally ever'time. It was funny because back then 'at was th'worst thing a boy and girl could do would be caught kissin'. That's th'worst thing you could do!

Ever'body'uz invited. Wasn't nobody skipped. They invited th'young and old. They all come together. And you never seen such corn shucks in your life. And if we got done at midnight'r'somethin' like that, why we'd have a big dance from then on to towards daylight. We never counted none on sleepin' that night. No way when we was havin' them big corn shuckin's 'cause we *knowed* it'd take th'biggest part a'th'night.

'Bout all th'way we had a'havin' fun was at them shuckin's. But I thought it was mighty nice a'them t'have things like that. I wish they'd have'em now back like they used to. There'uz lots a'fun in that.

WILL ZOELLNER: Sometimes th'first one that got a red ear'ud get a ten-dollar prize. That's what they called pokeberry corn. Looked like poke come in it. And ever' once in a while you'd get a plumb red ear. And th'girl that got th'red ear, she chose her partner t'dance with later.

One I went to—was about fifteen families lived over there, Ledfords and Penlands and Duncans—whoever got th'first red ear got a Jersey cow. Nicest thing you ever looked at. Well, we got t'shuckin' around there, and finally got in a fight throwin' corn east and west. Somebody socked me with a ear down th'side a'th'head and I caught th'thing, and it'uz a blood-red ear! When it hit my head, I seen th'red corn fly. I cracked it right quick—pulled th'shuck off—and says, "Look what y'done! Gimme good luck!"

So I got that—'bout a two-year green-colored Jersey heifer. I sold it—got about a hundred dollars fer't.

MRS. HARRIET ECHOLS: Used t'be all these areas in here was big farms. Mr. Cabe would haul up wagon loads of pumpkin, watermelons, and corn. Well, they and all their neighbors'ud get their corn gathered in, and then they'd start'n'they'd go from place't'place—maybe twice a week they'd have a corn shuckin' at a different place. And all th'men'ud get in th'barn and shuck, and if there was too many women, they'd go help shuck too. And then th'others'ud cook supper—have a big supper just like we have goin' t'a church supper'r'-somethin' like that.

And then they'd put th'corn in log cribs made where th'air could go through and finish dryin' th'corn they'd gathered in from th'fields. And they'd store th'pumpkins in a barn and cover'em with th'shucks and th'leavin's from th'corn t'keep them through th'winter.

And, well, it's just fascinatin' how they did.

AUNT ARIE: Well, Pappy'ud raise a big crop a'corn—maybe two hundred bushels—and put it in a crib shed. On a certain day they'd have a corn shuckin' and get all th'neighbors from ever'wheres t'come in here. If we had'em like we used to, we'd have ever'one a'you younguns come down here and we'd have th'best time.

PLATE 357 While gathering research for this chapter, we either tried or watched others try many of these activities. We enjoyed some of them so much we're still doing them. Every year, for example, a bunch of us get together and go up to Aunt Arie's to plant, and then later to harvest and shuck her white corn and popcorn . . .

PLATE 358 . . . dig her potatoes . . .

PLATE 359 . . . and help her string leather breeches beans for the winter.

They'd always come at dinner time—some of them before dinner. Well, they'd sit down t'eat, and then they'd go on t'shuckin'. Sometimes they'd shuck till twelve at night before they'd ever get up, and sing and holler and hoop and all th'devil! And they'd take th'shuck and hide people in'em and do ever'thing. Why they had ever' kinda fun in th'world. That made people love t'go to'em. If you'd been contrary or hateful, wouldn't a'been nobody'd wanted t'go.

When they got th'corn shucked, they'd put th'man of th'house on a rail and carry him t'th'house and set'im down and comb his head— comb th'lice off his head down on th'floor and stomp'em with their feet. You know, that wadn't so, but they just done that fer th'devilment and fun!

MARINDA BROWN: I always got th'biggest thrill out a'that—just th'children and me. Just th'very smallest children would get in and shuck corn and always look for th'red ears. Ever'body that found a red ear had t'be kissed. I didn't like that too much, though!

They'd come all day and just spend th'day, y'know, and go up into th'night. And then they'd have a dance. We'd have our lanterns and lights around, y'know, and we'd shuck up into th'night and have a big feast with tables loaded with all sorts of good foods.

MRS. E. H. BROWN: That was just a good time for us all. We enjoyed bein' together and doin' somethin' t'help somebody, too.

HOUSE AND BARN RAISIN'S

MRS. HARRIET ECHOLS: If they was goin' t'build a new barn, they got all th'logs t'gether, and all th'neighbor men got in and put up th'barn. They'd build a barn in a day—put in th'sheds and stalls and ever'thing. And if they didn't finish, they'd come back th'next day and cover it. And they didn't have any pulleys'r'anything t'horse those logs up. Three'r'four men'ud get on each end of a log and they'd just come up with it.

Of course, th'kids at that time was usually at school, y'know. And th'women gathered there and cooked, and they'd have up a quilt and be sewin' on it.

They got all th'material t'gether and had ever'thing there, and they'd set a certain day fer'em all t'meet, and then they went t'work.

ANNIE PERRY: This house was built that way. Th'neighbors'ud cut

PLATE 360 When Wig was building his log cabin, we all went out and helped cut and drag the poplar logs up to the foundation. We made a real party out of an otherwise tough job.

th'logs and split th'logs. Then they'd cut th'notches in th'corners t'keep'em from rollin' off. My grandma said that th'logs this house'uz built out of was right out of our woods—cut right around in rollin' distance. This house'uz built in 18 and 69. My grandmother moved here in August and she didn't have a fireplace t'cook on, and she didn't have a cookstove.

After th'raisin's they'd put th'stock in if it was a barn, and they'd have a dance if it was a house. Called it a house warmin'.

LAWTON BROOKS: Most of'em we built was log houses, and we'd pitch in and in a couple a'days we'd have a man a house built. Ever'-body'd just go in and help a man. Wasn't countin' on gettin' a dime out of it. 'Course they'd have a big supper, and when we got done we always had somethin' at th'end—some kinda big party'r'dance in th'house 'fore they ever moved in when they wasn't nothin' in th'way.

You take fifty men and it didn't take but a little bit t'build a dad-blame house. It went up fast. Some done th'notchin'. Some done th'layin' up. Some carryin' th'logs. Some peelin' th'logs. They'uz always a job fer every bunch, and ever'body'uz on their job and they kep' ever'thing goin', y'know. God, it didn't take long t'build a *big* house. Puttin' down th'floorin' was th'biggest job in it. 'Course they didn't get matched floorin'. They just got rough plankin', and they'd jam'em down as close as'ey could and go on about their business.

But it was lots a'fun.

AUNT ARIE: We had a house raisin' t'raise this house, and we had a barn raisin' t'raise th'barn. We had t'go t'th'mountains and get th'logs, and then get th'nails and whatever we needed t'have ready, and then we asked a whole lot a'men t'come in and raise th'house.

You'd need four men with good axes, and they'd have t'know what t'do. Each one took a corner of th'house, and th'others stood on th'ground and got th'logs ready and rolled'em up there where they notched'em and put'em down. Next thing y'know, they'd got up th'square of th'house.

And somebody'ud lay them rafters off a certain way and cut th'notches in th'rafters and nail'em t'gether at th'top and put'em up. I've helped do all of that.

Th'house ain't hard t'raise like th'barn. See, th'house is made out'a little logs, and th'barn is made out'a big logs. And th'barn's got four big stalls in it—maybe more. It took eight men for four stalls. You hardly ever got a barn raised in one day. No sir. It was too big. Too much.

There's not many people knows how t'put a roof on that won't leak. If y'don't get th'shingles on right, it'll leak. Now I've helped put on shingles.

MRS. ADA KELLY: A new couple'ud start t'build them a house, they'd have a house raisin'. Th'men all around th'community'ud go in and get th'framin' of th'house up and all they could that day, and then they'd have a house coverin'—meet and cover th'house and go on with it till they finished. Then th'couple was ready t'move in.

You couldn't get anybody t'do that fer y'now, could you? But they wasn't any vacant houses around then. My father built his house. I'uz born in a log house. Had two rooms downstairs and two rooms upstairs and a big old fireplace.

RICHARD NORTON: When somebody went t'build a house, ever'body flew in and helped'em. T'get th'logs up, most of th'time they used what we called skid poles. They'd lay up poles against th'house, and four'r'five men'ud get ahold a'them logs and roll'em right up them poles on th'house.

Sometimes they got'em up there first and notched'em after they got'em up there. They generally used smaller logs, and they'd turn'em up and notch'em and then turn'em back over t'fit.

QUILTIN'S

MARGARET NORTON: People'ud work all fall piecin' quilt tops, and when they got'em all pieced, they'd invite in all th'neighbors and have a quiltin', and that quilt'ud be for th'person that invited'em in. And whoever they had th'quiltin' for furnished all of'em dinner. If it'uz at your house and it'uz for you, you'd furnish th'whole dinner— even if they'uz twenty women there.

They could quilt one out in a day easy. Lots a'times we've had quilts out at breakfast and quilted two.

MARINDA BROWN: People used t'get t'gether and they'd just put up one. They could make as many days out of it as they wanted to. They'd piece one fer one family, set in and draw another one fer another family, y'know; just kind'a kept it goin'.

PLATE 361   We went to several quiltings. This one was on Betty's Creek where a lot of our contacts had gotten together to make two Poplar Leaf quilts for their Home Demonstration Club. For this quilting, each lady had pieced one square at home. When they were done, another lady gathered up the squares and sewed them together with borders to make the two tops. Then they all got together for the actual quilting.

ANNIE PERRY: They had quiltin's, but I never could quilt. My stitches were s'long you'd have t'keep your toenails broke off t'keep from gettin'em hung!

People were neighbors. They all helped each other t'do things. If you got anything t'do *now*, y'do it yourself or you let it go undone—whichever y'want to.

PEA THRASHIN'S

LAWTON BROOKS: Ever'body planted these old clay peas. I ain't seen'em in over twenty years. Th'seeds of'em's about t'run out. People used t'always plant'em in their cornfield.

Well, they'd go and pick'em and carry'em and pile'em up in great big ol'piles. Put'em on big sheets, y'know. Then we'd all cut us a pole t'beat with and you'd just beat, then you'd stir up a while, and then you'd beat again. Th'hulls'ud pile up on top. Then you'd stir t'get y'some more up that hadn't been hit, y'know. Then you'd beat'em again.

They'd grow lots a'them back in 'em'days. They'd grow'em and sell th'things. You could buy'em fer nothin' nearly a bushel. But still, that was a way a'gettin' some money. You had t'do th'best y'could. They growed them peas, and what they didn't eat, they sold. And they'd get out there and we'd thrash'em out fer'em. Thrash'em old peas out—have th'goodest old time y'ever seen.

SINGIN'S

MARGARET NORTON: When you'd have a singin', you'd usually have a group of people get together and sing and have refreshments like tea and coffee and ice cream, y'know. They'd gather at different persons' houses, or at th'church—whoever had a pianer'r'organ—and they'd play and sing just like any other get t'gether.

Usually y'sung religious songs, but sometimes they'd have like a sports party where you'd just sing sports songs. But usually it was religious songs, and we'd sing for two'r'three hours and have a few refreshments and go home.

And then sometimes they had'em all night long. You'd start at eleven o'clock and then go th'rest of th'night. As fer me, I'm not a good hand t'set up till all hours. I'd go t'sleep!

HARRY BROWN: They'd have'em in their houses, and then some-

PLATE 362 An all-day singing and dinner-on-the-grounds at Aunt Arie's church.

times they have'em up there at Andy Cope's fish farm. He's a great singer, and this fella' from Lakemont—Horace Page—all them go up there and sometime they sing all night.

I'd just go t'listen t'it. I never did sing. They used t'have old-time songs, y'know, like, "Walkin' in th'King's Highway," but they don't sing anymore. Oh, and, "They're Namin' th'Prophet, That Honorable Man," and, "On Down t'th'River Jordan." But th'songs they sing now is different from when I'uz growin' up.

And sometimes at th'church we'd have what they called an "all day singin' an' dinner on th'grounds." That was good too.

FLORENCE AND LAWTON BROOKS: Lord, yeah. People used t'have singin's at their houses. Sometimes we'd walk ten miles t'one. They'd have songbooks, y'know, with gospel songs, and th'house'ud be *full* a'people. They used t'do that *lots*—move all over th'settlement. When me an'Florence was married we done 'at fer a long time. Fer years after we'uz married we went nearly ever'night. Lots a'times people'ud have t'walk four'r'five miles, but they'd *go*. They'd be there. They'd all go.

That was about th'only thing that went on durin' th'week, and that'ud give th'young people a place t'go, and they'd always go. If a old boy got him a girl, he'd have her come t'th'singin', y'know. Had a nice time. Always had a nice time. No joke about it—it was nice. I think there ought t'be lots more. Wouldn't be half as much meanness done.

But they quit all that now, I reckon. Don't hear tell a'that no more.

LOG ROLLIN'S

LEX SANDERS: In log rollin's, you'd go all over th'community and gather up maybe twenty-five men. Then they'd cut logs and clear land and do a whole lot a'work in a day.

It'uz like th'old workin's. Lot a'th'women'ud come t'th'workin' and get dinner. And as a general thing, when they had a log rollin', they'd be eight'r'ten women there that'ud have a quiltin' too, and maybe make one'r'two quilts while th'men'uz cuttin' and rollin' th'logs.

RICHARD NORTON: They had log rollin's when they cleared th'land. I remember when they'd go t'what they called "new ground" and they'd clear it off, y'know. Then they'd have big log rollin's, and they'd pile all them logs up and burn'em. Th'women'ud always cook dinner, and they'd be twenty-five men maybe, and they'd clear a big field in a day—roll it up and burn it, y'know.

CANDY PULLIN'S

MRS. ADA KELLY: When they made syrup, th'last run of th'syrup they'd cook up a whole lot of, and they'd cook it down till it got real thick. And just along toward th'last before it got ready t'take up, they'd put some soda in it. I really don't know what that did to it, but it seemed t'make it get whiter or something.

And a boy and a girl would usually butter a dish and cool it off some and then get it up in their hands, y'know, and work it till they could get it in a ball. Then th'boy would get at one end and th'girl at th'other, and they'd pull backwards and forwards till they got it so it'd pull out in great long pieces.

Then they'd divide some of it and pull it out in long pieces sort of like stick candy and lay that out on a platter'r'something. When it got cold, you could just take a knife and crack it all, and it'd be sort'a like yellow stick candy. It was real good.

PLATES 363–364 One night, Florence and Lawton Brooks invited us over to see what a candy pull was like. We did something wrong and the candy came out a little sticky, but it tasted good.

And they always had boys and girls doing it together. That was all th'fun there was in it. Just invite th'young folks in t'make syrup candy.

WILL ZOELLNER: Y'grease yer hands with lard so it don't stick on yer hands. If y'ain't got no lard on yer hands, it gets all over yer hands and gets warm.

And y'go out there and get yer partner and cut that syrup out in big pieces, and then y'pull that and keep a'pullin' around and around till it gets plumb yella'.

Sometimes we'd go and have a corn shuckin' and candy pullin' and a all-night dance on New Year's. Dance th'old year out and th'new year in, and have stuffed turkeys and have a midnight supper. Then we'd have a drink outside. Had all kind'a cider where we were there. And once in a while had some blackberry wine—take a little swig a'that.

MRS. E. H. BROWN: They'd have those candy pullin's, and they'd have it all braided and in all kinds of shapes, y'know. They'd get it t'where they could pull it out and shape it any way they wanted to.

MAUDE SELLERS: Oh! I've pulled candy till I had blisters on my hands!

CANDY BREAKIN'S

MRS. E. H. BROWN: They'd have a dishpan fulla stick candy broke up into little pieces, and they'uz different colors, y'know. And th'pan was covered. And a girl and boy would pair off and go and reach under there and get a piece a'candy. If they each got a piece alike, why they could keep it, but if they didn't, they had t'put it back.

Last one I believe I remember ever bein' at was at my husband's home, and he carried me home that night after th'candy breakin'.

RICHARD NORTON: We'd just buy this peppermint candy—all kinds a'candy. Somebody'ud take a dishpan and cover it up and you had t'reach in there. If you and your partner didn't get th'same kind'a piece, you had t'pay it back, but if you did, you kept it.

There'd be twenty-five, y'know, sometimes; and it'd circle 'round and 'round, and you'd see who got th'most candy—who was th'luckiest, y'know. And boy would they have fun when y'had t'put your candy back!

MISCELLANEOUS

MRS. HARRIET ECHOLS: We had ice cream parties too—usually on Saturday night. See, most ever'body had four'r'five cows, and we'd make boiled custards (you know that's fixed with milk and eggs and sugar and flavorin', and it's delicious; but where y'put a lot a'eggs in it, it's s'rich y'can't eat much of it). And we'd get about five ice cream freezers and invite th'youngsters in, and we'd get in th'parlor and get around th'organ'r'piano and sing and play games. See, we didn't have anywhere t'go. And that's what we did for our recreation was our parties.

And we had our singin's, and we'd meet during th'week and we'd go t'prayer meetin' on Wednesday night and sing and practice songs fer th'choir and fer church on Sunday. And then on Saurday nights we'd have our ice cream supper—and in th'wintertime a candy pullin'. And we'd gather nuts and have a nut crackin' t'make our candy if we wanted t'make fudge'r'anything like that.

And three'r'four of th'girls would get t'gether and make five'r'six cakes, and we'd have cake and ice cream.

And we went t'dances in th'wintertime, and we'd have apple bobbin's, and we just had th'best time. We never went to a dance without our parents, and we'd just roll back th'rug if they had a rug; and if they didn't, we'd put meal on th'floor. And th'band would come in from th'little town. There was several of th'old men could pick a guitar or banjo or fiddle. And, well, we just had a good time!

MARGARET AND RICHARD NORTON: People used t'help each other kill hogs, too, when they had hogs t'kill. Th'neighbors'ud come in and help. Ever'body got a mess a'meat and went back home. You had four'r'five hogs t'kill, and half a dozen'r'more'ud come t'help y', and they'd do it for a combination and a mess a'meat.

R.: We just give'em a mess a'meat a lot of times. Me and my uncle, we'd gather together and kill big hogs. We'd always dress one out then, and then we'd kill two'r'three more for th'other feller, and two'r'three more for th'other feller till we had'em all killed and dressed out. We could get it all in one day.

M.: We had square dances, too. They'd get all th'furniture out of th'room, and had somebody a'callin' and somebody a'pickin', y'know.

R.: We always had Bill Lamb play th'fiddle, and had some banjo and guitar pickers, too, y'know. They was a lot a'young people around here then.

PLATES 365–366   This fall we helped Clark Norton and Jerry Ayres slaughter, dress, and salt down two hogs. Here we try to help scrape the hair off after scalding the hog with hot water. They got a lot of laughs at our clumsy attempts to help, but we tried—and enjoyed just being together.

M.: We had th'whole place covered up with young people. They hadn't got this crave then t'go up t'Atlanta'r'some big city. They just stayed on and helped farm in th'summer time and then go t'school in th'wintertime and have fun.

M.: Had barbecues, too.

R.: We just dug out a square place and piled it full'a hickory wood and burnt it down t'coals. Then we'd take poles and gather that hog— 'course his innards took out and ever'thing, y'know—and we'd run 'em through his hind and shoulders. Th'poles'ud be long enough t'reach across that hole, and we'd put him down over it and we'd have t'turn it ever' so often. Cook'im all night.

M.: They'd sit up all night, and next mornin' th'stew'ud be made—th'Brunswick stew.

R.: We cooked generally two sheep and a hog.

M.: Th'other people'ud bring th'vegetables and th'bread and th'things that went with it.

And we used t'get in t'gether and have bean stringin's and pea shellin's, too. We did that here last summer.

R.: We pile up a big pile there on a paper on th'floor and we all get around it, y'know.

M.: And ever'body gets'em a pan and a chair and a place t'put their hulls. First thing you know, you're finished.

And at Christmas time here we have a Christmas tree for all our children on Betty's Creek. Th'women all come and we fix up th'presents there. So that's a get-together. We still do that. And we *have* got together and preserved strawberries.

R.: All th'old people used t'double up like that. One'ud need some work done, and they'd all just pitch in.

And even that doesn't exhaust the list. In addition to the above, people grouped together for box lunches (each girl filled a cake box with a picnic lunch for two and decorated its exterior. The boxes were then auctioned off, and the boy with the highest bid shared the lunch with the girl who had made it) ; wool cardings and spinnings; and workings (when a man was sick, the neighbors would gather to plant or tend or harvest his garden and do his chores until he was well again). And *that* probably isn't all, either. The sense of community and interdependence was so highly developed that there was simply little people *didn't* do together. That amazes us now, but it also attracts us in some mysterious way. Perhaps that interdependence is the source of part of our nostalgia for a simpler time.

MRS. E. H. BROWN: I believe people enjoyed themselves more. They didn't have very much for entertainment, y'know, and when we did have some little something, we really enjoyed it. And ever'thing was nice. Ever'body behaved themselves. I used t'go to country dances, too. I never went t'a public dance in my life. It was always t'some neighbor's house. And ever'body had better behave themselves. If they didn't, they was invited t'go home.

My daddy was always th'fiddler. I've often told people I cut my teeth on a fiddle bow!

KENNY RUNION

"Put these riddles 'fore th'school and see if there's anyone in there can answer 'em!"

Round as a ball
And sharp as an awl;
Lives all summer
And dies in th'fall.

It goes all over th'field,
Through th'creek;
It has a long tongue
But it never drinks.

Big at the bottom,
Little at the top,
Little thing inside
Goes flippity-flop.

Black up and black down,
Black and brown
Three legs up and
Six legs down.

"Next time y' come back, tell me if anyone can answer 'em. I don't know. I don't believe they'll ever get that first 'un." (See Appendix, p. 407, for the answers!) KENNY RUNION

PLATE 367

Kenny Runion is a craftsman. He makes everything from laurel wood rocking chairs to belts to wooden necklaces bespangled with dime store jewels. He loves his work, he loves people, and he loves to talk.

Kenny has always lived in the mountains and sometimes spends hours each day tramping through them for his own enjoyment and in search of old wood, rocks, and relics to use in his craft work. We asked him how he learned to make such a variety of things: "Well, I just studied it out. I'm about a third Indian and it just comes to me. That belt there was hard to figger out. See, I'd never seen nary'un. I'd never seed anything like that." He just uses his imagination.

Kenny lives alone in a tiny frame house. We interviewed him a number of times, and he was always ready and willing to talk—even if he was in the middle of carving a chair leg. He'd pop up his hand in a friendly wave and, grinning, say, "I'uz wonderin' when you were goin' t'come see me again." Then he'd begin to talk about anything from witchcraft to "whuppin's." Kenny's conversation is as well spiced with wit and serious philosophy as his carving is with ingenuity and imagination.

JAN BROWN

People now's a'havin' a good time. Now whether it'll last . . . I'm a'feared it ain't. They'll be somethin' happen. People ain't thankful no more. They don't 'preciate what they got.

And ever'body's in a hurry. Where they goin'? Where they goin'? Back then you could meet an ol'feller with an ol'ox wagon and he'd stand there a half day if you wanted t'talk. Stand as long as you'd talk. You meet a feller now, he'd run over y'. Where's he goin'? Just ain't got no patience.

Yeah. Back then he'd just stop his two oxen in th'road and git off. Talk as long as y'wanted t'talk. Maybe he'd give y'a drink a'liquor. But now people's a'gittin' there fast, ain't they? People now, they go more in a week then they went in a year back then. They go more places now then they did in a year. They go more'n'more ever' week. They's people raised around here—*old* people—never seed a train. And now they're ever'where, ain't they? If they'd seed a airplane, they'd run in th'house and shet th'door.

People made their livin' back there. They had a woods full'a hogs, sheep, and cattle. Chestnut trees bent with chestnuts. All they had t'do was go out in th'fall and go t'killin' hogs. Bring'em in just as fat as they got'em. They seen a good time, but they didn't have th'cars and money. You'd see fellers goin' up and down th'road 'fore tax-payin' time tryin' t'sell three bushel a'corn for a dollar.

We got fifty cent a day—or my pa did. I didn't get that; I was just young, y'know. Fifty cent from sunup to sundown. It was a lot a'hard work. We got th'hardest jobs in th'world. Why, times then was tough. You know what snuff is? You could get three box for a quarter. Y'could buy you a big fried chicken fer fifteen cent. Dozen eggs fer a dime—all y'wanted. Th'stores wouldn't buy'em. There wadn't no demand fer'em. And all that stuff was as cheap as nothin'—but you couldn't git nothin' fer your labor.

Buy you as good a cow as ever milked fer fifteen dollars. I'm talkin' 'bout th'*best* now. Git all th'liquor y'wanted fer a dollar a gallon. Good corn liquor. Corn, fifty cent a bushel.

I guess it was better back then. A dollar ain't worth more'n a quarter now. Back then, if you got a'hold of a dollar hit'd *buy* y'somethin'. You'd git twenty pound a'meat fer a dollar.

I learnt how t'build fences, split wood, hoe corn. Worked just as hard then as I do now. I was raised poor and still poor. Me and my daddy'd work just anywhere we'd get a job. And we had fun. You had people meet up, y'know, and drink and dance and have all kind'a fun. No fights much. You could go down th'road in broad daylight with five gallon a'liquor on your back and not be bothered. Shore you could. You could go down with a five-gallon jug on your back and never be bothered. It was twelve mile t'th'sheriff and there wadn't no phone. Had t'walk it, and wadn't nobody goin' t'do that, y'know. They'd just let y' go on.

Ever'thin's different. Ain't nothin' now like it was then. You didn't go ever' time you sneezed then to a hospital. There wadn't nary'un. Back yonder, th'doctor made a twenty-four-mile trip. He'd come here and stay with y' about an hour. Doctor y' and give y'ever what you needed. And when he got ready t'go and y'asked what y'owed him, said five dollar. Five dollar. And what would that cost now? Cold or hot, he'd come. He'd come cold or hot. He'd have a big gray horse and a big bird dog'ud come lopin' right in with him.

And sometimes if y'got sick they'd have *old* granny doctors'at'ud come see y'. Doctor y'up. If y'had th'flu—they called it th'grip then —they'd go out and get some boneset, some penny royal, and put a big ol' pot on. Had fireplaces. They'd fill'er about half full; boil'er down and give y' a teacup full of it and put y' in th'bed. You'd just wet a sweat up. Few minutes and you'd be knocked out. You've took quinine, ain't y'? 'At ol' boneset's as bitter as it. Those old'uns would

PLATE 368

come and doctor y'. Wouldn't cost you a dime. They'd stay all night with y'.

And I never heard tell of 'pendicitis till I was growed. I watched ol' Doc Lyons operate on a woman in Towns County fer one. I didn't know there was such a thing. People called it th'cramp colic. They'd lay down just as close t'that fire as they could get and bake that place. Almost burn it.

Biggest thing they had was what they called dropsy. Yer feet go t'swellin' down here and it just goes up. Other words, yer blood just goes t'water is th'best way I can explain it t'y'. But la-a-a-aw, there's ten t'heal y'*now* when there wasn't nary'un then.

If y'got yer leg broke, they'd know just what t'do. They'uz a feller ridin' on a wagon and he'uz settin' down on th'couplin' pole. Don't know *what* he meant 'less he'uz drunk. And his feet was just about 'at fer from th'ground [about a foot], and he hung his foot there again' a stump and broke his leg square in two. Just broke it. Way they done when 'at happened, they just rolled his breeches leg up and go out there and split some wood pieces and commence right here around yer leg. They'd place it back th'best they could and go plumb around yer leg with them little pieces. Then they'd tie it with a rope or a good

PLATE 369

stout string and there you'd set fer about twelve month. And that's what y'got. No doctor medicine. Didn't have no doctor medicine at all. It'uz just pull and take it. No dopes. No dopes at all. No shots. No *nothin'*. You'uz just there in th'chair.

Same way with yer arm. They'd take them little strips and go around yer arm there. Then when they got plumb around it, they'd tie it. Didn't need no sling. Couldn't get out'a there nohow fer them strips. Now that's th'way they done with that cripple business. *Law.* People back then shore didn't get it good. Wadn't a thing in th'world. Not even asprin tablets.

Times are different now—*great* goodness, I reckon! They used t'be an ol' Indian doctor come t'stay with us a long time. If I ever hear anything, I've got her. I'll remember it. Said that poke root, it's as poison as strychnine. You dig up th'root of it and roast 'at stuff like a sweet 'tater, lay it down on somethin' like a clean cloth and cut it up and put it t'th'bottom of yer foot. If you got a risin' here anywhere, hit'll draw her out. I don't care how black yer foot is; when you pull it off it's as white as cotton.

If y' had t'have a tooth pulled, you come in to a feller name of J. Garrett. Say, "Lay down on 'at floor, feller." You'd stretch out here on th'floor. He'd put one knee here [on your chest] and catch you just like 'at [around your head]. He'uz stout, too. He'd put one of'em homemade pullers in there and give her 'at [yanking]. If it broke off, 'at's all it wrote. If it broke off, he couldn't get it. But if it didn't break, he'd bring it. You couldn't get up. He'd have one knee here [on your chest]. Caught y' with his left hand and got in yer mouth. Take his pocket knife and cut around it 'bout that deep [about a half inch]. Little blade of a knife. You could just hear that a'squrshin' in there. Sometimes his pullers'ud slip off. *Great* goodness! You'd hear all kind'a racket in your head. Just like bustin'. He'd say, "Oh. My pullers slipped off." They'uz old homemade'uns from th'shop. Sometimes they'd get slick and slip off. *Great* goodness! Might'nigh bust yer head. He'd go back again. Keep on till he got it, unless it busted off.

But now when all 'at was over, you didn't owe him a dime. Didn't owe him a thing. Didn't charge a dime. He'd pull half a dozen fer each one of us. Not a cent. You had t'hold yer mouth wide or prop it open with a stick. After it'uz pulled, you'd fill your mouth full'a salt. You know how '*at* hurt now. Washed yer mouth out and th'next day it'uz feelin' good. You didn't go around with yer lip swellin' down here with 'at old poison, y'know. Just looked like y'always did—if he didn't bust it. If he busted it in yer mouth, then he'd have t'pull it out by pieces. You didn't have many shots, either. Now boys, you had t'have th'nerve. That tooth'ud ease about th'time you got on his porch it'ud scare y' so blame bad. Then you might start home and it'ud start hurtin' 'fore you got home. Hit'uz just pull it or let it hurt. Just suffer on or he'd get it out. Now it's five bucks t'pull'em, ain't it?

[We asked Kenny to tell us the best advice his father ever gave him.] Stay out of meanness. He raised me right. I've never been arrested in my life. Never been in jail except goin' t'see my folks. Never been locked up. Yeah. He raised me right. My mother, of course, was tight on me too. I don't drink. Don't cuss. Don't do none a'that. If I see I'm goin' t'meet bad company, why, if I have t'go by, I just say, "Howdy," and go by. I don't fool with'em. Bad company'll get you in trouble. 'Course, I ain't a'feared when I get mad. I ain't scared of'em. But I'd rather stay out of trouble.

Kids today do as they please. You know that? Mother'll tell'em t'bring her a bucket a'water. Says, "Ain't goin' do it. You go get it yourself." Boys, when I'uz raised up, my daddy told me t'do somethin' and I done'er. I done'er. I tell'em now that a hick'ry don't hurt like it used to. It don't hurt now.

I used t'get more whuppin's than anybody. Boys, I'm tellin' you th'truth. Back then, people had their children under control. One word and you'uz gone. My daddy used t'whup me and Gus fer fightin' back when we was six, seven'r'eight year old. He didn't whup me with a second handed hick'ry. He'd go out and get two. Now when he got through with us, we'uz dressed out. And it wouldn't be long till we'd get'er again.

I had a teacher in school. He'uz a fine feller. He sat in a new cane-bottom chair sort'a in th'corner a'th'house. Guess he had twenty-five hick'rys there. He'uz blame lazy when he whupped y'. He wouldn't even get up. No, he wouldn't get up. But now you'uz dry cleaned when he got through with y'. Boy, that'uz a mean teacher. About six foot high and stout t'go with it. I couldn't whup nobody in a chair, could you? He'd bring 'at hick'ry around 'at'a'way. Mankind! He'd whup girls. It didn't make no difference. Anybody 'at'ud come up there and disobey or didn't have their lessons.

But in a way, hit'uz worth somethin'. It'uz worth somethin'. Mankind, you had t'have 'at lesson. Ever' time you'd have—examination, I call it—we all get in them seats plumb across. Not a dadgone book. Nothin' but a tablet. And when they'd get askin' y'somethin', you had t'put'er down. You had t'put'er down. You didn't have no book t'go by, and you couldn't ask nobody, either.

You had t'buy yer books. They didn't get y'nothin'. Had t'buy yer

PLATE 370

books, yer pencils. We used a slate lots. Ever seed a slate? Then they'd put out a pencil with that. Use that. Went t'school 'bout eight hours a day. In at eight and give us an hour at dinner and got off at four. You didn't skip nothin'. You took it from th'floor up. After school'uz out, if you could complete th'seventh grade you could teach school. But I want you t'know, 'at old Sanford workbook was a bad'un. 'At old speller. 'Bout that thick. I guess you've seed'em. Words in there 'at long.

[Kenny has much longer hair than many of the people we interview, so we asked him what he thought of young people wearing long hair.] I think it's nice. Other words, it's hippie-like, ain't it? I believe we ought t'be good to'em, don't you? I shore do. I like t'see'em with long hair. My folks is all again' me wearin' it. I'm th'only one that wears it. I've got a brother—he shaves ever' mornin'; has his hair cut ever' week. 'At's his pride. Want t'look good, y'know. Look pretty. Well now, 'at's what it's for.

You ought t'seed me. I cut my beard off. 'At beard was *way down*. You wouldn't'a'knowed me if I'd a'come in th'street. It got t'botherin' me—people a'laughin' at me, y'know—and I just cut it off. Yeah. I really ought t'have some beard with m'hair t'look good. Long mustache. Back when I was a boy, you never seed a man but what he didn't have a beard way down t'here, or a mustache one. And long hair like mine. Ever' one of'em. I don't believe it's wrong t'wear it. I've got pictures down there at home of Jesus and his hair's way *down* here hangin', fallin' 'round on his shoulders. That's what I told my folks. Said, "Look 'at picture. You believe that?" I said, "It's not wrong. Christ wore it, didn't he?" And Samson wore it till he cut it off, and what'd he get into when he had his hair cut off? Makes y'stouter. It does!

I don't think it makes much difference what y'wear. If y'want t'wear shorts, mini-skirts, or wear your hair long I don't think that bothers y'. Do you? I ain't again' none of it. I've had big arguments. People said, "Runion, you'll just argue anything."

I said, "I think it's nice."

I don't think it makes much difference what y'wear ner nothin' 'bout it. It's how yer heart is.

Yeah. Why, I ain't again' a hippie. Why, he's just a man just wearin' his beard. I ain't again' him. But now, people'll talk. Sometimes when I go through Clayton I can hear'em back behind say, "There goes another ol'hippie." They don't know me hardly.

Yeah. I ain't goin' have mine cut no more. I can't marry nohow, and I'm just goin' t'let my hair grow.

[We knew Kenny had been married before, so we asked him why he didn't feel he would ever marry again.] Scared I'll get in trouble. Scared I'll get up in th'mornin' and she'd hit me with a stick'a'stovewood! Well, it's all right t'have yourself a woman, but I've stayed with myself many a day. I've got used t'it. If I want t'get up at midnight, I can. If I want t'lay to ten o'clock, I can. When I go in of a night, I wouldn't mind havin' one. But it's ten or eleven o'clock 'fore I get through sometimes. Trouble of it is, I might have t'go in and cook her supper!

It'd be better if women stayed at their homes. I believe in a woman stayin' at her home. I may be wrong, but they're really needed at home. There's a lot t'do about a place, you know that? She's got a job t'keep her house up. 'Course I don't keep my house up, but I keep it in th'best shape I can. Housework's a job. Man don't know what a woman goes through with. Beds t'make up. Dishes t'wash. And th'yard t'sweep. Time you get that done, why it's just about ready for dinner and all t'do over again. Woman's got a job if she keeps her house goin'.

If you marry twenty-five times, you'll study about your first wife. It'll be on your mind in spite a'all you can do. You know how long it'll be on it? Five long years. Five years y'can almost imagine her. And you're liable t'mistreat your wife; say, "You ain't as good as my first'un was. I'm sorry I married y'." First thing you know, you'll leave her.

Now you know if you ever marry, an' I guess y'will . . . anybody 'at marries ought t'study a whole lot before they marry. Now I'm a'tellin' y'th'truth. You get married, of course you can get a divorce, but that ain't worth fifteen cent. It shore ain't. It ain't worth fifteen cent. That'll loose y'from th'law, but it won't do yer mind no good. You'll still worry 'bout that woman.

And y'get out there in court tryin' t'get a divorce, and you'll say, "Well, she'uz t'blame." And she'll say you'uz t'blame and it'll take forty lawyers t'tell who's right. But they will listen to a woman more'n they will a man. They will now. Woman's got way yonder better a chance, and a man don't stand none. Man'll speak and sell y'a line. Says, "Well, she wouldn't stay at home with me or cook for me ner wouldn't do a thing." Shoot y'a line.

She'd get up there and say, "Well, he mistreated me. Hit me with a stick'a'stovewood 'fore breakfast." 'At'll pass [the jury will believe that]. 'At's A number one, see?

[Knowing Kenny to be a religious man, we got on the subject of religion and what proof there was for him of a God.] Well, it's right here a'fore your eyes. You can see things a'happenin' ever'day. Different things. I was sittin' here th'other day and a ol'hen was comin' through here that had chicks. She'd go a little piece. Then she'd cluck. Now what cause her t'do that? I studied about that. Just sat here and watched. She'd go a little piece; then she'd cluck again. Now what makes her do that? 'At's Nature. 'At's Mother Nature.

And they'll sit there on those eggs three weeks, and 'at's Mother Nature. Three long weeks. And they'll stay there, too. Well, there's somethin' behind that some'ers, or she'd get off and leave. There's somethin'r'other keepin' her there.

Why, you *know* that there's a power if y'just look out. Now they talk about goin' t'th'moon, and they may of went. I don't know. But that moon. Is it standin' still, or movin', or what about it? Rises here [he points], and th'next mornin', it's here. Plumb across th'world. What d'y'think about that now? And when it goes, it's dark nights. And when it starts up, it's a bright light thing. It's little and gets bigger and bigger. What changes that? They's somebody—somethin'—behind it. It'll change. Then it'll get fuller and fuller till it's a full moon.

There's a whole lot to study about in this world, boy, when y'get right on t'th'business. Shore is. Some says when y'die, if you're a sinner, you'll go t'Hell and burn forever. Some says you won't do it. You'll just burn up like paper. So that's another question. Well, I kindly believe you'll suffer. You just got t'take all'em old things and figger'em out. Figger'em out.

[Kenny is a devout believer in keeping the Sabbath. He gave us many reasons why the Sabbath should be a day of rest.] Now I don't know fer shore if they's anybody in this world that keeps th'Sabbath. If you read th'Bible, it's pretty close. It says t'do nothin'. What is nothin'? Now do you know what nothin' is? I believe it's wrong t'drive a car on Sunday. Now I may be wrong. I'm just tellin' y' my belief about it. I asked as good a mechanic as ever lived in this country, I said, "I have arguments on drivin' cars on Sunday." I says, "Hit work?"

He says, "If 'at ain't work, 'here ain't none."

'At's th'reason I say mighty few keeps th'Sabbath. I don't believe in workin' then. I can say somethin' very few men can say. I never worked fifteen minutes on a Sunday in my life. I never have. I tried once and my brother jacked me up. I took a lot a'this stuff down t'th'road t'sell it, and boy, he come down on me! He said, "Why, Kenny, don't you know better'n'that? Today's Sunday, man." I took t'th'house and never did come back n'more.

Yeah. You know way back then, they wouldn't even cook. They'd have ever'thing cooked and lay it back t'eat on Sunday. No cookin' at all. They'd have ever'thing ready.

I've hit tough luck. I know that's a self-learnin'. Fella' come up one Sunday when I lived up yonder. I'uz fixin' t'go t'church. He'uz old— about eighty-two year old—and said he wanted t'go back yonder where he was raised. Well, I didn't want t'go. He said, "I'll have y'back again before th'singin's over."

Well, you know when we come back we was in a wreck and just both about killed. I just drawed plumb over. Couldn't even straighten up. Three months 'fore I got good breath. We passed two churches goin' over th'mounains, and he had a twelve-hunerd-dollar pickup and it wouldn't a'brought fifty dollars. Tore it lit'raly all to pieces.

I tell y'now, you gotta notice. Lotta folks say, "Well, now, if I don't work I'll lose m'job." That ain't a'gonna he'p you a bit. It didn't he'p ol'Eve none when she eat that fruit. She said that ol'serpent got her t'eat it. Did that he'p her? No. Didn't he'p her. And because his wife told him t'eat it, that didn't do *him* no good and they was both drove out of th'Paradise. Excuses has been from that day t'now. Excuses.

Lotta folks now, they mebbe say, "Well, I got a good excuse; th'car didn't run right," or somethin'. But now you take it on this here latest business. I don't believe that will he'p you a bit in this world. Yer either right or wrong. Am I right or wrong?

[The Bible is one of Kenny's favorite topics of discussion. He has his own colorful version of many stories, such as this one of Samson.] Now a preacher argued me that Samson just had one wife. He argued me down, but he *had* two. They burnt.

After his first wife, he decided he wanted another one a'them ol'Philistines, and he went down and got'im another'n. And that's th'one that had his hair cut. She kept on and on and then cut them seven locks off and he wasn't more'n just a boy in strength then.

Then he went t'work pullin' a syrup mill. You ever see how they grind cane? All kind'a jobs like that.

But it passed on and he got revenge. He didn't ask fer revenge in only one thing: said he wanted revenge fer his two eyes. They gorged'em out. It's a side a'rich people, I guess, t'have big times; and ol'Samson, I'm satisfied he'uz up there in prison chained. "Come on around! Go up and git Samson! Go up and git'im!"

'Course th'lad, he went and got'im. I'm satisfied he led'im with a chain; brought'im back down. Sit around awhile and said, "Let's walk out around th'buildin'."

Walked out there and Samson said, "Would you mind me a'stoopin' down?"

'Course that lad, I reckon, told him yes. But when he reached down he got aholt of each one a'them pillars and over she went. Killed him and thousands. Five thousand on top of it.

Now you know it took strength and power t'do that. But he got revenge fer his two eyes. That's all. This whuppin' and beatin' and dealin', he didn't rest w'that. He just revenged his two eyes. Them ol'Philistines—they'uz rough.

Bible's a good thing t'read.

PLATE 371

[Out hiking with Kenny on several different occasions, we noticed his keen communication with and love for nature. We asked him why he liked to live out in the country.] 'At's where ever'thing's quiet. Ever'thing is quiet. I hardly ever do go t'Clayton. You never see me in Clayton hardly; unless I go a'ter some material fer m'job. I don't like a town. Why, if I'uz t'go t'Atlanter, I could get a good job. Them womens come up a'ter me from Floridy. But I just can't stand a town. I'd ruther be in th'woods. I get t'feelin' funny'r'somethin'. I don't feel right. I go t'town and I don't stay but just a little bit.

If I had children, I'd raise'em like this. In th'back woods. Sure is better. Sure is. Stay out a'towns all y'can. Stay out a'towns.

[We asked him what he thought the difference was between people who lived in the country and those who live in the city.] Well, I believe they get along better, and seem like they're more different. You meet'em—they'll speak howdy to y'. You take these big towns, they just go on by y' like you was a mile post. They're a lot more kinder. More kinder.

A big town, they won't speak hardly at all. 'Course, I never saw a stranger in my life. I go t'Atlanter, I talk t'somebody. But th'people in th'country is more friendlier'n they are in town. They can't see so much meanness goin' on.

You take like this here now, it's perfectly quiet. We hardly have anybody t'come up here. But you take Atlanter. Gosh it's rough! Too many cars bumper t'bumper. This world's full a'cars, you know it? What you goin' t'do with'em? If they'uz all piled up, they'd be a hunerd miles. Higher than trees!

I believe we'd live longer if we'd go back. We'd go slower, y'know, and study as we go along. Back then, you could meet a man with a yoke a'steers and they'd stop and talk t'you a hour at a time. Long as you wanted t'talk. We couldn't do that now. She's too fur gone. No. They's no hope.

[Relaxing in a rocker on his old front porch, Kenny looks across a field of grazing horses toward a clear pond.] Me? I'm just goin' through this world th'best I can. Don't bother nobody. Don't bother nobody. I work out what I get; just gettin' through th'best way I can. I don't claim t'be good, but I'm just doin' th'best I can. 'At's about all anybody can do, ain't it?

S ince the publication of the first volume of *The Foxfire Book,* we've come across additional information on some of the topics covered there.

1. CHIMNEYS

PLATE 372   A beautiful stick-and-mud chimney on a cabin near Brasstown, North Carolina. Note also the gable of hand-split shingles and the wooden shutter with wooden hinges covering the window. Such shutters were used in place of glass, which was not available at the time.

2. JOINING WHITE OAK SPLITS

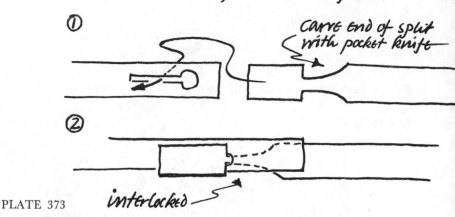

Another way to join white oak splits together as demonstrated by Thomas Barnes. The same lock can be used with wood split barrel hoops.

① *Carve end of split with pocket knife*

②

PLATE 373   *interlocked*

3. BASKETS AND HAMPERS: A FRIDAY AFTERNOON

Only a few generations ago, a close and strangely beautiful inner kinship existed between the people of this region. Neighbors were friendly, reliable, and eager to help and teach each other. Times have changed, though, and apparently so have people. Now such warm traits are rarely found, but sometimes it still happens.

In *The Foxfire Book* (pp. 119–27), Aunt Arie and Beulah Perry each showed us how to make different kinds of white oak split baskets. Not long after that, Beulah said she wanted to try her hand at making one of Aunt Arie's baskets, so we all got together at Aunt Arie's for another lesson.

The day held its share of fun and confusion. Aunt Arie had another gigantic meal to cook. Beulah struggled with splits too big and rough. A car got stuck in the mud. And three copperheads showed up. Yet Aunt Arie's meal was as delicious as ever, Beulah good-naturedly yanked and pulled and laughed while we tried to resplit the splits, we pushed the car out, and the snakes didn't bite. Beulah and Aunt Arie made a basket and became friends. A lot of working, learning, and laughing went on that day, and somehow that old tradition of friendliness, kindness, and respect reappeared.

Article and photographs by JAN BROWN

PLATE 374 Aunt Arie, left, watches carefully as Beulah Perry, middle, makes the first tentative weaves in her basket. Mary Garth helps.

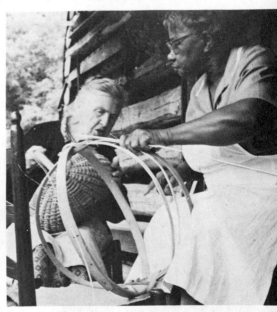

PLATES 375–377 "Well, look a'there what you've done!"

4. A CORDED BED

This photograph illustrates the rope wrench used to tighten the ropes on a corded bed (Vol. 1, pp. 139–41). You can make a duplicate easily for your own corded bed. To tighten the ropes, simply follow the path the man used who wove the rope through the bedframe in the first place. Work with the loops that appear on the outside of the frame. Start with the first loop the rope makes, "foul" the forked wrench in the loop, twist until the first length of rope is tight, drive the wooden peg into place in the hole in the bedframe to hold that first rope length tightly in place; then move to the second loop at the opposite end with the forked wrench, twist the second length of rope tight, have your helper free the wooden peg from the first hole and bring it up to you to be driven into the second hole to hold the second length tight while you move to the third loop down at the opposite end of the bedframe, and so on until the whole web is the desired tension. Retie the knot at the end of the rope that holds the whole web in place so that you won't lose that tension, and you're in business.

PLATE 378   PLATE 379

5. QUILTING

A Quilting Frame:

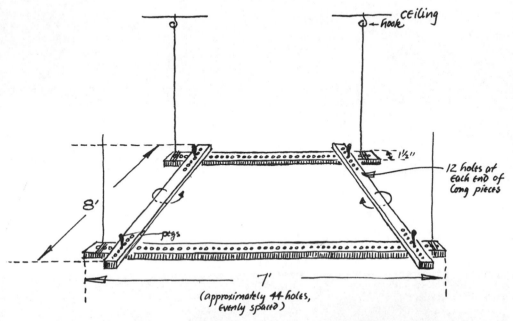

1. Ends of quilt's cotton lining are lashed to 7' end pieces of frame, which is suspended from the ceiling so as to be at a comfortable height when sitting.

2. Sides of quilt (batting + top) are lashed to 8' frames. As rows are quilted from the sides, the pegs are removed from the corners and the finished work rolled under to get at the unquilted portion.

PLATE 380

PLATE 381   As Aunt Arie hangs her frame, the corner construction is obvious.

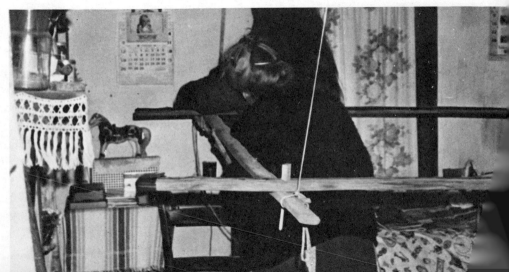

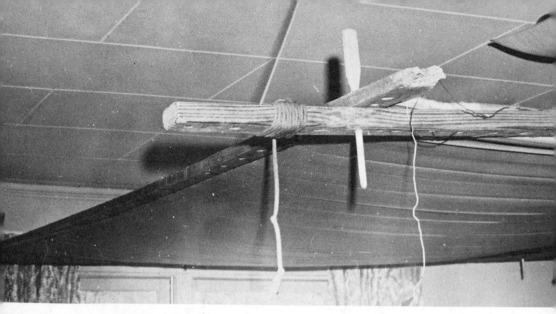

PLATE 382   The corner of Harriet Echols' frame from underneath, with a quilt lashed in place.

PLATE 383   Edith Darnell displays a "Double Wedding Ring" pattern quilt she made

6. SOAPMAKING

Martin Pilgrim's family has an ingenious method for testing soap which we have just learned about. As the melted fat was mixed with the boiling lye [Vol. 1, pp. 155–58], a feather would be stirred briefly in the mixture. If it ate the bristles off the feather, there was still too much lye in the mixture. Fat would be mixed in slowly until the solution could no longer damage a feather. At that point the liquid was ready to pour out into a container to harden into a jelly-like soap.

Millard Buchanan's recipe for soap is as follows: Use five pounds of grease, one box of Red Devil Lye, three tablespoons of borax, two tablespoons of sugar, one tablespoon of salt, one-fourth cup of ammonia and one-half cup of boiling water.

Mix the lye in a pan with a quart of hot water and stir until the lye is dissolved. Let it cool, and add the lukewarm, dissolved grease. Mix the borax with a half cup of boiling water, and add it along with the other ingredients. When all the ingredients are dissolved and well mixed, pour the solution into flat, shallow pans to harden into soap. When hard, the soap can be cut into bars for use.

7. RECIPES

AUNT ARIE'S RECIPE FOR LEATHER BREECHES BEANS—
—Take good, full green beans ("If they're nothin' but slabs, they ain't fit t'eat"), and string them on ten or twelve spool thread and break off the ends. Don't hang them out in the open air or they'll mold. Aunt Arie hangs them from the rafters in the warm, still dark air of her attic. She doesn't like to put them in the sun for fear it will make them brittle and tough.

To cook them, she takes down as many strings of beans as she needs and soaks them overnight. In the morning, she parboils them for an hour on the wood stove, with a little soda added in to soften them up. She doesn't use over a teaspoon of soda as too much makes them yellow.

When they've parboiled for an hour, she takes them out, washes and rinses them, puts them in a pot with clear water and several large chunks of fat meat (pork) and cooks them for two or three hours more until they're soft and done.

ADA KELLY'S RECIPE FOR CORNBREAD——Cook one quart of corn meal mush until thoroughly done. Salt to taste. Remove from heat and add cold water until you can bear your finger in it. Then add ¾ cup sugar, ¾ cup lard, and meal enough to make stiff as cornbread. Set aside until it ferments (overnight). Add meal to make medium batter. Bake in well-greased pan in slow oven. Remove from pan when cold.

Margaret Norton's pickling recipes (Vol. 1, pp. 176–80):

ICICLE PICKLES——Use two gallons of cucumbers, one pint coarse salt, one gallon of boiling water, one walnut-sized lump of alum, two quarts of vinegar, four quarts of white sugar, one grain of saccharine (one tablet), one tablespoon of pickling spice, two tablespoons of celery seed, and two tablespoons of cinnamon buds.

Split cucumbers lengthwise, no matter how small they are. Add the salt to the boiling water and pour it over the cucumbers. Let it stand one week.

Then drain, cover with boiling water again and let stand twenty-four hours. Then drain, dissolve the alum in boiling water and pour it over the pickles. Let stand twenty-four hours.

Then drain the pickles and take two quarts of vinegar and four quarts of sugar and all the spices and boil them together and pour them over the pickles. Do this for four mornings, each time pouring off the liquid, reboiling it, and pouring it back over the pickles again boiling hot.

Then seal them in a can. (They will also keep in an open jar, but most people seal them for the winter.)

LIME PICKLES——Use seven pounds of cut-up tomatoes (green) or cucumbers to make seven quarts. Also use three cups of builder's lime and two gallons of cold water.

Let all soak together for twenty-four hours. Then let the pickles soak in clear water for four hours, changing the water every hour.

Then make a syrup of three pints of vinegar, five pounds of white sugar, two tablespoons of pickling spice, and bring it all to a boil. Add the cucumbers and let them stand overnight. Then boil them for one hour, pack them in glass jars, and seal.

SPICED GRAPES——For this relish (used with meat, bread, etc.), use seven pounds of grapes (Concord or wine grapes), one cup of fruit vinegar, two teaspoons of cinnamon, five pounds of sugar, one teaspoon of cloves, and one teaspoon of allspice.

Wash, stem, and pulp grapes. Put pulp with seeds over fire and cook until the seeds come free. Add skins and pulp together, and also add the sugar, vinegar, and spices. Cook until thick and can.

PICKLED GREEN TOMATOES——Wash and quarter green tomatoes. Pack them raw into pint jars, adding to each jar two–three small whole pods of hot pepper and one quartered pod of bell pepper.

Make a brine of two parts vinegar, one part water, and one part sugar and heat it until the sugar melts. Pour into the packed jars leaving a half-inch at the top. Put on the lids and rings and process fifteen minutes in a water bath.

PICKLED PEACHES OR APPLES——Peel apples or peaches, quarter, and put in a pot. Make enough brine of two parts vinegar, two parts sugar, and one part water to cover the fruit. Add ground cinnamon, nutmeg, and allspice to taste, and cook until tender. When done, lift the fruit out and pack into jars. Keep brine simmering and pour into jars over the fruit leaving one-half inch at the top. Seal immediately.

Others:

AUNT ARIE'S RECIPE FOR EGG CUSTARD (cooked on a wood stove)—— Line a small pie pan with plain biscuit dough rolled thin. Then, in a separate bowl, mix up one egg (beaten well), one cup of sweet milk, a handful of flour, a teaspoon of nutmeg, a half a teacup of sugar.

Mix it all up well, pour it into the crust, and, using just a little wood so the fire won't be too hot, bake it slowly until it "sets." It will "blubber up"—or bubble, and then the bubbles will settle.

At this point, it is ready to eat. Serves four.

SWEET POTATO PUDDING——Mix together two cups of cooked and mashed sweet potato, one-half cup brown sugar, one cup sweet milk, two eggs, one teaspoon vanilla, and one-half cup each of raisins and grated coconut. Bake in a casserole dish in a moderate oven for about a half-hour, or until firm. Serve hot or cold.

IRISH POTATO DUMPLINGS——Peel and quarter about a

quart of potatoes. Put them in a pot, cover with one and one-half to two quarts of water, add salt and pepper to taste, a tablespoon of butter and a cup of sweet milk. Boil until the potatoes are tender.

Roll biscuit dough out one-quarter-inch thick, cut in two-inch squares and drop into the rapidly boiling water the potatoes are in. Cook dumplings about one minute, take the pot off the heat, and the whole thing is ready to serve.

PEPPER SAUCE——Use fourteen large onions, one dozen green bell peppers, one dozen ripe bell peppers.

Chop ingredients up fine, pour boiling water over them and let stand for five minutes, and then drain. Put back in a kettle and pour on more boiling water, let boil two minutes, drain, and then put back in kettle again.

Add two–three pints of vinegar, two cups of sugar, and two tablespoons of salt and boil for fifteen minutes. Then can.

JAKE WALDROOP'S RECIPE FOR BLACKBERRY WINE—— Gather six to eight gallons of wild blackberries, wash them well, and put them in a big container. Mix in five pounds of sugar, and then cover the top of the churn or container with a cloth, tied down so air can get in but insects can't. Let the mixture work for eight to ten days.

Then strain the mixture through a clean cloth, squeezing the pulp so that all the juice is removed. Measure how many gallons of juice you have. For every gallon of juice, add one and a half pounds of sugar. Let it work off. When it stops (when the foaming and bubbling has stopped on top), strain it again, measure the juice, and again add one and a half pounds of sugar to each gallon of juice. When it finishes working this time, it is done and can be bottled. Jake keeps his in an earthenware jug with a corn cob stopper.

He makes grape wine the same way.

8. CURING PORK

Recently Jake Waldroop told us of a method of curing pork that was quite different from any that we had published so far (see Vol. 1, pp. 199–201). It is as follows:

"The way we used t'do it, m'daddy an'all of us. Fer years an'years, we'd salt it down an' let it git cured out good, y'know. We had a big smokehouse an' it never had no floor. It'uz just dirt. Just on th'dirt.

"Well, he'd save his ashes all winter. He wouldn't burn nothin' but hickory wood. An' if he seed anybody spit in that fireplace, why he'd kick their hind end nearly. He wanted them ashes kept clean.

"An' he had'im a big ol'tub of steel, kind of a iron tub of a thing in under his shed. He'uz just as careful. He'd take them ashes out yonder an' he had'im a big ol'sifter. An' he'd sift them ashes through there an' if they's any coals'r'anything, he separated'em; but them ashes went down in that.

"Along up in th'spring 'bout last o'March, first o'April, why he'd put'im down a layer of them ashes an' he'd put down a layer o'that meat. Then he'd cover that first layer of meat with ashes, on thataway. Sometimes I've seen'im with a thousand'r'twelve hundred pound

PLATE 384   Jake Waldroop was able to show us how meat was hung. First it would be salted down well. Then the pieces would be put into individual cloth bags, tied shut, and hung from the rafters of the smokehouse. Here Eddie Bingham helps.

o'meat there in one pile of ashes. An' you could go any time in th'summer you wanted t'git that an'they wadn't no strong edges. It'uz just as good an'sweet bacon as any breakfast bacon y'kin buy now. Better. Oh, it was real good. Put it up in hick'ry ashes."

We were also able to get Martin Pilgrim's method demonstrated recently. His family (from Lookout Mountain, Tennessee), immediately after slaughtering, made a mixture of brown sugar and salt. They used two cups of brown sugar to every cup of salt. The hams would be disconnected at the last joint, and all joints packed with salt to keep them from souring down inside the meat. Then the pieces of meat would be rubbed down thoroughly on both sides over a period of several days with the sugar/salt mixure. When they were well saturated, they would be wrapped individually in brown paper, sewn up in handspun cloth, and hung from the rafters by wires to keep them safe from rats.

PLATE 385

PLATE 386   Cracklin's.

In the spring, to keep skippers out, Martin's family would rub the meat with a mixture of boric acid, salt, sugar, black pepper and red pepper. Martin also said they would boil the backbones down with the liver and some onions. When the meat loosened off the bones, the bones would be removed and the mixture boiled again with sage—then canned.

We also are now able to offer photographs of rendering lard immediately after slaughtering. The scrap pieces of fat from meat and intestine are boiled down into liquid form in an iron pot (*Plate 385*).

When the fat is all melted, Nelson Cabe dips it out of the pot and strains the liquid through several layers of white cloth into the containers in which the lard will be kept. As the lard is strained, the cloth catches hard, granular pieces of cooked skin and meat (*Plate 386*). These are the "cracklin's." They are set aside to mix up in dough for cracklin' bread.

PLATE 387

ANSWERS TO KENNY RUNION'S RIDDLES

(1) A chestnut.
(2) A wagon.
(3) A churn.
(4) A person carrying a milk stool upside down riding on a donkey.

INDEX OF PEOPLE

THE KIDS:

Glenda Arrowood
Pat Arrowood
Walter Beals
Eddie Bingham
Rhonda Black
Danny Brown
Jan Brown
Judy Brown
Laurie Brunson
George Burch
Andrea Burrell
Tony Burt
David Bush
Jimmy Carpenter
Dickie Chastain
Carla Coleman
Bill Colsen
Eddie Connor
Mike Cook
Karen Cox
Barbara Crunkleton
Patti Darnell
Bradley Davis

Kathy Dickerson
Opal Dickerson
Buzzy Dotson
Stan Echols
Jimmy Enloe
Susan Farr
George Freemon
Mary Garth
Paul Gillespie
Gail Hamby
Phil Hamilton
Frank Hill
Russell Himelright
Steve James
Diane Kimbrell
Sue Kirkland
Ken Kistner
Kathy Long
Ray McBride
Don MacNeil
Billy Maney
Carol Maney
Wayne Mason

Chris Moon
Eddie Moon
Susan Mullis
Lois Nix
Ernie Payne
Paul Phillips
Mike Pignato
Mary Rhodes
Mary Jane Shepard
Danny Spivey
Dennis Spivey
Greg Strickland
Barbara Taylor
John Turner
Sheila Vinson
Gary Warfield
Rose Wells
Betse Whilden
Frenda Wilborn
Craig Williams
David Wilson
Carlton Young
David Young

THE CONTACTS:

Lester Addis
Jule Anderson
Mamie Arrendale
Mrs. Robert Avery
Mr. and Mrs. Thomas Barnes
Dean Beasley
Grover Bradley
J. S. Bramblett
Josephine Brewer
Florence and Lawton Brooks
Mrs. E. H. Brown
Marinda and Harry Brown
Mary Brown
Minnie Buchanan
Mrs. Don Burnette
Sam Burton
Doris Cannon
Aunt Arie Carpenter
Bertha Carpenter
Harley Carpenter
Jud Carpenter
Mary Carpenter
John Conley
Minyard Conner
Clifford Connor
Ethel Corn
Fidel Crisp
Edith and Claude Darnell
Fred Darnell
Mimi Dickerson
Effie and R. M. Dickerson
Carrie Dixon
Sarah and Happy Dowdle
Belle Dryman
Harriet Echols
Jim Edmonds
Bob Edwards
Mrs. R. L. Eliott
Aunt Nora Garland

Carrie Dillard Garrison
L. B. Gibbs
Ruth Gibbs
Simone Gonzales
Ardilla Grant
Irene Gray
Hillard Green
Marian Gregory
George Grist
Deffie Hamilton
Blanche Harkins
John Henry
Ral Henslee
Jim Heuser
Laura Holman
Mrs. John Hopper
Kate Hopper
Mrs. Selvin Hopper
Anna Howard
Alex Justice
Gertrude Keener
Mrs. Hershel Keener
Ada Kelly
Lovey Kelso
Farish Kilby
Fanny Lamb
Myrtle Lamb
Alvin Lee
Elb McClure
Fern MacDowell
Jan MacDowell
Mr. and Mrs. Tom McDowell
Daniel Manous
Pearl Martin
Myrtle Mason
Marie Mellinger
David Mize
Roy Mize
Lawrence Moffitt

Dr. Rufus Morgan
Algie Norton
Lula Norton
Lester Norton
Mr. and Mrs. Mann Norton
Margaret and Richard Norton
Mrs. Tommy Lee Norton
Ethel Parker
Eula Parker
Elizabeth Patterson
C. R. Pennington
Annie Perry
Beulah Perry
Martin Pilgrim
Esco Pitts
Fannie Powell
Harvey Reid
Lon Reid
Kenny Runion
Mrs. Lex Sanders

Walter Shellnut
Maude Shope
Pansey Slappey
Mr. and Mrs. Lake Stiles
Calvin Talley
Nearola Taylor
Polly Teat
Harley Thomas
Hoyt Thomas
Well Thomas
Mrs. Dillard Thompson
Grady Waldroop
Jake Waldroop
Les Waldroop
Ed Watkins
Mrs. Andy Webb
Mrs. Al Webster
Delia Williams
Will Zoellner